DE HAVILLAND
MOSQUITO

1940 onwards (all marks)

COVER CUTAWAY:

de Havilland Mosquito B XVI. *(Mike Badrocke)*

First published in October 2013

A catalogue record for this book is available from the British Library.

ISBN 978 0 85733 360 5

Library of Congress control no. 2013941311

Published by Haynes Publishing,
Sparkford, Yeovil,
Somerset BA22 7JJ, UK.
Tel: 01963 442030 Fax: 01963 440001
Int. tel: +44 1963 442030
Int. fax: +44 1963 440001
E-mail: sales@haynes.co.uk
Website: www.haynes.co.uk

Haynes North America Inc.,
861 Lawrence Drive, Newbury Park,
California 91320, USA.

Printed in the USA by Odcombe Press LP,
1299 Bridgestone Parkway, La Vergne,
TN 37086.

Acknowledgements

The authors wish to thank the following for their kindness, help and enthusiasm. Without them this book would not have been possible.

Ian Thirsk, Head of Collections, Royal Air Force Museum, London, for allowing us to draw on his encyclopaedic knowledge of the Mosquito, for his advice, patience, and always finding the time to help. We owe him a huge debt of gratitude.

Roger de Mercado, of the de Havilland Aeronautical Technical School Association, for advice and archive material. His support has been invaluable.

Barry Guess, BAE Systems Heritage Department, Farnborough; Ralph Steiner, Director, de Havilland Aircraft Museum Trust Ltd; Dick Bishop, son of R.E. Bishop; David Newman, Mosquito design team; Capt Eric Melrose Brown, CBE, DSC, AFC, RN, former test pilot and author; Kim and Mike Ingram, Victoria Air Maintenance, Vancouver, Canada, for their kind permission to reproduce photographs of the restoration of Mosquito B 35, VR796; Warren Denholm, Avspecs Ltd, Ardmore, New Zealand, for his kind permission to reproduce photographs of the restoration of Mosquito FB 26, KA114; Glyn Powell, Drury, New Zealand, for kind permission to reproduce photographs of his fuselage building; Jerry Yagen, USA, for his support for this book; Paul Le Roy, Wellington, New Zealand, for his generous contribution of words and pictures; photographer Gavin Conroy, New Zealand, for permission to use his stunning air-to-air photographs of KA114; Alan Allen, Paul Blackah and Keith Wilson, for permission to reproduce copyright photographs; René J. Francillon and San Diego Aerospace Museum, USA; Peter Watts, Rachel Watts, Rob Gardner, Retro Track and Air (UK) Ltd, for their help and support willingly given; Imperial War Museum, London; Mark Postlethwaite and ww2images.com; airrecce.co.uk; Lee Barton, RAF Air Historical Branch; Matthew Marke; Francis Cooper for allowing us to use his recollections of his time as a 'sparky' on 230 OCU; Cliff Streeter and Stuart R. Scott, for their kind permission to allow us to reproduce copyright material from *Mosquito Thunder*; Mike Badrocke, creator of the superb cutaway drawing; the late Robert Converse; Clair M. Waterbury; Robin Matson; Mike Packham; Ken Haynes; Alison Holmes; the Reid family; and last but not least Penny Housden, and Louise McIntyre and James Robertson at Haynes Publishing.

DE HAVILLAND
MOSQUITO

1940 onwards (all marks)

Owners' Workshop Manual

An insight into developing, flying, servicing and restoring
Britain's legendary 'Wooden Wonder' fighter-bomber

Jonathan Falconer and Brian Rivas

Contents

OPPOSITE Man and machine: a thumbs-up and a smile from Geoffrey Raoul de Havilland as he prepares for a Mosquito test flight. Geoffrey, the eldest son of Captain Geoffrey de Havilland, was chief test pilot of his father's company and is remembered for his blistering displays in the Mosquito. *(Getty Images)*

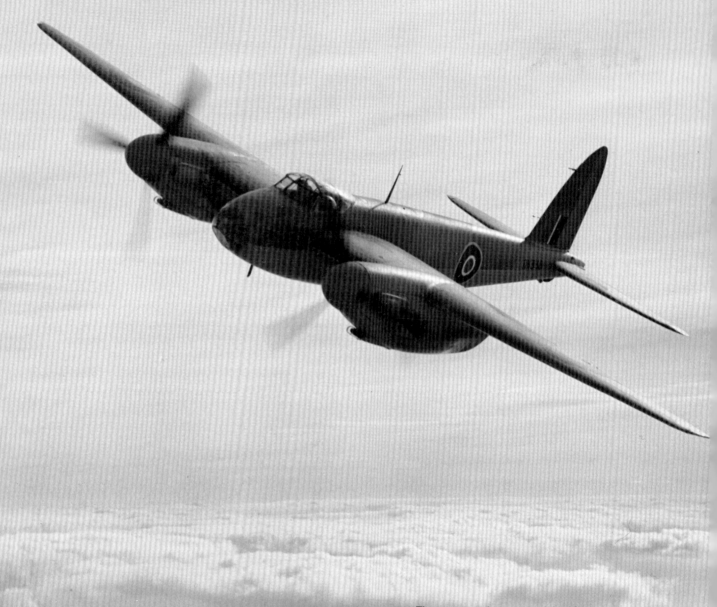

'Probably man's highest engineering achievement in timber.'

Ralph Hare, de Havilland

The power and purpose of the Mosquito are captured in this classic shot by the famous aviation photographer Charles E. Brown of a B IV Series 2 (DK338). Serving with 105 Squadron, this aircraft took part in Operation Oyster, a successful low-level raid on the Phillips radio factory at Eindhoven in December 1942, but crashed at Marham five months later after an engine failure. The crew of two were killed. *(RAF Museum/Charles E. Brown).*

Introduction

With its slippery lines and crackling snarl from its twin Merlins, the de Havilland Mosquito looked and sounded as though it meant business. And it did. When it went into service this charismatic and devastatingly effective British warbird could show a clean pair of heels to everything else in the air, whether fighter or bomber, Allied or Axis. It became a jack of all trades and master of them all, and as such became the most versatile multi-role combat aircraft ever built.

Not bad from a company that didn't particularly want to build a military aircraft in the first place.

Being manoeuvrable, tough and fast, it was loved by its crews and to them it was the 'Mossie'. It also had other affectionate nicknames, such as 'Freeman's Folly', 'Wooden Wonder', 'Bamboo Bomber' – even 'Termite's Dream'. But perhaps the most succinct summing-up came from Ralph Hare, who was on the original design team and who later became chief stressman at de Havilland: 'Probably man's highest engineering achievement in timber.'

Even Hermann Göring paid a tribute, though of a slightly different kind: he was furious every time he saw a Mosquito. He was 'green and yellow with envy' that we were able to knock together a beautiful wooden aircraft with such a performance. 'There is nothing the British do not have,' he said. 'They have the geniuses and we have the nincompoops' – a comment that may not have endeared him to his glorious leader.

The DH 98 Mosquito was an extraordinary undertaking, with no less than six different kinds of wood being used in its construction, each of which had to undergo evaluation tests to determine its effectiveness. But the aircraft wasn't made entirely of timber: there was plenty of metal used as well, such as a total of about 30,000 brass screws in the wing assembly. 'Never glue without a screw' was the motto.

One of the most astonishing statistics is that

BELOW 'Aloft incumbent on the dusky air' – this resonant quotation from Milton's *Paradise Lost* was used by Hilary St G. Saunders, author of the official wartime HMSO publication *Bomber Command,* to accompany a photograph of an RAF Wellington bomber high in a moonlit sky on its way to bomb an enemy target. It seems apt here to reuse Milton's words to evoke the atmosphere of this photograph of a de Havilland Mosquito B XVI, set against the sprawling cloudscape of a dusky sky. The Mosquito was truly a multi-role combat aircraft, equally at home at high level as a pathfinder or on a photo-reconnaissance sortie as it was at deck height blasting U-boats, or in precision bombing. *(Copyright unknown)*

MOSQUITO
Fastest Aircraft in
Service in the World

Another triumph by

DE HAVILLAND
Leading Builders of Transport Aircraft
in the British Empire

de Havilland Aircraft   de Havilland Engines
de Havilland Propellers   Components and
Accessories   Light Alloy Engineering
Flying Training   Technical Education

In the attack today – on the trade routes of the future

it went from a few pencilled sketches to first flight in less than a year – but it had a bumpy ride just getting off the drawing board.

The Air Ministry thought it was too radical, especially coming from a company that had little inter-war years' experience on military designs. And it went completely against the RAF policy of big, heavy, multi-engined metal bombers bristling with armament.

Had the top brass visualised the Mosquito's potential earlier it is almost certain that a larger four-engined version would have been built, giving huge extra impetus to our bombing capability. As a result of Whitehall's resistance, the prototype Mosquito didn't even take to the air until after the Battle of Britain in 1940, and had it not been for the support of one high-ranking official it may never have got that far. In the event it went on uncompromisingly to fulfil a multiplicity of roles that has never been equalled – although this could not have been foreseen by the Ministry, and it is all too easy to ridicule them now for what looks like shortsightedness.

But as things settled down the Mosquito quickly found roles in every aerial theatre of war, roles that it fulfilled superlatively, from fast bomber to night-fighter, pathfinder, high-speed photo-reconnaissance, weather reporting, fighter-bomber, intruder – and even as an airliner for BOAC. It could fly at great altitude in safety from attack, it could sneak fast and low under enemy radar, it discovered V-weapon sites, it

ABOVE One of the more unusual tasks assigned to the Mosquito during the Second World War was to test an anti-shipping variation of Barnes Wallis's bouncing bomb, code-named 'Highball'. A Mosquito Mk IV Series 2 was converted to carry two 'Highballs' in tandem. In the end the weapon was never used. *(Copyright unknown)*

carried the Barnes Wallis Highball bomb (albeit not in anger), and took part in a number of high-profile operations. There was nothing of importance that it couldn't do, and as well as the RAF it served with the Royal Canadian Air Force, the Royal Australian Air Force, the US Army Air Force, and more than 12 other air forces, all of whom recognised its outstanding capabilities.

And there was more, for being made almost entirely of wood, Mosquito production allowed hundreds of trades outside the aviation industry to play a vital role as parts were subcontracted all over the country – trades which would otherwise be making no contribution to the war effort, such as furniture makers. Even housewives played a part, so not only did Britain have a remarkable warplane but one that was a real morale-booster, which made everyone involved feel useful.

It is a delightful irony that a man who didn't want to build warplanes was later to receive a knighthood for his contribution to the war with an aircraft that still commands the deepest awe and respect and, in some cases, fanatical dedication. If ever an aircraft deserved the title 'legend' it is the Mosquito.

Unlike the Spitfire and some other famous warbirds, there were never going to be many owners – although there are about 30 examples preserved in museums, the most famous being the yellow prototype W4050 in the de Havilland Heritage Centre at London Colney. The reason is simple: wood and glue are not as durable as metal, and the attrition rate over the years from deterioration due to climatic conditions, especially in the Far East, was inevitable. It was

LEFT With its reputation for derring-do, perhaps it's not surprising that the Mosquito and its crews have found their way into film and literature (see page 93). They also became the subject of dozens of comic-book stories in the popular 'Commando' war comic series of the 1960s and '70s. *(Jonathan Falconer collection)*

designed as a war machine, and structural integrity over decades was not the prime consideration. As for airworthy examples, the last one in the UK was lost in 1996 when it crashed at a Manchester air show.

Although that seemed like the end of the story, it was not. The ultimate dream had always been to get another Mosquito where it belongs – in the air. New Zealand warbird restoration specialists Avspecs took on the fitting-out of one man's extraordinary undertaking: Glyn Powell's almost impossible-sounding build project, virtually from the ground up – including constructing new fuselage moulds – of an FB 26 (KA114), which culminated in its momentous first flight in September 2012.

So after a gap of 16 years, a Mosquito, phoenix-like, has taken to the air once more. It will not be the last.

BELOW On the far side of the world in New Zealand, Glyn Powell and Warren Denholm of Avspecs gave wings to the idea of returning a Mosquito to flight. The stunning result is a rebuilt FB 26, KA114, owned by American collector Jerry Yagen. *(Paul Le Roy)*

'The Mosquito was a wonderful thing.'

W.J. Ince, de Havilland electrician

Chapter One

The Mosquito story

The concept of the Mosquito cut through all conventional thinking. No wonder the Air Ministry were sceptical, but no wonder de Havilland persevered, for they knew that their idea of a streamlined high-speed bomber with no clumsy gun turrets would be a winner, one that could go in fast, bite hard, and then show the enemy a clean pair of heels.

OPPOSITE Up where she belongs: rebuilt Mosquito FB 26, KA114, is put through her paces in New Zealand skies in January 2013. *(Paul Le Roy)*

Beginnings

When Geoffrey de Havilland left school he was expected to enter the Church and follow in the footsteps of his ill-tempered father, who was vicar of Nuneaton. Thankfully for the future of the British aviation industry, Geoffrey had other ideas. Spending summer holidays on his grandfather's farm, he developed an abiding interest in engineering and nature, and his love of the natural world is echoed in the names given to some of his most famous creations – although 'Mosquito' had an appropriately more aggressive and venomous ring to it than, for example, the gentle-sounding Puss Moth and Hummingbird.

A single-minded man of great ability and determination, he built and piloted his own rudimentary aircraft in 1909 before he had even seen another aeroplane fly. And, such was his self-belief and tenacity that, with his background in engineering, he also built the

engine for it, convinced that nothing else was good enough. This energy and drive was to be at the heart of Geoffrey and, later, the de Havilland Aircraft Company. During the First World War he designed some landmark machines, among them the DH 4 day bomber, which foreshadowed the Mosquito by being

able to out-fly all German fighters – a lesson from history that the Air Ministry would have done well to heed some 20 years later.

After hostilities ended he turned his attention to civil designs, and thus began a golden period of unforgettable aircraft, epitomised by the immortal Moth series, which introduced thousands of people to the delights of private flying. He steered well clear of military aircraft: Captain de Havilland – this was his rank at the end of the First World War – was wary of Air Ministry specifications, which he believed were flawed and outdated, but design and construction innovations that were featured on some of the later DH designs, notably the record-breaking DH 88 Comet Racer and the graceful four-engined Albatross airliner, were to stand the company in good stead when the Mosquito finally got the go-ahead.

Both of these aircraft came from a team led by chief designer Arthur Hagg, whose position was taken in 1936 by the brilliant Ronald Eric Bishop. Hagg had taught Bishop the art of wooden construction, and Bishop was to expand upon this to great effect with the Mosquito, a design that he looked on in later years as his finest achievement.

LEFT With the Mosquito and Comet jet airliner to his credit, chief designer R.E. Bishop had much to be proud of – yet he hated having his photo taken. This classic portrait of him alongside the Comet is one of the few in which he looks relaxed and at ease. *(Dick Bishop)*

BELOW Looking at these Mosquito fuselages at the de Havilland plant in Sydney, Australia, one is reminded of a line of fish – and that is no coincidence, for chief designer R.E. Bishop drew his inspiration from a most unusual source, and demonstrated that beneath his austere appearance he had quite a sense of humour.

Mounted on the wall of a lavatory at Salisbury Hall when the Mosquito was in the design stages was a splendid stuffed pike in a glass case, a pike that had been caught in the moat before the 1914–18 war by no less a person than Winston Churchill.

As Bishop was seated on the pedestal one day, the design of the Mosquito very much on his mind, his eyes wandered to this fish and, contemplating its graceful and purposeful contours, he felt that it would make an excellent shape for the fuselage of the Mosquito, and so, pulling an envelope from his pocket, he made a quick sketch of the creature.

In this unlikely but unforgettable setting began one of the most famous designs in the history of aviation, one that was to be marked with Bishop being made a CBE in 1946. *(Milton Kent)*

Genesis

With the threat of war growing in Europe, de Havilland's thoughts turned reluctantly to studying the Ministry's military requirements, but while other manufacturers stuck to conventional designs with guns sprouting from every available location, other ideas were afoot at Hatfield based on minimal surface area and aerodynamic cleanness, which they believed were just as relevant to a bomber as a fighter. And they wanted to build it from wood, like the Comet Racer and Albatross.

There were strong arguments for using wood: except in torsion it was as strong as duralumin or steel, it was readily available, would lead to quick and simple construction, would be easy to repair and would not eat into the valuable reserves of metal for other weaponry. The Mosquito itself had not even been contemplated at this stage, although the principles were there when a military version of the Albatross was discussed.

With the Munich crisis in 1938, war looked almost certain and thoughts about a bomber design intensified. Based on the philosophy of lightness, aerodynamic efficiency and speed, Geoffrey de Havilland and chief engineer Charles Clement Walker went to the Air Ministry with their proposals and drawings for a twin Merlin-powered wooden bomber with no armament whatsoever and just a two-man crew – a bomber with the speed of a fighter. Using wood would save about a year in getting the prototype airborne, would give it a super-efficient aerodynamic surface with no overlapping metal panels, and without any armament it would be fast enough to outpace any aircraft in the world.

It seemed to have everything: speed, efficiency, manoeuvrability, and a far more favourable crew-to-bomb load ratio than the big, heavy, multi-engined, multi-crewed conventional bombers. But it was so out of line with current RAF thinking that the men from the Ministry couldn't see beyond official policy and barely glanced at the drawings. However, they had a suggestion: forget all this wooden bomber nonsense and instead build wings for current aircraft. Angry and frustrated at this patronising response, the two men returned to Hatfield, bowed but not beaten.

Geoffrey de Havilland had a creed: 'In life you must never give up.' He didn't – not then, not ever – and he found a staunch ally in high places to support his speed bomber plans in the form of Air Marshal Sir Wilfred Freeman, who had been appointed Air Member for Development and Production. It took just one letter and one meeting for Sir Wilfred to see the merit of de Havilland's revolutionary concept, and from then on they had his wholehearted support. But even that wasn't enough, for Sir Wilfred met considerable opposition from the diehards who were still hidebound around a heavily armed bomber built from metal – diehards not just in the Ministry, but in the RAF and Bomber Command as well.

They could not get away from their obsession with armament, and they did not believe de Havilland's drag estimates. One of the design team, David Newman, recalled how he had to spend a Sunday at Salisbury Hall writing out 'in words of not more than two syllables for the benefit of the Ministry, a detailed analysis of the known and measured drag of the Albatross and an estimate of the drag of the Mosquito using the same methods and comparable detail'. His estimates showed that the Mosquito would have a top speed of 388mph.

Gradually, after further meetings and continued backing from Sir Wilfred, the Ministry became more convinced and at a meeting on 29 December 1939 the go-ahead was given to the unarmed format and a prototype was ordered, with some interest expressed in reconnaissance as well as bomber roles. But de Havilland needed a specification, so at a further meeting on 1 January 1940 specification B1/40 was drawn up there and then by John Buchanan, Director General of Aircraft Production, and John Connolly, senior engineer on the Air Registration Board.

Birth

The design team were ready for an immediate start, as in October 1939 – a month after the outbreak of war – they had been packed off to Salisbury Hall, a moated country house at London Colney a few miles away and safer from the attacks that were likely to be targeted on Hatfield. In this pleasant and

quiet setting, steeped in associations with Nell Gwynne and the Churchill family, Bishop now had a free hand and set to work with a will. His team, which totalled nearly 25, consisted of many of de Havilland's legendary names, such as Tim Wilkins, William Tamblin, Richard Clarkson, Bob Harper, Fred Plumb, Ralph Hare and David Newman.

Not only was it to be designed at Salisbury Hall, but the prototype would also be built there in a hangar disguised as a barn that was erected on a cabbage patch. It was all very British. Design work proceeded apace after the Ministry, with some trepidation, placed an order on 1 March 1940 for 50 bomber-reconnaissance aircraft straight off the drawing board under specification B1/40 without waiting for a prototype to be built.

The hours and dedication put in by Bishop and his team were heroic, but the setbacks weren't over: after Dunkirk in June, Minister of Aircraft Production Lord Beaverbrook ordered the Mosquito project to be dropped for at least 18 months so that de Havilland could concentrate on Tiger Moth and Airspeed Oxford trainers. He considered it far more important to get pilots trained to fly Spitfires, Hurricanes, Wellingtons, Whitleys and Blenheims, and Freeman was told three times by Beaverbrook to order de Havilland's not to continue with the Mosquito.

But Freeman was canny, never actually issuing any firm order, and a month later the project was back on course – although to get it there de Havilland had to promise that the 50 bomber-reconnaissance aircraft, including

ABOVE Design characteristics which would feature in the Mosquito can be seen in the thin tapered wings and tailplane of the famous DH 88 Comet Racer (G-ACSS) *Grosvenor House*. This unusual view was captured as pilot George Ellis was being strapped in for a display at Hatfield Open Day in 1987. After the demonstration the aircraft made a normal touchdown, but near the end of its landing run it swung to the left and then, on correction, swung to the right and ground-looped, causing the port main gear to collapse. A free-castoring tail wheel had been responsible, but the aircraft was restored and today is part of the Shuttleworth Collection. It had been a distressing accident, as earlier that year the aircraft made its first flight for 49 years after a massive restoration project at Farnborough and Hatfield. This is the actual DH 88 that won the MacRobertson Air Race in 1934 when it flew from England to Australia in 70hrs 55min crewed by Charles Scott and Tom-Campbell-Black. *(Ken Haynes)*

the prototype, would be completed by July the following year, a promise they knew was virtually impossible, but rash commitments seemed the only way forward. Small wonder that it was already being known as 'Freeman's Folly' – and there was little thawing of the Ministry's scepticism, for the Mosquito must not hold up more important work such as repairing battle-damaged Hawker Hurricanes, producing trainers, and even a sort of aerial equivalent of Dad's Army by fitting bomb racks to Tiger Moths for attacking troops should the expected invasion happen.

The Mosquito was to be constructed from numerous different woods – Spruce, Birch, Balsa, Ash, Douglas Fir, and Walnut. All these had to be tested for stress and strength, and Ralph Hare made daily journeys in his little Austin 7, carrying test samples from Salisbury Hall to the de Havilland materials lab at Stag Lane in Edgware.

Several mock-ups were built at Salisbury Hall

before the DH 98 was finalised. One of these dispensed with a conventional cockpit and had the crew seated in the fuselage behind a transparent nose, similar to the Heinkel He 111 bomber, but this was soon discarded in favour of a more conventional approach, which had the advantage of making the nose adaptable for armament.

Meanwhile, the Ministry couldn't shake off its doubts, still uneasy at the unarmed bomber concept, and began to think in terms of a fighter, so they altered the order for 50 aircraft to 20 bombers and 30 fighters. Although de Havilland's intention had been for an unarmed bomber, Bishop had always planned to leave space in the nose section to house four 20mm cannon

below the cockpit floor for other possible roles, so this in itself was not an issue – but many half-finished spars and wings at Hatfield had to be modified to take the higher stresses of the fighter role, and 28 completed noses had to be taken apart and altered. Had it not been for this, the rashly promised original order would have been completed almost on schedule

Then came a tragic blow: the airfield came under surprise attack on 3 October, a day of mist, low cloud and appalling visibility, when a Junkers Ju 88A, 3Z+BB of Stab 1/KG77, dropped four bombs from very low level which, more by chance than design, bounced on to the 94 Shop, where the DH 94 Moth Minors were built, but which was now a sheet metal shop that contained large quantities of Mosquito materials. It was a terrible day: 21 people were killed, 70 more were wounded and nine months of Mosquito output was destroyed.

By this time the prototype was nearing completion, and if ever an aeroplane looked right, it was the Mosquito. Painted bright yellow so that it would be conspicuous to anti-aircraft gunners who might otherwise confuse this new shape with a hostile aircraft and get trigger-happy, it was dismantled and taken to Hatfield on Queen Mary trailers on 3 November, there to be reassembled in readiness for its first flight. The twin Merlin 21s were run up and tested in a blast-proof building, and on 19 November 1940 the prototype, briefly bearing the Class B registration E0234 before adopting the military serial W4050, was rolled out for engine runs, well camouflaged with sacks and tarpaulins. This aircraft was neither bomber nor fighter – although in appearance it resembled a bomber.

The prototypes

W4050

Six days later chief test pilot Geoffrey Raoul de Havilland, captain and Louie de Havilland's eldest son, took it on its first flight, accompanied by engine installation designer John Walker. The performance was immediately impressive, with a potential speed nearly twice that of any previous DH design, but for this flight Geoffrey did not exceed 220mph and was very happy with the handling, manoeuvrability and feel of the aircraft. Leading edge slots were kept shut, and in fact were never fitted to production Mosquitoes as the stall was benign, with no tendency to drop a wing.

The Mosquito had gone from drawing board to first flight in just under 11 months, an extraordinary achievement in the best of circumstances, let alone in the midst of frequent air-raid alerts. But fear of bomb attacks was never far away, and between September 1940 and the following March more than a third of Hatfield's workforce, tooling and jigs was spread throughout other premises nearby that had been hurriedly requisitioned, from sweet factories to film studios, and these were fitted out for work on Airspeed Oxfords and Tiger Moths – but also with the Mosquito in mind.

Meanwhile, Geoffrey continued flight-testing W4050 and on 29 December gave an impressive demonstration to Lord Beaverbrook. Result: a mightily impressed minister and an order for a further 150 Mosquitoes to add on to the original 50, and in January de Havilland were told to produce a reconnaissance prototype. Now things were moving at last, but the best was yet to come when W4050 went for flight trials at A&AEE Boscombe Down, where in February 1941 Geoffrey clocked a speed of 387mph – 23mph faster than a Spitfire, and just 1mph short of David Newman's extraordinarily accurate estimate.

ABOVE The first flight by a Mosquito. The prototype, with its early E0234 serials, comes in to land at Hatfield after a successful maiden flight on 25 November 1940. *(BAE Systems/ DH479D)*

RIGHT The tall figure of chief test pilot Geoffrey de Havilland Jr chats with de Havilland guests after a demonstration flight of a new B IV Series 1 at Hatfield in November 1941. *(BAE Systems/DH9218)*

ABOVE David Newman worked for de Havilland as an aerodynamicist. The nacelle-type intake forward of his hand is the original exhaust manifold exit duct positioned on the engine side cowling. This arrangement proved very troublesome and was replaced by the double ejector 'saxophone' configuration (enclosed within a flame-damping shroud) or individual exhaust stacks situated in line with the engine exhaust ports. The photograph shows an experimental fillet sited on the exhaust exit duct top section (and blended into the side cowling) in an attempt to reduce the tail buffeting problem experienced with W4050 in its initial 'short' engine nacelle configuration. (Copyright unknown)

BELOW Now with its W4050 serial, the first prototype takes off on 10 January 1941. (BAE Systems/DH492)

For a completely new design, the Mosquito had few vices. One problem was some mild buffeting from the tailplane at speeds greater than 240mph causing some handling difficulties, but this was cured by extending the nacelles beyond the trailing edge to give a smoother flow over the tailplane – although some variants went into service with short nacelles, as production had been sanctioned before the prototype flew.

However, W4050 did have one major setback at Boscombe: on 21 February 1941, with Flt Lt C.E. Slee at the controls, the castoring tail wheel caught in a rut while taxying over rough ground and fractured the rear fuselage. Repair was not practical, so the fuselage from the photo-reconnaissance prototype, W4051, was substituted. By mid-March, W4050 was back in the air and a new fuselage from the production line was used for W4051.

Later there was a second, less serious, fuselage fracture on the port side aft of the wing while on the ground, and this was patched up. That repair is still evident today where the aircraft is on display at the Mosquito Museum. The weakest point of the fuselage was in the region of the rear access door on the starboard side,

an area that was to suffer from serious water soakage on early production aircraft, and both problems were cured by the fitting of a longitudinal strake, which added strength and helped get rid of water. This became a standard fitment.

In May 1941 invitations were sent out to numerous top-ranking officials at the Ministry, including Beaverbrook, to see the Mosquito put through its paces. Geoffrey did not disappoint. He was a skilled demonstration pilot and on this occasion gave one of his most extravagant displays: blisteringly fast runs a few feet above the ground, high G turns with audible vortices streaming impressively from the wingtips, high-speed vertical climbs to 3,000ft, loops, rolls, dives – and then upward rolls with one propeller feathered, followed by a very slow flypast. If any scepticism lingered, this demonstration banished it forever.

The Mosquito was at the start of a glittering combat career.

W4052

Meanwhile, the fighter prototype, W4052, construction of which was overseen by Fred Plumb, had been completed at Salisbury Hall and was ready for its first flight in May 1941. Plumb looked at the field beside the hangar and wondered if it could be flown straight off, without having to be dismantled and taken to Hatfield. This would save about a month's work. It was tempting, and he asked Geoffrey Jr what his feelings were. Geoffrey, who was generally game for most things, made a careful study of the field: even with a hedge removed, there

BELOW **W4052, the fighter prototype, on a test flight from A&AEE Boscombe Down. The early type exhaust ejector duct can be seen on the starboard engine.** *(Copyright unknown)*

ABOVE The design team on 28 April 1943. Chief designer Ronald E. Bishop (left); Fred Plumb, experimental shop superintendent; Bill Tamblin, senior designer; Percy F. Bryan, chief draughtsman; Richard M. Clarkson, head of aerodynamics and assistant chief engineer; D. King; J.K. Crowe; G.W. Drury; Tim Wilkins, assistant chief designer; Reg Hutchinson; C.F. Willis; Rex King; Bob Harper, chief structural engineer; David R. Newman, aerodynamicist; Frederick T. Watts; Ralph M. Hare; Maurice Herrod-Hempsall; F.J. Hamilton; J.P. 'Phil' Smith; E.H. King; R.J. Nixon; Alan G. Peters; G.C.I. Gardiner. *(BAE Systems/DH982)*

BELOW The sorry sight of W4052 after a forced-landing. Geoffrey de Havilland Jr had been on a test flight on 19 April 1942 when the port engine failed. Lining up for a single-engined landing at Hatfield, he suddenly saw a Proctor taking off, so retracted flaps and gear, carefully opened up the live engine and did a belly-landing at nearby Panshanger. Damage was minor and the aircraft was back in the air less than a month later. *(BAE Systems/DH643E)*

were still only about 450yd. Plumb bet him £1 he wouldn't do it. 'I'll do it,' said Geoffrey, then turned to Fred, 'but you come with me.' Plumb could hardly refuse, and there was indeed just enough room for the take-off run.

Designed to specification F.21/40, W4052 featured extended engine nacelles and sported four 0.303in Browning machine guns in the solid nose, plus four 20mm Hispano cannon under the fuselage with 300 rounds per gun, part of the installation being in the bomb bay. The weaponry meant that the crew entrance had to be moved from directly under the cockpit to the side of the fuselage, but with all the armament concentrated in the nose area, this machine could pack one powerful punch. It also had a flat bullet-resistant windscreen as opposed to

ABOVE **A display to remember. Coming in fast and low with the starboard prop feathered, Geoffrey gives the cameraman a dramatically close view of W4052 during Press day at Hatfield in April 1943. At this point in its career, W4052 sported the standard night-fighter scheme of medium sea grey with dark green camouflage on the upper surfaces. The cine film of Geoffrey's display is preserved at the Imperial War Museum.** *(BAE Systems/DH996)*

BELOW **The third prototype, W4051, which featured the original short engine nacelles, on a test flight.** *(Aeroplane)*

Less than a month later the remaining prototype, W4051, flew on 10 June. With a slightly greater wingspan of 54ft 2in – 20in more than W4050 – it was powered by Merlin 21s and featured the original short engine nacelles. It was unarmed and could carry a wide variety of photographic equipment depending on the mission, including an arrangement whereby two cameras pointing

vertically downwards were synchronised as one unit with the picture areas slightly overlapping to give a stereoscopic image. The PR 1 had a maximum speed of 382mph, could operate up to 35,000ft, and had a range of 2,180 miles.

A month later W4051 bore the distinction of being the first Mosquito to enter RAF service, joining No 1 PRU at Benson on 13 July. The unit later received all 10 of the PR 1 Mosquitoes.

Continuing as the mainstay of experimental flight tests, a mock-up turret was fitted to W4050, and it flew with this in July 1941 – but it robbed the top speed by about 20mph. This aircraft went on to achieve a level speed of 437mph in August 1942. Powered then by the Merlin 61 and piloted by Geoffrey Jr's brother John, also a DH test pilot, this remains the highest speed ever reached by a Mosquito.

Production

Britain

When the first Mosquito deliveries were made to the RAF in July 1941, production was ordered to be stepped up even further in Britain, with large-scale building also to be started at de Havilland Canada at their Downsview, Ontario, premises. Suddenly no one could get enough of the Mosquito, which had now graduated from 'Freeman's Folly' to 'Wooden Wonder'.

Huge expansion for Mosquito production was implemented, with more than 400 subcontractors being brought in from the length and breadth of the country, from furniture manufacturers to piano makers, from small engineering companies to housewives – and this in an era long before the age of mass and instant communication. It was a highly complex operation for the production planners, and the co-ordination involved was extraordinary. The Mosquito may have seemed simple, with its liberal use of wood, but there were 10,000 drawings involved and any mistakes by the subcontractors, many of whom knew nothing about the construction of aircraft and had to be specially trained, could cause great disruption to the schedule.

As the *de Havilland Gazette* put it: 'The drive to increase and expand went out like a great crusade, carried into the byways by teams of car-driving contact men who, despite fires, blast and craters, poor tyres and petrol coupons, struggled to build up the output from hundreds of suppliers. Everyone worked very long hours.'

But the schedules themselves, especially in the early stages, were constantly moving targets. Indecision by the Ministry over the numbers of Mosquitoes needed meant that when an order was finally forthcoming it was so urgent as to be almost impossible to meet, as there had been no opportunity for any forward planning.

In England, fuselage shells were made mainly by the furniture companies Ronson, E. Gomme, Parker Knoll, and Styles & Mealing. Much of the specialised wood veneer used in the construction of the Mosquito was prepared by the Roddis Veneer Company in Marshfield, Wisconsin, USA.

Wing spars were made by J.B. Heath and Dancer and Hearne. Many of the other parts, including flaps, flap shrouds, fins, leading edge assemblies and bomb doors were also produced in High Wycombe, which was suited to these tasks because of a well-established furniture manufacturing industry. Dancer and Hearne processed much of the wood from start to finish, receiving timber and transforming it into finished wing spars at their High Wycombe factory.

Many smaller – and, on the face of it, unlikely – companies were involved in the production of detail parts, including bicycle manufacturers and a firm of craftsmen whose speciality was making ecclesiastical ironwork. Groups of housewives were contracted to make simple parts in garden sheds that had been turned

BELOW Millions like us: Mrs Judd was one of the huge army of factory workers that built the Mosquito. This photograph was taken inside the de Havilland factory at Hatfield in May 1943. *(Imperial War Museum (IWM) TR930)*

into workshops, while other components were made in garages and church halls.

Everything, large or small, had to be produced to the required standard of interchangeability, so inspection techniques had to be set up in accordance with Aeronautical Inspection Directorate requirements. This task was undertaken by the indefatigable Harry Povey, chief production engineer.

British ingenuity and resourcefulness were in full swing – but it wasn't all plain sailing, for there were many difficulties. For example, some of the plywood did not meet specifications and there were problems with a number of the glued joints.

Although Hatfield produced 3,054 Mosquitoes, they couldn't handle everything themselves, so further production was split between their Leavesden factory turning out 1,390, Standard Motors 916, Percival Aircraft 245 and Airspeed 122. But there was more to the operation than just building Mosquitoes: although a carpenter might get out in the field and hack out a damaged piece of Mosquito to splice in some new woodwork, more seriously damaged ones had to be repaired at the factory, with 1,252 being refurbished at Hatfield alone before going back into service.

Other aircraft also came to de Havilland for repair at Hatfield and their factory at Witney in Oxfordshire, including 470 Hurricanes and 335 Spitfires. The total number of aircraft of all types repaired was 2,962 – and all the while production of other machines was going on, in addition to the Mosquito.

All this was against a background of new orders, revision to existing orders, and new combat roles for the Mosquito, which culminated in a staggering total of more than 40 variants made up of photo-reconnaissance types, bombers, fighters, night-fighters, fighter-bombers, and trainers. Workers were averaging 53 hours a week, executives were consistently putting in a 12-hour day, and engineers were constantly on the road introducing programme changes to subcontractors. Everyone was stretched to the limit and de Havilland's engine and propeller divisions were equally hard-pressed, overhauling 9,022 Merlin engines and repairing 40,708 propellers.

It was this British momentum, doggedness and staying power that won us the war.

USAAF MOSQUITOES

'On our way from Hatfield to Boscombe Down, doing 260mph, a USAAF P-38 Lightning fighter pulled alongside us 50 feet away. The pilot made a rude gesture. Duffill, who was piloting me, opened the throttles and just steamed away from him. I could see his surprise, even under goggles' – David King, de Havilland.

Although the Americans didn't want to start building a British aircraft, the appearance and performance of the Mosquito could not be denied. A demonstration by Geoffrey de Havilland Jr to Lord Beaverbrook and Maj Gen Henry 'Hap' Arnold in April 1941 left an indelible mark.

Arnold's aide, Maj Elwood Quesada, remarked how all aviators were affected by appearances, and that if an aeroplane looked fast it usually was fast. 'The Mosquito was, by the standards of the time, an extremely well streamlined aeroplane,' he said later. 'It was highly regarded, highly respected.'

Reflecting to some degree the Air Ministry's scepticism and prevarication, there was little initial enthusiasm for the Mosquito in the States, but Arnold had been greatly impressed and urged the USAAF to take a closer look. But in those early years of the Mosquito, no one – either at home or abroad – was aware of the huge impact the aircraft would have upon the war.

Arnold asked de Havilland to provide plans, data, and photographs of the Mosquito, which were studied by Beechcraft, Hughes, Fairchild, Fleetwings, and Curtiss-Wright, with engineers from Curtiss-Wright spending nearly a month at Hatfield making a detailed assessment.

BELOW *The 'Spook' was originally KB315, an early B VII, and the third* **Mosquito received by the USAAF, as 43-34926. She was one of 40 Mossies delivered to the USAAF in 1943 (and designated F-8) as photo-reconnaissance aircraft.** *The 'Spook' was ferried across the Atlantic for* **delivery to the 32nd Squadron, 5th Pursuit Group, US 12th Air Force, at Oran in Algeria, joining Lockheed F-4 Lightnings and RAF Mosquitoes in the photo-reconnaissance role.** *(US National Archives)*

Not only was there little interest, but the report from Beechcraft was scathing – almost rude: 'It appears as though this airplane has sacrificed serviceability, structural strength, ease of construction and flying characteristics in an attempt to use constructional material which is not suitable for the manufacturing of efficient airplanes.'

The Americans were confident that their forthcoming Lockheed P-38 Lightning would be able to handle all photo-reconnaissance needs, and the last thing they required was some outdated wooden thing. Or so they thought.

Rather like Sir Wilfred Freeman's lone voice against the powers-that-be, Arnold did not give up and believed that, even if they didn't build the Mosquito, the Americans had a lot to learn from it.

But a few days later events overtook

them with the attack on Pearl Harbor on 7 December, and they realised that they were entering the war without a high-performance dual-purpose reconnaissance aircraft, and promptly ordered one Mosquito for evaluation. From then on, as always, the Mosquito's performance and abilities banished all prejudice about wood being no good.

Arnold's steadfast faith in the aircraft had been vindicated, and although none was built in the States, the USAAF ordered 120 Mosquitoes for photo-reconnaissance duties. But only 40 were delivered, made up of 6 Canadian-built B VIIs and 34 B XXs. They were given the US designation of F-8.

The RAF provided 145 PR XVI aircraft to the Eighth Air Force between 22 April 1944 and the end of the war. These were used for a variety of weather, photographic, and night reconnaissance missions, as chaff dispensers and as target-finders for the heavy bomber force. At first pilots were not over-keen on the Mosquito, with its pronounced swing on the take-off run, and some were involved in accidents – but once this characteristic was mastered everyone wanted to fly them.

Operating with the 653rd Bomb Squadron (Light) of the 25th Bombardment Group at Watton, Mosquitoes carried out 1,131 'Blue Stocking' meteorological flights, penetrating deep into Germany and Austria. They also flew scouting missions ahead of bombing raids to report on weather conditions and enemy activity, homing in after the raids to obtain photographic evidence.

In the latter months of the war US Mosquitoes went on American OSS (Office of Strategic Services) 'Red Stocking' missions as part of the high-security operation to obtain intelligence from inside the Reich. They were used as H2X Mickey platforms by the 802nd Reconnaissance Group (Provisional), later renamed the 25th Bomb Group (Reconnaissance). Mickey was an American development of the British H2S radar, the first ground-mapping radar to be used in combat (see page 61).

The 25th Bomb Group lost 29 PR XVIs on operations, including those destroyed in landing or take-off accidents. It was a record that reflected the Mosquito's superiority in hostile airspace.

Canada

Even before the war, de Havilland thought that their Canadian operation would be suitable for building military aircraft, and the Mosquito seemed ideally suited. There was also talk about production in the United States, but negotiations fell through as the Americans didn't want to start building a British design, feeling the P-38 Lightning would handle the role just as well, and in many ways de Havilland were thankful, as it would have been difficult to spare engineers for the USA as well as Canada.

However, Packard had arranged in 1940 to manufacture the Merlin, and their variants of the engine were later installed in Mosquitoes, with adverts such as 'Who puts the buzz into Mosquitoes?'

The Downsview factory near Toronto was engaged on a big order for Tiger Moths and Ansons in 1941, but this was rescheduled, and after discussions agreement was reached on producing the first two Mosquitoes by September 1942, with production reaching 50 a month the following year. An order would be placed by the British Government, but the option was also there for the Royal Canadian Air Force (RCAF) to have their own Mosquitoes.

Thousands of drawings were sent off from Hatfield, while fuselage and wing jigs were prepared for shipping. All did not go smoothly: some of the drawings ended up in Montreal, others found their way to Washington, and tracking these down wasted valuable time. By

the time the fuselage jigs arrived Downsview had made their own, so the British ones were shipped off to Australia – only to be sunk on the way by the Japanese.

It was another nightmare for Harry Povey, who had gone over to organise production in Canada. But later another problem became apparent: a combination of moisture from the glue, the application of heat to speed up the bonding process, and the high humidity of the Toronto climate, was causing variations in the fuselage moulds. Povey suggested concrete moulds. The manufacturing process for these was complex, as great accuracy was needed, but it solved the problem.

The Ministry of Aircraft Production, who would be buying the aircraft from Canada, had ordered 400 bombers, but the RCAF wanted fighters, so Hatfield asked the MAP to revise

ABOVE KB300 was the first Canadian-built Mosquito. She is seen here at de Havilland Canada's Downsview airfield on her maiden flight on 24 September 1942, flown by the company's chief test pilot Ralph Spradbrow. *(BAE Systems)*

LEFT Crowds gather outside de Havilland Canada's Downsview factory on 14 May 1944 to see Hollywood actress Joan Fontaine (a cousin of Geoffrey de Havilland Jr) unveil Mosquito B XX, KB273, specially named 'Joan' in her honour. KB273 can be seen on the right of the picture with the Union flag draped over her nose ready for the actress to unveil. *(BAE Systems)*

ABOVE Canadian-built B 25, KB424, went on to serve the RAF with 608 and 162 Squadrons. *(Copyright unknown)*

the order to 300 bombers and 100 fighters – but then this was cancelled and a Canadian contract was drawn up for fighter-bombers. As in Britain, subcontractors were brought in: General Motors made fuselages, Massey Harris produced wings, Canadian Power

Boats worked on flaps, and Boeing Vancouver constructed tailplanes.

The initial difficulties and setbacks, which were expected in such a massive operation, were eventually ironed out and production settled down. A total of 1,032 Mosquitoes were

LEFT On 13 August 1943 the first Canadian-built Mosquito arrived at Hatfield after a 3,280-mile flight from de Havilland Canada's Downsview, Ontario, factory. B XX, KB161, christened *Acton, Ontario,* **was piloted by Flg Off J.G. Uren, RCAF, with Flg Off R.C. Bevington, RCAF, as his navigator. The first five Canadian-built Mosquitoes were named after cities that had donated the most money in a Canadian Victory War Bond drive. The aircraft named** *Acton, Ontario; New Glasgow, Nova Scotia; Moose Jaw; Saskatoon, Saskatchewan***; and** *Vancouver, B.C.,* **were unveiled on the tarmac at Downsview in July before they were ferried over the Atlantic to England. KB161 went on to serve as a pathfinder with 139 Squadron, but was lost ten months later returning from marking Ludwigshafen when a flare that had hung up in the bomb-bay caught fire, causing the Mossie to crash near Cambridge, killing the pilot.** *(BAE Systems/DH1087)*

built at Downsview – although there is some uncertainty about the exact figure – made up of nine different variants, with 420 going to the RCAF. The initial deliveries to Britain of Canadian-built Mosquitoes were two B XXs in August 1943, and the first operational sortie was a bombing raid on Berlin in December.

Ferrying Mosquitoes from Canada across the Atlantic earned the pilot $1,000 a trip. This was a lot of money in those days, but it was a hazardous operation and there were a small number of losses. Although de Havilland Canada addressed production problems with engine and oil systems, and introduced an extra five hours of testing on production aircraft, the cause was never fully established, although ice forming at high altitude was later a prime suspect.

A batch of B 25s from Canada was adapted for Royal Navy duties in the Far East, while 162, 163, 139, 608 and 627 Squadrons also operated Mosquitoes built in Canada. By 1945 production had outstripped demand, but one surplus fuselage was put to good use by a woman who saw it as the ideal location for her trade, and 'second fuselage from the end' did brisk business for a while. It took the concept of multi-role to an interesting and unforeseen dimension.

After the war, about 200 surplus Canadian Mosquitoes were sold to the Chinese nationalists in 1947 to bolster their civil conflict with the Communists.

Downsview Mosquito production was made up of the following:

B VII: Canadian version based on the Mosquito B V. Two 1,418hp Packard Merlin 31; 25 built.

B XX: Canadian version of the Mosquito B IV. 145 built, of which 40 were converted into F-8 photo-reconnaissance aircraft for the USAAF.

FB 21: Canadian version of the Mosquito FB VI. Two 1,460hp Rolls-Royce Merlin 31; two built.

T 22: Canadian version of the Mosquito T III trainer.

B 23: Unused designation for a bomber variant.

FB 24: Canadian fighter-bomber version. Two 1,620hp Rolls-Royce Merlin 301; one built.

B 25: Improved version of the Mosquito B XX. Two 1,620hp Packard Merlin 225; 400 built.

FB 26: Improved version of the Mosquito FB 21. Two 1,620hp Packard Merlin 225; 338 built.

T 27: Canadian-built training aircraft.

T 29: A number of FB 26 fighters were converted into T 29 trainers.

Australia

The distance for shipping engines, components and materials to the other side of a world at war would be a major undertaking, but in November 1940 Hatfield submitted a report to the authorities in Australia suggesting that Mosquito production might be possible at de Havilland's Bankstown plant near Sydney. However, it wasn't until a year later when it looked as though the Packard Merlin could be supplied from America that the project was given more serious consideration.

Facing logistical problems similar to those in Canada – but with much greater distances involved – the plan finally received the go-ahead from the Australian Government, and de Havilland Sydney were instructed to produce FB 40 fighter-bombers for the Royal Australian Air Force (RAAF). One obstacle which caused delay was the fact that Canadian birch wood

BELOW Australian Mosquito FB 40 production at de Havilland's Bankstown factory in New South Wales, 22 January 1945. The aircraft in the middle foreground is undergoing a quality control check by the Aeronautical Inspection Directorate (AID). *(Copyright unknown)*

was not available, so Australian coachwood was used instead. Shortages of components and a change from Casein to a formaldehyde-based adhesive were to cause further delays in the early stages of production, and after the 22nd aircraft was built there was a serious problem

with a gap occurring on a cemented joint in the wing. Modifications had to be made to 49 other wings, and this caused a lengthy hold-up.

The first Australian Mosquito was delivered on 23 July 1943 and accepted by the RAAF in March the following year. Capt de Havilland's

second of three sons, John, also a test pilot at Hatfield, was planning to go to Australia in August 1943 to familiarise pilots with test-flying procedures, but before he was due to leave tragedy struck. While testing a Mosquito, he and fellow DH test pilot George Gibbins in another Mosquito collided in scattered cloud. The accident took not only the lives of two very fine pilots, but also killed flight-test foreman Nick Carter and aerodynamics department flight observer John Scrope. John de Havilland's place was taken by Pat Fillingham.

The FB 40 was equivalent to the RAF's FB VI, and although 212 were built at Bankstown, only 209 served with the RAAF because three were destroyed in crashes before acceptance. By VJ Day on 15 August 1945, just 108 had been built and so the Mosquito saw very limited service with the RAAF, although it played a brief but effective role in the Pacific War and served with No 1 Photographic Reconnaissance Unit, Nos 87 and 94 Squadrons, No 78 Wing, No 1 Aircraft Performance Unit, Aircraft Research and Development Unit, Central Flying School, No 5 Operational Training Unit, and Ferry-Survey Flights. Six FB 40s were converted for photo-reconnaissance as PR 40s, and were so effective that 28 other FB 40s were converted to PR 41s. These were similar to the PR 40, but had extra

radio gear and were powered by the two-stage supercharged Packard Merlin, whereas the PR 40 used the Merlin 31.

After the war, photo-reconnaissance Mosquitoes were used between 1947 and 1953 on survey flights in Australia. They were phased out in 1954, although a few were transferred to the Royal New Zealand Air Force.

Bankstown Mosquito production was made up of the following:

FB 40: Two-seat fighter-bomber version for the RAAF. Packard Merlin 31 and 33; 178 built.

PR 40: FB 40s converted into photo-reconnaissance aircraft; six built.

PR 41: Two-seat photo-survey version for the RAAF; 28 built (all conversions of FB 40s.

FB 42: Two-seat fighter-bomber version. Two Rolls-Royce Merlin 69. One FB 40 aircraft was converted into a Mosquito FB 42.

T 43: Two-seat training version for the RAAF; 11 FB 40s were converted into Mosquito T 43s.

By the end of the war a total of 6,710 Mosquitoes had been built in Britain, Canada and Australia.

ABOVE T 43 dual-control trainer, was converted on the production line from FB 40 A52-17, served with the RAAF as A52-1052, and was later passed to the Royal New Zealand Air Force as NZ2306. (Jonathan Falconer collection)

'I always felt very proud to have helped the Mosquito to fly.'

A.E. Hurren, de Havilland drawing office

Chapter Two

Building the Mosquito

The fact that the Mosquito was put into production less than two years after the first drawings remains a tribute to de Havilland's unswerving self-belief. They may have had little hands-on experience of military aircraft design, but they knew what was needed and they knew how to do it. Building the Mosquito was an object lesson in ingenuity.

OPPOSITE The assembly track at Hatfield showing a line of wings in the final stages of assembly. To the left of the picture is the rear of a PR IX (MM256), which served with 60 (SAAF) Squadron, and was shot down over France on 13 May 1944 by the famous German ace Horst Hippert. The pilot, Lt W.C. Joubert, and observer Lt C. Mervis, were killed. To the left is an FB VI (LR264), which went to 69 Squadron RAF. *(IWM TR1426)*

Fuselage

The fuselage construction followed the form pioneered on the beautiful and luxurious de Havilland Albatross airliner and was one of the simplest, quickest and most effective methods of producing a monocoque unit, being basically a very strong ply–balsa–ply skin over wooden bulkheads. The division of the fuselage into vertical halves split along the centre line also simplified the installation of hydraulics, electrics and other services, as these could be attached to each section before final assembly, thus giving the ultimate in accessibility. Both halves were built at the same time so that temperature variations affected them equally.

Each half of the fuselage was formed horizontally with the joint line facing downwards and would be built around a male mould of concrete or mahogany, shaped to the contours of the interior. The procedure was similar to that used in other industries for moulded plywood, but in the case of the Mosquito it was done without heat or a pressure chamber. The stiffening and bracing components were constructed integrally with the skin, and the first part of the process was the location of these in slots and recesses in the mould.

Then six of the seven bulkheads were positioned in transverse slots to locate them longitudinally, while laterally they were retained by stops as they were pressed inwards when the skin was applied. Each bulkhead was built from two plywood skins separated by spruce blocks. In highly stressed areas the plywood was placed diagonally, but in less demanding areas it was put on straight to use less material. There were also slots in the mould to attach the bomb-aimer's floor-bearers.

Bomb doors and fuselage lower side panels were made as part of the fuselage halves and later cut out as separate assemblies before attaching the various fixtures and fittings, their stiffening members already provided in the mould. The pick-up points for the one-piece wing were also moulded into the shell halves. Walnut, an extremely strong hardwood, was used where the steel fuselage-to-wing attachment bolt loads were distributed. The walnut carried bearing pads from the bolts and these loads were distributed to the supporting structure.

RIGHT A line of moulds for the fuselage shell halves. The one in the foreground is having sections of the inner ply skin applied, following the insertion of bulkheads through slots in the mould. *(BAE Systems/DH587F)*

The next stage was placing the inner plywood skin of three-ply birch over the structural members. This skin was 1.5 and 2mm thick and applied in relatively large sections, with only the bomb doors being preformed. The vertical joints between panels were arranged to fall between bulkheads, while longitudinal joints were made on spruce stringers forming the stiffening structure between the skins. For the tighter compound curves of the nose section, narrow strips of wood were scarfed and glued together.

The skin was laid over the mould, making contact with the bulkheads and other structural parts to which glue had been applied, and then held tightly in place by broad, flexible, steel bands tightened down by turnbuckles to exert a very high pressure on the structure during the curing process. The bands were placed very close together, almost touching each other, so that an even pressure was applied over the whole skin. The bands had perforations on them so that the skin could be stabbed to allow excess adhesive to ooze out.

Before the ⅜in balsa sandwich pieces were fitted, the inner skin was stiffened with laminated spruce strips screwed through the skin and on to the bulkheads, and then longitudinal stiffening members of spruce gave reinforcement in specific locations. Doors and other access points were given a cemented surround of spruce doublers before being cut out.

Next came the fitting of the balsa filling between the skins. Sections were cut to size until the whole surface had been covered, cement being applied after dry fitting. Once again the steel bands held everything good and firm as the glue dried, but the bands were lightly greased on the inner surface to prevent the balsa sticking to them. When the adhesive had cured the bands were removed and the balsa smoothed before the outer skin was cemented and held tightly in place as before.

Fitting out

The next stage was for the two fuselage halves to be removed from the jig, cleaned up and sent to the assembly department to be prepared for the installation of ancillary equipment. Templates were used for fixing

ABOVE Fuselage halves in various stages. The middle one has had the inner ply skin applied and is having the inter-layer of balsa blocks fitted before the top skin is glued on. *(BAE Systems/DH933I)*

LEFT Interior of starboard fuselage half. This method of construction made the installation of fittings and services much easier than on conventional metal airframes. *(BAE Systems/DH522A)*

LEFT Bare fuselage shells. These were built in pairs to avoid temperature variation. (BAE Systems/DH3354H)

CENTRE Lines of fuselage halves awaiting installation of equipment. In the background are two de Havilland DH 89 Dominie fuselages. (BAE Systems/DH511)

BOTTOM Port fuselage half with some cockpit fittings installed. (Copyright unknown)

ferrules at specific points on the interior, and this work had to be accurate as many of the fittings came with jig-drilled mounts. Then the bomb doors and side panels were cut out to be completed and furnished with metal parts in the wood detail shop.

While the fuselage was still in two halves, as much equipment as possible was fitted before they were joined. This made the operation so much quicker and more simple than on conventional metal aircraft. The assembly was also simplified by having control cable runs down the port side of the fuselage and hydraulics on the starboard. The control column was also installed on the port shell and connected to the rudder and elevator cables before the halves were joined, and all metal fittings were grounded with copper strip. Well over half the installation process was completed in the half-shell stage, which represented a huge saving in assembly time, for there was not the restricted space of an enclosed fuselage where only a limited number of fitters could operate.

The work was carried out carefully and efficiently, for there was a tremendous atmosphere of dedication and teamwork at Hatfield – and the hours put in were extraordinary, with workers often accruing 100 a week. Everyone knew that they were playing a big part in the war effort and producing one of the RAF's finest aircraft. Working conditions were rather unusual in that the blackout was enforced morning and night, so for much of the year people arrived in the dark and went home in the dark, but twice a day for half an hour the BBC's *Music While You Work* was played on the radio and relayed round the factory. It was something to look forward to, it was

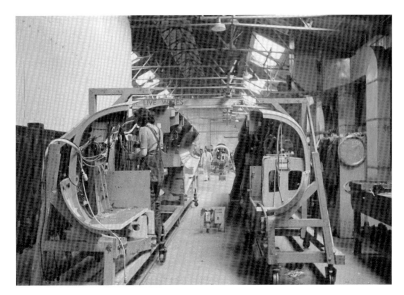

RIGHT **Fuselage half-shells being fitted out before being bonded as a single unit.** *(Copyright unknown)*

CENTRE **A basic fuselage nearly ready for the doping stage.** *(Copyright unknown)*

BOTTOM **Cockpit canopies being assembled.** *(BAE Systems/DH1210C)*

appreciated, and was a far cry from today's ceaseless music.

When all possible fittings had been installed it was time to join the fuselage halves, a process known as 'boxing up'. Both sections were placed on trunnions with levelling pads for precise longitudinal and transverse alignment using a clinometer. Plumb bobs suspended from the midpoints of the bulkheads were aligned with datum markings on the floor to maintain the position of the fuselage centre line. The large gap for the wing assembly was temporarily strengthened with a jury strut to prevent distortion during assembly of the fuselage.

The two halves were drawn tightly together by using circular laminated wooden cramps, tightened with turnbuckles, the join being achieved by scarfing together with V-cuts on the starboard side interlocking with V-recesses on the port one. The skin was then rebated on both sides of the centre line for a plywood strip to be placed flush with the fuselage skins. On the inside, this strip was then covered with a further strip twice as wide before everything was glued and screwed into place.

With the two halves joined lobster-shell fashion, further equipment was installed, such as instrument panels and more wiring and plumbing. At the rear of the fuselage the remaining bulkhead, number seven, was fitted, and this carried the rear fin and tailplane attachment components. Bulkhead number six, in front of it, carried the front fin fastening and slots were cut in the top of the fuselage to take the fittings. Careful levelling and accuracy was necessary at the rear. For example, where bulkhead seven was fitted the tolerance between it and the skin had to be no

MOSQUITO WOMEN

Whether working at home or on the factory floor, women played a major role in the construction and fitting-out of the Mosquito, many having to combine the traditional domestic role of housewife with long hours on the production line.

1 Running through the checklist for bomb-bay fittings. *(Copyright) unknown)*

2 Dope being applied to a fabric tape around the nose cut-out. *(Copyright unknown)*

3 The installation of hydraulics and other cockpit services. *(Copyright unknown)*

4 Drilling a Mosquito's port engine inner side cowling. *(BAE Systems/DH754B)*

5 Aileron assembly. The one on the right has been skinned and the trim tab fitted. *(BAE Systems/DH754C)*

6 An RAF roundel being sprayed on the port wing with the aid of a template. *(BAE Systems/DH959F)*

7 Dope being applied to the rear of a Mosquito fuselage. *(BAE Systems/DH1846D)*

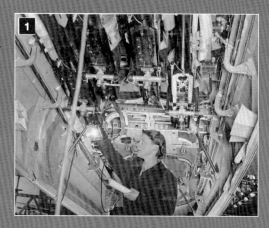

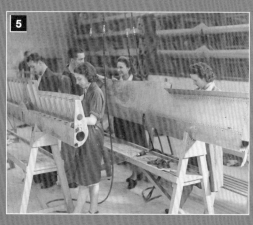

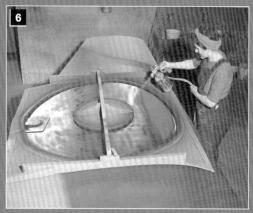

ABOVE Wrighton Aircraft produced many Mosquito fuselages and wings, often operating under very difficult conditions in Walthamstow, a heavily bombed part of London. Here, the staff celebrate the production of their 1,000th fuselage. *(BAE Systems/DH18400D)*

RIGHT Another fuselage shell leaves the premises of High Wycombe furniture makers Styles & Mealing. *(BAE Systems/DH1940E)*

more than 0.015in – a very exacting figure for wood. Checking this was difficult for a person of average height and build, owing to the restricted space inside the rear of the fuselage, so this was a job for very small people.

With the cockpit opening cut out from a template and the edges brush-painted, the canopy itself was lowered as a sub-assembly and bolted into place. With the fitting of the instrumentation, radio equipment and all hydraulic and electrical circuitry possible at this stage, the fuselage was ready for the final assembly line.

Wing

The wing, which had been designed primarily by Bill Tamblin, bore more than a passing resemblance to other de Havilland creations – in particular the DH 88 Comet Racer, with its tapered wings terminating in a narrow tip. It was built in one piece with an exceptionally smooth surface, free from the rivets of a metal-skinned wing, and at its heart was a conventional two-spar construction with inter-spar ribs. But a wing able to take the stresses of combat flying put huge demands on the design team and stretched them to the limit, with many tests having to be done to measure the performance properties of the wood, method of construction and optimising the stress distribution. Eventually two spars with tip-to-tip top and bottom booms of laminated spruce boxed with plywood webs were selected as the ultimate. The section chosen was RAF 34 with modified camber, which gave a low maximum lift coefficient resulting in a flat landing approach.

Spruce was the ideal wood for aircraft manufacture. The trees are very tall, thus allowing long uninterrupted lengths, have few knots, a straight grain, and low density for the

RIGHT Wooden
panels and strips
being prepared at
Walter Baker of High
Wycombe. *(BAE
Systems/DH1940J)*

BELOW Construction
of the rear wing spar
and booms, a complex
assembly combining
forward sweep and
dihedral. *(Copyright
unknown)*

best strength-to-weight ratio. But selection of trees was critical, and in fact only one in ten Canadian spruces was suitable for the Mosquito's 50ft spars. And that wasn't the end of it, for Air Ministry specification DTD 36B detailed the parameters for moisture, density, brittleness and straightness of grain, plus how to test for these, as well as other requirements.

Although de Havilland were the leaders in wooden construction, the Mosquito was going to be subjected to far higher stresses than any of their previous designs, and they knew that the diagonal spruce wing planking used on the Albatross would not be up to the job

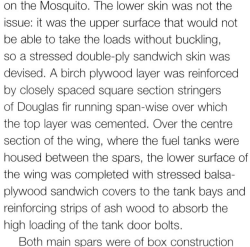

on the Mosquito. The lower skin was not the issue: it was the upper surface that would not be able to take the loads without buckling, so a stressed double-ply sandwich skin was devised. A birch plywood layer was reinforced by closely spaced square section stringers of Douglas fir running span-wise over which the top layer was cemented. Over the centre section of the wing, where the fuel tanks were housed between the spars, the lower surface of the wing was completed with stressed balsa-plywood sandwich covers to the tank bays and reinforcing strips of ash wood to absorb the high loading of the tank door bolts.

Both main spars were of box construction with spruce booms of three laminations and plywood webs on either side. In theory, the booms could have been solid spruce beams, but laminations made construction easier and were the best use of spruce resources – and they were just as strong, if not stronger, as tests showed that the wood fibres tore before the glued joints. During production these three laminations became ten, which saved considerably more wood. And laminating had a further advantage in that it eliminated the shrinkage and warping to which a single long piece of timber would be prone. The front spar laminations were arranged horizontally, the rear vertically, and this gave a torsionally very stiff box structure.

New glue

A technique was developed for sawing laminations to an extraordinary accuracy of 0.010in, the edges left rough so that the glue had a better key. The glueing operation was critical, and the first type used was Casein, a milk-based adhesive which de Havilland had used for years. But it had one unfortunate problem in that it encouraged fungal growth, and a Mosquito full of fungus was not an ideal scenario, so a search began for something better. Aero Research Ltd at Duxford, headed by Dr Norman A. de Bruyne, who listed 'inventing' as his recreation in *Who's Who,* had developed a synthetic resin known as Beetle glue and this proved entirely satisfactory, being exceptionally strong and the forerunner of ReDux (ReDux being a contraction of Research at Duxford). Beetle, which was introduced in 1942, was more resistant than Casein to humidity and the kind of huge temperature variations that would be experienced by Mosquitoes operating at very high altitude and in climates all over the world.

The upper and lower spar booms were constructed differently. With the top boom the centre and main outer sections were built to full depth and then Beetle resin was applied to the faces of the laminations with a rubber squeegee before the whole assembly was placed in a screw press for bonding. With the thinner lower spar each lamination was built to its full span by scarfing and glueing a number of shorter lengths. The dihedral was formed by a specially shaped section in the centre, and then the laminations were coated with resin before being moved to a purpose-made block to give the exact angle of forward sweep. Screw clamps were used to force the assembly hard against the base of the fixture, and as the glue cured the assembly dried to the correct shape. This was followed by rough machining and then final finishing, checked by straight edges against datum blocks.

Next came the plywood spar webs, which were short lengths spindled to shape and drilled for fixing to the boom in wooden jigs. Scarfing of these lengths to make the complete web was done by machine and the sections were then precisely aligned on a table between pads so

ABOVE Rear spars and booms under construction at the Kingsbury premises of coach builders Vanden Plas. After the war the company made parts for the de Havilland DH 100 Vampire. *(BAE Systems/DH1127C)*

that the scarfed ends overlapped. Beetle glue was then applied and the joints were allowed to cure under pressure.

Final assembly of the spars was done on special sloped platforms to accommodate the forward sweep of the rear unit, and security was provided by wedges driven against their inner faces and the locating blocks. Throughout the whole procedure up to this stage an astonishing

BELOW Construction work on a rear spar and boom at Parker Knoll, who also produced wing leading edge assemblies. *(BAE Systems/DH1940D)*

tolerance of 0.02in was maintained on each half of the boom.

Spruce spacers between the upper and lower boom were positioned with templates, and Beetle cement was applied to booms, spacers, and the underside of the web, which was then positioned and screwed down, sufficient pressure for setting coming from the screws. But Beetle cement had one disadvantage, and that was the time it took to cure at ambient room temperature. This would cause a long delay, as no further work could be done on the spar until the adhesive had fully set, so it was decided that electrical heating would have to be devised to speed things up. This was not as easy as it may sound, as it was not possible to apply heat directly to the cement line, and the glued area varied considerably over the span. Another difficulty was applying heat evenly, because a door at

one end of the wing made that part of the shop floor cooler than the other end, which was near the canteen.

A solution was found with the expertise of the Northmet Power Company from north London, who devised a scheme whereby a number of wooden heating panels were placed on the spar web while it was on its platform. These panels had wire heating elements in the base and they were connected to the AC mains. Current was then supplied from bus bars carrying about 40 amps, while balancing resistors kept each panel to the correct heating figure. An ingenious thermostatic control maintained the temperature to within 1.5°F throughout the length of the spar, regardless of room temperature variations, and thermometers could be plugged straight into the glue line as a double-check.

When bonding was complete the spar was turned over and the webbing fixed to the other side, followed by the rib posts, which were bonded and screwed into place. The completed spars were then ready for the drilling jig in preparation for the various steel or metal components such as undercarriage mountings and hinge brackets for the ailerons.

Methods for constructing the skin panels were very similar to those for the spar booms. Stringers were made up from scarf-jointed shorter lengths of Douglas fir. The lower surface was a single skin with stringers, while the upper was a ply–stringer–ply sandwich. The stringers

were placed in slots on a table, the cement was applied to them and to the underside of the skin, and then the skin was laid in place determined by metal location stops. Screws were used to give extra strength and to apply the necessary pressure for the glue to bond. The motto for Mosquito construction was 'never glue without a screw' – although there is some uncertainty as to the origin of this. The result was that a complete wing assembly contained about 30,000 brass screws.

Assembly

The wing was assembled on a jig with the leading edge at the base and the trailing edge at the top, so the work was done with it in a vertical position. Locating blocks ensured that the spars were in the correct place, and in the case of the front spar this was achieved by attaching the engine bearer fittings, which were secured by pins to the pick-up points on the jig. The undercarriage radius road attachment brackets were used in a similar way for locating the rear spar.

With the spars forced firmly into place by special jacks, the wing was ready for the inter-spar ribs to be fitted – 16 for each half. But the ribs were not all the same: rib number one, nearest the centre line of the aircraft, was a sturdy L-section made up of a heavy three-ply web with a top boom of five spruce laminations

and a bottom boom of Douglas fir. Ribs two to six were of conventional box section with spruce booms and plywood webs, while rib seven and the remainder were of half-box construction with the web attached only on the inboard side.

Outboard ribs were simply glued and tacked to the rib posts on the inner faces of the spars, ribs two, five and six were glued and screwed, while ribs three and four, which were the engine bearing ribs, were bolted to metal fittings on both sides of the spars. These fittings were part of the undercarriage structure.

With all ribs in place, it was time to attach the bottom wing skin by drilling and screwing through the rib booms – but at this stage only from rib six to the tip, as the inner part of both wings would be taken up with fuel tanks, the engine nacelles and undercarriage, which were yet to be fitted.

ABOVE Construction of the engine mounting frames at furniture manufacturers Evertaut. (BAE Systems/DH1210A)

BELOW A partially completed airframe, showing engine mounting frame and undercarriage legs and struts. (BAE Systems/ DH582E)

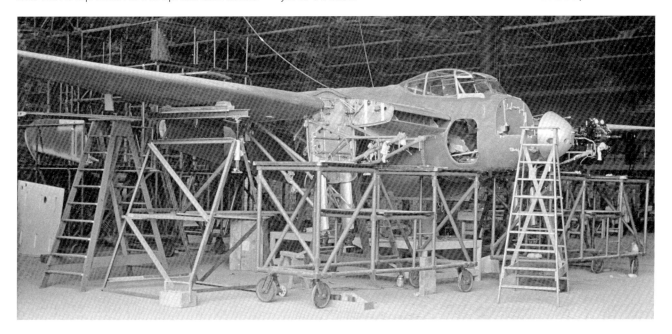

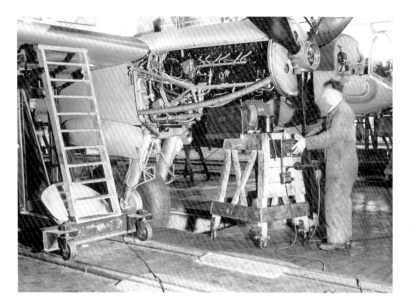

ABOVE A fitter at work on the starboard Merlin. The channels in the factory floor to accommodate the lowered undercarriage can be seen. *(Copyright unknown)*

BELOW A Merlin mounted in the starboard wing receiving attention from the fitters. *(Copyright unknown)*

The inner top skin, with its stringers already glued to the outer surface, was known as the inner shell and was offered up and secured before the fitting of the top skinning. The outboard sections were the first to be assembled on to the wing, and after being fitted on the spars the shell was laid on trestles and drilled for attachment along the edges and and on the rib joint lines from templates. This shell section was then offered up to the wing structure and held in place temporarily with a few screws while the spar booms and rib booms were counterbored to depth for the fixing screws.

The skin of the outboard sections of the inner shell extended beyond the inboard end of the stringers, and the centre section was made up simply as a narrow panel of skin to form the surface between the port and starboard number one ribs, the stringers projecting beyond it on each side. The ends of these stringers were tapered off to make a scarf joint between the centre and outboard members.

The centre section was then dry-fitted and the edges drilled for temporary attachment before wedge cramps were fixed to the scarfed ends of the stringers to hold them in place. The cramps were simple, ingenious and highly effective, and were designed by one of the shop personnel. Each consisted of two parallel jaws connected by a bolt, which allowed some play. The jaws would then be placed over the two components to be compressed, and a tapered wedge would then be driven between the jaws from the back, forcing them to clamp very tightly at the front.

The skin attachment screws were inserted from the interior of the fuel tank bays, and at this stage spacers were placed between the stringers at various points over the outboard panels and around access and inspection cutouts on the skin surface.

Glued and screwed

The centre section, which had been only dry-fitted, was then taken down and Beetle glue applied before it was replaced and screwed onto the wing structure. Attachment booms in the form of spruce strips were screwed on to the spar booms, and finally the stringer scarf joints were glued and held under pressure with the wedge cramps for the duration of the curing process.

Water-resisting white cellulose paint was brushed on to the new wood assembled in the inner shell, and then the top surface of the stringers was faired and all excess glue removed to provide a good, clean surface for the top skinning to be applied. This consisted of three panels that were pre-drilled for fixing to the inner shell, and after it was lined up in position it was used as a template for counterboring the stringers and booms.

Rather than applying cement to the stringers, the whole of the inner surface of the

top skin was coated with Beetle glue to double up as adhesive and a waterproof coating for the plywood. The skin was lifted by several men and placed on to the wing structure, which was still in its vertical assembly fixture, and then screwed into place through the spar booms and inner skin stringers. More than 4,000 brass screws were used to secure just this one skin surface and battens were cramped along the edges of the skin over the spar booms to give maximum bonding. Additional security was provided from run stations one to six by anchor bolts through the skin and inner shell into the rib booms. Then the very strong and hard walnut mounting pads were fitted over both number one ribs to mate with the fuselage wing pick-up points.

To give a super-smooth wing surface, all screw heads on the skin were covered with filler, and the wing assembly was then ready for removing from its fixture, this being done with special purpose-made bogies fitted with a vertical framework to hold the wing. The whole assembly was wheeled out for the wing to be picked up by a crane and lowered, upside down, on to cradles for the fitting of the leading edge, flaps and aileron shrouds.

Apart from the undercarriage bays between ribs three and four, the whole interior of the wing between rib six on each side was taken up with fuel tanks. The bottom surface over this part of the spar was stressed, but was

detachable for the installation or removal of the tanks. The tank covers were fitted and assembled when the wing was in the cradle, and attachment angles were fixed round the inside of each tank bay and drilled from

ABOVE A consignment of fuel tanks being prepared at Gallay Ltd of Willesden, London. *(BAE Systems/DH1127E)*

BELOW Proudly lined up in front of rows of Mosquito drop tanks are the staff of W.L. Thurgood, coach-builders of Ware in Hertfordshire. They had much to be proud of: dispirited as demand for custom-built coach bodies dried up with the outbreak of war, they then suffered a far greater tragedy when a German bomb demolished their premises – yet within five months they had it rebuilt and up and running. They were soon working flat-out producing fuselage components and jettisonable wing tanks for the Mosquito, and after the war they returned to coach-building. *(BAE Systems/DH1899C)*

ABOVE A Mosquito B 25 nears completion on the assembly line at Downsview, Canada, in September 1944 as men and women work on the wing fixtures. The complex radiator piping and ducting can be seen on the starboard wing. *(Copyright unknown)*

BELOW B IV airframes nearing completion. *(Copyright unknown)*

templates for GKN aero-tight anchor nuts. The tank doors were plywood and balsa sandwich units with a spruce stiffening structure and were glued together in screw presses.

The remainder of the undercarriage fittings on ribs three and four were installed at this stage, along with the corresponding part of the fuselage pick-up on the walnut blocks on rib one. The wing leading edge was also attached, and was built conventionally from formed plywood skin with internal stiffening nose ribs. It was fixed to the wing by lapping the rear edges of the skin into the rebates on the front spar booms. It was glued, screwed and held securely while curing by canvas bands drawn back tightly over the wing and gripped in place by cramps mounted on the rear spar.

Aileron hinge brackets were attached to pre-drilled locations on the rear spar with shims for accurate alignment. The ailerons were then swung on their hinges to ensure free movement and to check that they cleared the shrouds. At this point the wings were almost ready for doping; there were just the engine and radiator fairings to fit on the upper surface and the installation – but not connection – of the flap control cables. Then the wing was lowered vertically by crane on to bogies and taken to the paint shop where two coats of red nitrate dope were applied.

When this was dry the whole surface was laid over with a close-weave fabric known as Madapolam, which took its name from a village in India, where Britain had a cloth factory. This covering was shrunk tightly with three coats of red dope and two of aluminium dope, and was similar to the techniques used in traditional balsa-and-tissue aeromodelling. The fabric was pulled tight in all directions and gave great surface strength. Finally, camouflage paint was applied.

Electrical and hydraulic services, coolant piping, control runs and undercarriage mountings were then completed, fuel tanks were installed, engine support struts assembled, and the wing was ready for the tips to be attached. These were small and simple structures that were skinned with ply, with a cut-out at the front corner for the navigation lamp. They were attached to the wings by

means of screws through a Bakelite-reinforced strip on the inboard edges, thus completing the wing structure.

Tailplane and fin

The Mosquito's tailplane looked like a smaller version of the wing – but reversed, with a swept-back leading edge as opposed to the wing's swept-forward trailing edge. The tailplane's format was reflected in the fin and rudder, which was mounted slightly in front of the tailplane.

Construction of both units was very similar to that of the wing, the tailplane being made in one complete piece incorporating spars that were miniature versions of the wing. As with the wing, the tailplane was built up on a vertical fixture – but in this case in two sections, with the leading edge constructed first at a comfortable working height.

The front spar was located to datum centre lines on the front web, and locations were also on the fixture for the outer end ribs to govern the overall length. This was critical, as the elevator horn balances would overlap the tips

of the tailplane, so there had to be enough clearance for their operation. Datum lines on the spar and ribs were used for the accurate positioning of the ribs, which were glued and pinned in place. The curve of the leading edge was also set by a datum line before being cemented and screwed in place, with final shaping being done by hand with templates used at each rib station to check for accuracy.

Construction of the main section of the tailplane began with the attachment of fittings to the rear spar, such as elevator hinge brackets, and the spar was then located on to the building fixture for the fitting of the inter-spar ribs. These were of box construction and were assembled by sliding them over rib posts mounted on the inner web of each spar and then glueing and pinning them in place. At the outer ends, templates were used for locating the ribs, all rib profiles were faired by hand, and incidence of the tailplane in relation to its fittings was checked with a clinometer.

Skinning on each side was done as single panels scarfed from smaller pieces, with inspection apertures cut out and reinforced with ply. After the first skin was attached in the usual way with Beetle cement and screws, all metal fittings were completed and the whole of the interior sprayed with white water-resistant paint. With the second skin fitted, all imperfections were stopped up before the application of Madapolam, dope and camouflage paint, thus completing the assembly.

Construction of the fin followed almost exactly the same procedure as the tailplane.

Flaps

Because the engine nacelle fairings extended beyond the trailing edge of the wing, the flaps had to be made in two sections linked by a torque tube that passed through the nacelle. This tube was itself in two parts joined in the centre by a cranked fitting that incorporated the centre hinge and connecting lug for the hydraulic jack, which was pivoted on the rear spar of the wing. The ram of the jack operated through the gap in the torque tube formed by the cranked centre fitting.

Construction was conventional, but unlike the wings and tailplane, which were assembled on a vertical fixture, the flaps were built

BELOW Wing flap assembly, which was split either side of the engine nacelle. *(Copyright unknown)*

horizontally and consisted basically of a nose section formed by the leading edge and spar and connected to the trailing edge by ribs. The two nose sections with torque tube were built as one unit, the first step being to fit the tube attachment spools to the inner ribs of each flap section. Location for the tube was taken from the jack connection and centre hinge bracket.

The remainder of the nose ribs were then located and faired in before the application of Beetle cement for the fitting of the preformed leading edge skin, after which the assembly was removed for the gluing, screwing and pinning of the spar to the nose ribs. The leading edge section was taken to a second assembly fixture where, as before, it was located from the hinge and jack fittings on the torque tube.

As with the wings and tailplane, the inside of the flaps were sprayed with water-resistant paint, the second skin was cemented and the whole assembly went for doping and covering with Madapolam. A final check on hinge alignment was made with a template.

Undercarriage legs

The undercarriage of the Mosquito, with its rubber compression blocks for suspension, was an exercise in simplicity, economy of materials and ease of repair. However, what made it unusual was its use in an aircraft of that size: until then, rubber for the oleo had been confined to lightweight types such as primary trainers. It was also quick to manufacture, as there was no need for the kind of precision machining necessary on the tubes of oleo-pneumatic units, and servicing was minimal with no hydraulic joints to maintain.

The leg was extremely simple, the casing being split on the centre line and each half comprising a semi-elliptical pressing formed from 16-gauge DTF 124 steel, complete with joint flanges. The operational part of the leg consisted of a piston tube connected at the base to the wheel axle, and at the upper end to an elliptically shaped piston of laminated and fabric-reinforced Bakelite, which worked inside the casing. Immediately above this, and bearing down upon it, were the rubber compression units made up from 12 separate pieces packed vertically with separators

between each one and rubbed with graphite powder to act as a lubricant. There were ten full-size and two half-size blocks in the assembly. A guide block, also of Bakelite, in the lower part of the casing served as a bearing and guide for the piston.

Each rubber block was moulded with two locating lobes on its upper face and two recesses on the underside, so that the whole assembly was self-aligning. A rebound rubber block was mounted at the lower end of the leg between the piston and the guide block. It was found in service that there was very little loss of resilience in the rubber, and it could easily be restored by replacing just one half-size block, rather than the whole pack.

Assembly of the leg was quick and straightforward. When the casing halves were received from the press shop, their flanges were drilled for joining, which was done on a bench-mounted squeeze-riveting machine.

Each wheel and brake assembly was held between two compression legs, a mudguard was mounted on the rear of the frame some distance from the tyre, and retraction was backwards into the nacelle, actuated by a jack.

BELOW Completed undercarriage installation on the starboard wing of W4051. *(Copyright unknown)*

LEFT Mosquito production well under way at Downsview in Canada. The placard in the background says: 'Bay 3. Weekly production of Mosquitos. This week's objective – 10; production to date – 4.' *(BAE Systems)*

CENTRE A proud moment as the first Canadian-built Mosquito, a B VII (KB300), is towed out of the factory. It is being pulled by a Ford N Series tractor. *(Copyright unknown)*

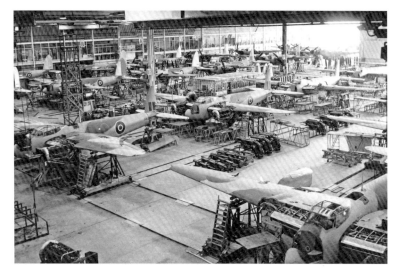

BOTTOM Mosquitoes in the latter stages of assembly at Leavesden in 1943. Some are awaiting fitment of engines, which can be seen on the factory floor, while others require rudders and elevators. HK290 in the foreground is an F II. It went to Marshalls of Cambridge in June 1943 for conversion to Mk XVII with AI Mk X/SCR 720 radar before it joined 456 (RAAF) Squadron later that year. *(BAE Systems/DH1048D)*

Final assembly

With all the various components completed, it was time for final assembly, and for this two special U-shaped track systems were laid out – one for fighter variants, the other for bombers and PR types. The aircraft would start at one end and move round for various stages of assembly until it ended up at the paint shop. For ease of working, the aircraft were supported at a very low level throughout the process.

First, the wing assembly was mounted on cradles, one under each wing outboard of the engine nacelles, with levelling adjustment provided by screw-jacks. Ladders were also fitted to the cradles for work on the wing's top surface. With the wing accurately set up, the fuselage was lowered on to it by an overhead crane for the five pick-up points to be bolted together – two on the top of the wing, three on the rear spar – followed by the fuselage side panels below the wing. Then the whole thing was moved sideways on the bogies for the next stage of assembly, which was the tailplane and fin. These were bolted to rear fuselage bulkhead number seven, followed by the tailwheel and its mudguard. Then came the main undercarriage, after which a levelling check was made on the engine mountings.

Two of the next items to be installed were the distinctive leading edge radiators, which incorporated engine coolant, oil coolers and cabin heaters, and for this operation a jig was made that was really a dummy radiator. This was located on the radiator pick-up points on the front spar, and at its inboard end the jig had a profile plate with holes representing the pick-up points on the radiator end rib on the side of the fuselage. This rib was aligned to the jig to give interchangeability of assembly when the radiator was mounted.

Then everything was wheeled on to the next part of assembly, which was the fitting of the inboard fuel tanks, radio equipment and bomb racks to take four 500lb bombs in two pairs. (This process varied for FB and PR variants). The bomb-bay doors were then hung in position.

Next was the fitting of the engines. These were installed as complete units with all accessories in place, and were lowered into position from an overhead conveyor track, followed by the connecting up of all engine controls to the cockpit. The engine nacelle fairings were attached to angle pieces on the bottom booms of the engine ribs and the undercarriage doors were hung.

At the end of the first half of the assembly process engine inspections were carried out and then the aircraft was moved to the return section of the U-track by an ingenious system of small tracked turntables that moved through 90° to line it up with the return. This last part of the journey was mainly for completing electrical connections and testing the various systems, including undercarriage operation. This was done without having to alter the assembly height of the aircraft, being achieved with pits sunk into

the floor below the nacelles so that connections and adjustments could be made at floor level.

The de Havilland Hydromatic propellers were lowered from overhead conveyors and positioned on to the engine shafts, the spinners were fitted, and then the aircraft was ready for the final stages before going to the paint shop. Bomb operating gear was tested, various AID (Aeronautical Inspection Directorate) inspections were made, the coolant system was tested, and a complete final check-over of the whole aircraft was made. This completed the construction and assembly operations.

ABOVE A day to celebrate as personnel from Downsview are photographed with the 1,000th Mosquito (FB 26, KA406) to roll off the Canadian production line. *(TopFoto/The Granger Collection, New York)*

BELOW The last Mosquito B 35 off the Hatfield production line, (TK656), with 56 of the men who built her. As she progressed through the assembly stages, many of them painted their initials on parts of the airframe and when she reached the paint shop she was covered with signatures. She was rolled out for this historic photograph on 27 June 1946. *(BAE Systems/DH2320)*

'What a beautiful little aircraft this is, I thought, looking at the trim silhouette of the leading Mosquito, its carpentered lines, slender, its tail cockily high, the big Roll-Royce engines gulping down the miles. The Mosquito: tough, belligerent, swashbuckling – fastest two-seater in the world.'

Pete Rowland, pilot, 105 Squadron

Chapter Three

Mosquito at war

Until it took off in anger, no one could have foreseen the effect the Mosquito would have on the war, or of the almost limitless roles it would fulfil. It was a spy in the sky, it was a bomber, it was a fighter, it was able to pack a crippling punch from guns, rockets or bombs, and it pioneered precision bombing with spectacular success.

OPPOSITE From mid-1943 the Light Night Striking Force (LNSF), an offshoot of 8 (Pathfinder) Group, used Mosquitoes exclusively for diversionary and harassing raids on Germany. This is B XVI, ML963, '8K-K', of 571 Squadron, pictured in 1944. Among the squadron's initial allocation of four aircraft from 692 Squadron, she failed to return from a Berlin trip on 10–11 April 1945, but her crew of Flg Off R.D. Oliver and Flt Sgt L.M. Young, RAAF, evaded capture and returned to their squadron before the month was out. *(RAF Museum)*

Photo-reconnaissance

At the start of the war Britain was short of effective reconnaissance aircraft. So was Germany – but we did something about it quicker than they did, recognising the urgent need for this role. Although the Spitfire had the necessary performance to bring back photographic information from enemy territory, it was let down by limited range. The Mosquito provided the perfect answer, able to perform equally well as an unarmed PR platform as an unarmed bomber.

In the early stages of the war, No 1 Photographic Reconnaissance Unit (PRU) at Benson in Oxfordshire had been operating Spitfires successfully, but the arrival of the Mosquito gave them so much more, such as greater range, the security of two engines, and an extra crew member to operate the navigational equipment and thus ease the load on the pilot. From the nose transparency he would also have an excellent view, which would ensure greater accuracy on PR missions.

The first Mosquito for No 1 PRU was the prototype, W4051, whose original fuselage had been used as a replacement for W4050 after the Boscombe Down tailwheel mishap. It arrived at Benson on 13 July 1941, followed soon after by W4054 and W4055. Pilots loved them, although many younger engineers were sceptical, thinking the wooden construction outdated. But they soon learned the error of

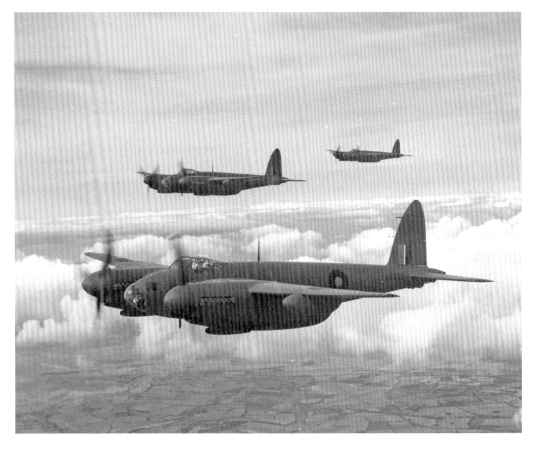

their assumptions and came to appreciate the strength and durability of the aircraft, plus the ease of repair.

As the initial PR machines were about to be delivered, the first order for bombers was issued, with the result that nine of the PR 1s had to be completed as the B IV Series 1 – another instance of the Ministry's constantly changing requirements for the Mosquito which caused so much disruption to the production schedule.

By September Benson had five PR 1s out of a total of nine built, two of which were later tropicalised for operation in the Mediterranean and Far East theatres. These had the original short engine nacelles, were powered by the Merlin 21 of 1,480hp, and had metal-skinned elevators.

The first reconnaissance mission for No 1 PRU was when old Etonian Sqn Ldr Rupert Clerke and navigator Sgt Sowerbutts, a former Margate barber, took off on the morning of 17 September in W4055 to photograph Brest and the Spanish–French frontier, flying at around 24,000ft. It was not a success, as the generator failed, leaving the batteries with insufficient current to operate the cameras, but on the way home they were jumped by three Messerschmitt Bf 109s. To the surprise of the German pilots, their 109s were humiliatingly outpaced by the Mosquito, which convincingly demonstrated that it didn't need armament.

The PR 1 prototype, W4051, was kept busy as operations intensified, bringing back pictures of the French coast before the Commando raid on St-Nazaire in March 1942, and Benson were

carrying out up to ten sorties a day during May, penetrating deep into Europe and scanning many targets as far afield as northern Norway and Czechoslovakia. Unlike the Spitfire, which was restricted by its range, the Mosquito had the fuel reserves to photograph three or more areas in one mission. Apart from targets on land, Mosquitoes kept a close eye on the movements of German battleships, W4051 taking superb shots with her 24in camera of the *Gneisenau* in dry dock at Kiel.

High-resolution cameras

So effective were the Benson-based Mosquitoes in their roles of pre-bombing raid reconnaissance, post-raid assessment, tracking down German warships and locating enemy tactical sites such as radar installations, that in October No 1 PRU was disbanded and re-established as five squadrons – 540, 541, 542, 543 and 544 – but on the last day of the squadron's operation as a single unit, W4058 flew to Oslo and never returned. However, losses were generally not high, the average being one per 470 hours of operational flying.

In November two Mosquito PR IVs that joined the squadron were fitted with multiple ejector exhausts instead of the saxophone-shaped manifolds enclosed in flame shrouds for night operations. These shrouds were a constant source of trouble with overheating issues, and as the stub manifolds produced enough thrust to give an extra 10mph top

ABOVE The PR XVI was used extensively in north-west Europe and the Far East. Watched by an erk, stripped to the waist in the sweltering heat at Alipore, India, the twin Merlins of NS645, 'P', of 681 Squadron are ground-run before flight. Note the open direct-vision window to help get some air circulating inside the cockpit (the Perspex canopy acted like a greenhouse), and the Pierced Steel Plank covering the ground of the dispersal, which heated up in the sun as the day wore on. *(San Diego Aerospace Museum, Jack Canary collection)*

The type of camera installed in a photo-reconnaissance aircraft of the Second World War period depended on the nature of the missions being undertaken. For the Mosquito PR I, II, IV, VIII, IX and XVI, the cameras used included split pairs of vertical F8 high-altitude daytime survey cameras with 20in lenses, or vertical F52 high-altitude day reconnaissance cameras with 36in lenses; or a split pair of vertical F24 14in lens universal cameras and a single oblique F24 camera with either an 8in or 14in lens. Small numbers of PR Mosquitoes were fitted with a forward-facing camera sighting through the clear vision panel of the bomb-aimer's window for use on extremely low-level sorties, operated by the pilot from a button on his control column. Some later versions of the Mosquito carried two F24 14in forward-facing cameras for low-level photography, with each camera fitted in a dummy 50gal under-wing drop-tank.

Later, the long-range PR 34 carried a split pair of vertical F52 cameras with a choice of 14in, 20in or 36in lenses, the 36in being mounted forward; two vertical F52 cameras in tandem in the fuselage behind the wing; and an F24 14in oblique camera mounted on the port side, also behind the wing, and sighted along the port wing by the pilot.

Earlier in the war the cameras were fitted inside the aircraft on steel mounts with rubber pads, but these were replaced by wooden mounts with rubber pads because it was found this reduced camera vibration in flight and thus increased picture quality. A detachable film magazine was clipped on top of each camera. The number of exposures varied according to the type of camera: F8 – 250; F24 – 125 or 250; F52 – 250 or 500.

Split pair vertical cameras were installed with each camera set at a slightly different angle to the other, which gave double the photographic coverage. To obtain stereo imagery of a target area, each camera had to produce a run of images with an overlap of 60% between frames. The F52 36in-focal-length camera flying at a height of 35,000ft would give a lateral coverage of three miles.

BELOW Instrument fitters line up aerial cameras at RAF Benson before installing them in a Mosquito PR IV. From left to right: two Type F24 (14in lens) vertical cameras, one F24 (14in lens) oblique camera, and two Type F52 (36in lens) 'split pair' vertical cameras. *(IWM CH18399)*

speed, it was considered this fact alone outweighed any advantages of flame suppression.

The most important requirement was always for extra ceiling, as high-altitude German fighters were starting to pose a threat, and conversions were made to 29 more PR IVs to make them lighter, even though they carried extra fuel tanks in the bomb-bay. Before the purpose-designed high-altitude PR IX version was delivered, the PR VIII appeared as a stop-gap measure. These were B IVs converted to carry two 50gal drop-tanks and were powered by the Merlin 61 inter-cooled engine with a two-speed two-stage supercharger – but only five of these aircraft were built.

Night sorties

Once PR IX deliveries began, the PR IV was switched to night sorties where it would be less vulnerable to attack. For these operations it used the American M46 photoflash, which enabled night-time photography to be carried out without the aircraft being limited to low altitude. The M46 looked like a conventional small bomb and was fitted with tail vanes closed off with a drag plate. The Mosquito could carry 12 of these in the bomb-bay. When dropped, the arming wire was pulled to activate a mechanical time fuse which then ignited the flashlight powder – an event that was dangerous to the naked eye,

BELOW Exposure problems from using long focal-length cameras in the Mosquito were solved by the adoption of the American M46 photoflash which, at 600,000-candlepower, was three times brighter than the British equivalent. Twelve of these photoflashes could be carried in a Mosquito's bomb-bay, allowing reconnaissance photographs to be taken at a shutter speed of 1/25th sec at the peak of flash intensity, which lasted for 1/10th sec. *(US National Archives)*

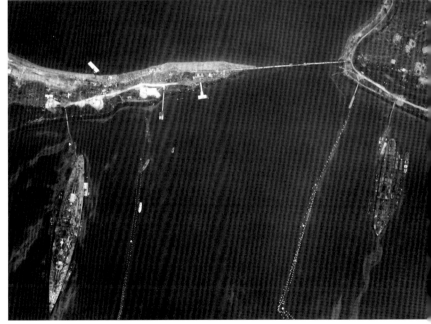

BELOW Attempts to sink the German battleship *Tirpitz* preoccupied Winston Churchill for much of the war. Dubbed 'the beast' by the premier, the *Tirpitz* was regularly photographed by the RAF's photo-reconnaissance squadrons to monitor its activity and to assess damage from the various attacks on the vessel by the Royal Navy and the RAF. The outstanding sortie that produced this photograph of the *Tirpitz* (seen left) was flown on 12 July 1944 by Flt Lt F.L. Dodd and Flt Sgt A. Hill in Mosquito PR XVI, NS504, of 544 Squadron, temporarily detached from Benson to Leuchars in Scotland. After refuelling at Sullom Voe in the Shetland Islands, Dodd and Hill flew to Kaafjord and back to Leuchars, to complete one of the longest photo-reconnaissance flights ever made, having spent 7 hours 40 minutes in the air. Dodd was awarded an immediate DSO for this achievement. The *Tirpitz* was finally sunk by Lancasters of 9 and 617 Squadrons four months later. *(IWM HU92979)*

The high-flyer

What looked like a new threat from Germany appeared in the summer of 1942 in the shape of the Junkers Ju 86P high-altitude high-performance bomber, which was a heavily modified version of the Ju 86 airliner. It didn't sound very exciting, and all it ever did was drop the occasional 550lb bomb, but one flew at more than 40,000ft over Hatfield on 5 September 1942, its contrail observed by chief aerodynamicist Richard Clarkson and other de Havilland executives.

If nothing else could catch this, maybe a modified Mosquito could, so to tackle these raiders five Mosquito B IV bombers were converted into high-altitude fighters (later designated NF XV) powered by two-stage inter-cooled Merlin 73s and 77s fitted with four-bladed propellers and drastically lightened. The first was MP469, which spent seven days in the de Havilland experimental flight hangar being converted. A group of workers was addressed by Fred Plumb, manager of the Experimental Department, who stood at the front of the aircraft and announced that the nose would be sawn off immediately and replaced with a fighter nose carrying four .303 Browning machine guns.

Then he paused for a moment, staring at the assembled workers: 'You're not listening to what I'm saying: I said we are starting straight away – hasn't anyone got a saw?' With that, a 'chippy' scuttled off, returned with a rip saw and began tackling the nose while Plumb continued to detail other modifications to reduce weight as much as possible, such as replacing the pilot's armoured steel backplate with a plywood one, removing some fuel tanks and extending the wingtips.

Just as he finished talking there was an almighty crash as the nose fell on the floor. This was a classic example of how quick and easy it was to make modifications to the Mosquito, and very soon Britain was ready to tackle any Ju 86P that cared to show its nose over England. Ironically, none did – but the ultra-light Mosquito gave a welcome edge in high-altitude interception, being 2,300lb lighter than standard and able to reach almost 44,000ft.

This aircraft, together with PR XVI prototype

ABOVE The German Army Research Centre at Peenemünde photographed on 23 June 1943 from a Mosquito PR IX of 540 Squadron flown by Flt Sgt E.P.H. Peek, using a Type F52 (36in) vertical camera. This detailed enlargement of the image shows Test Stand VII at the facility in northern Germany. Clearly seen at bottom centre inside the elliptical earthwork is a V2 rocket on its trailer. Two other trailers can be seen to the right.
(IWM C4783)

as it peaked with a massive intensity, lasted for about a fifth of a second, and was three times brighter than the British equivalent. These were hazardous objects to handle, being highly sensitive to friction, shock and temperature.

The RAF developed an extremely accurate technique that allowed a photo to be taken at the instant of flash intensity, and these bombs continued to be used on the PR IX, which, together with the PR XVI that had a pressurised cockpit, was the penultimate photo-reconnaissance version, powered by two-stage supercharged Merlin 72/73 engines.

From autumn 1942 until late 1943, PR Mosquitoes and Spitfires photographed the German Reich and northern France as part of Operation Crossbow, a campaign to pinpoint and eliminate Germany's V-weapons. Reports had come in that German scientists were developing a small, pilotless aircraft, and such a weapon was observed at Peenemünde on the Baltic coast. During the summer of 1943 a large number of ski-shaped launch platforms were discovered in France, and Mosquitoes continued to keep Peenemünde under observation. In November the link was made between Peenemünde, the V1 flying bomb and the ski sites, thanks to PR Mosquito pilot John Merifield.

(DZ540) that was also equipped for extreme high-altitude operation, underwent trials at A&AEE Boscombe Down. Both were fitted with pressurised cabins with blower drives operated from the Merlin. With an all-up weight of 17,465lb, MP469 was able to reach 44,800ft, while DZ450, tested with its maximum permissible all-up weight of 22,340lb, had an absolute ceiling of 36,700ft.

To operate safely and regularly at these altitudes, there were several technical issues concerning the interrelated matters of crew comfort and safety which needed resolving by the back-room boffins at RAE Farnborough and A&AEE Boscombe Down.

When flying at altitudes above 12,000ft the human body, if unprotected, will suffer serious physiological harm from the effects of altitude sickness and hypoxia due to the reductions in outside air pressure and oxygen saturation in the atmosphere as height is gained. An additional consequence of high-altitude flight for the Mosquito was condensation freezing on the insides of the Perspex cockpit canopy and on the glazing of the bomb-aimer's position in the nose, completely obscuring all vision. Once this problem got out of hand it was virtually impossible to rectify, particularly when external air temperatures could often be as low as minus 55°C.

Farnborough and Boscombe Down overcame these problems by pressurising the Mosquito cockpit and delivering oxygen to the crew through pressure-demand face masks. The condensation problem was solved by replacing the single-thickness Perspex panels of the main cockpit windows with Triplex double-layer glazing.

Higher and faster

Still greater altitude was sought for photographic operations generally, and in January 1944 a PR IX at Benson was fitted with Merlin 76/77 engines and paddle-blade propellers. By the end of February four conversions had been done and the result was more height and more speed. Four further aircraft were adapted, but the greater altitude brought other problems above 35,000ft, such as canopies icing up.

The PR XVI, which was delivered in late 1943 to 140 and 400 Squadrons, had a pressurised cockpit but no heating due to heat exchangers not being available. It was impossible for crews to function properly for more than an hour in the extreme cold, and most operations went on for three hours or more.

By this time 540 Squadron was engaged in up to seven missions a day photographing targets from Munich to Breslau, from the Zuider Zee to Toulouse and Foix-Grenoble. The Mosquito's virtual immunity to enemy action was plain for all to see. There was little that the envious Göring could do about it: in 1944 one Mosquito from 544 Squadron managed to evade even a rocket-powered tailless Me 163 Komet – a highly dangerous machine that caused more fatalities to its own pilots than to the enemy, mainly due to its volatile fuel.

Even when Germany put their twin-jet Me 262 into service, Mosquitoes were usually able to evade this much faster machine by virtue of their extreme manoeuvrability.

Throughout the war Mosquitoes were engaged in reconnaissance missions all over Europe, virtually immune to the best that Germany had to throw at them. In the first four months of 1945, 540 Squadron carried out 393 sorties for the loss of just one machine. The

LEFT Wg Cdr 'Steve' Steventon, DSO, DFC and Bar, was one of the RAF's top photo-reconnaissance Mosquito pilots of the war. He also commanded 541 Squadron (October 1942–July 1943) and 544 Squadron (November 1943–September 1945). He survived the war after extensive operational experience only to die tragically in a senseless flying accident years later. *(RAF Museum)*

106G 1569 21JULY44 F/10 //5445

aircraft were under constant development to give more height, more speed, and more range – but none of this required major structural work.

These round-the-clock missions by Mosquitoes were vital to the Allied offensive, much of that itself carried out by Mosquitoes. Yet Germany, to Britain's advantage, seemed to have made few inroads into the art of reconnaissance, thus ignoring the basic premise that knowledge is power.

Fighters

Although de Havilland's original concept for the Mosquito had been for a high-speed unarmed bomber, by the end of 1940 the RAF had a more urgent need for a fighter version.

Flight trials of prototype W4052 were completed by the end of July 1941 by Wg Cdr Gordon Slade, who was given command of 157 Squadron at RAF Debden in Cambridgeshire, the first unit to be equipped with Mosquito fighters. Towards the end of

the year experiments were carried out on W4052 with an unusual circular Youngman frill air brake, which operated round the circumference of the fuselage behind the wing and looked like a cake frill. It was designed to give rapid deceleration during combat, but was problematical and caused serious vibration and buffeting, which Boscombe Down believed could cause structural failure to the airframe. The device was discarded.

In January 1942 Slade delivered the squadron's first aircraft, an NF II (W4073), to their satellite base at Castle Camps, a bleak and gloomy place with very basic workshops and foul weather.

By this time the NF IIs were being equipped with the AI Mk V radar, and later the squadron developed flash eliminators for the machine guns in the nose. Without these the crew could be momentarily blinded when the guns were fired at night. But a more serious issue was the dreaded flame-damping shrouds on the exhaust manifold, which were the source of endless problems. In April the squadron grounded all its Mosquitoes after a cowling had burned through, but gradually the difficulties were overcome, although the penalty of the shrouds was a loss of about 10mph on top speed. The second Mosquito fighter squadron, 151 based at Wittering, also had to have the cowlings modified, but by mid-July all were fully operational. Another problem had been tailwheel shimmy, and this was cured by fitting Marstrand double-track tyres.

First kill

Who was going to claim the first kill – 157 or 151? There was keen rivalry. After some frustrating near misses, the honour fell to 151 on the night of 24–25 June. For their CO, New Zealander Wg Cdr I.S. Smith in W4097, it was a night to remember: he and his observer, Flt Lt Sheppard, spotted a Heinkel He 111 against the northern lights and opened fire. With its port fuel tanks ablaze the Heinkel pulled out of a dive, went into a stalled turn, jettisoned what looked like a torpedo, and then took another burst of fire from Smith. With large pieces falling away, it flew into cloud to be claimed as a 'probable'.

But the excitement wasn't over, as shortly before midnight Smith closed in on a Dornier Do 217 bomber and opened fire from about 100yd. The Dornier dived into the sea. A few minutes later Smith's radar picked up another Do 217 and he gave it a long burst of gunfire from about 200yd. With its wings well ablaze and its fate almost certainly sealed, the Dornier's gunner bravely returned the fire, but he missed the Mosquito, which closed in for the kill.

The following night, 151 claimed two more kills. Their operations had got off to a better start than 157, who had actually flown more hours, and as

BELOW Wearing the early sooty black night-fighter paint scheme, which was found to reduce the aircraft's speed, Mosquito NF II, W4087, 'RS-B', of 157 Squadron is pictured at Castle Camps during 1942. *(Andy Thomas)*

ABOVE AI Mk IV transmitting aerial and 0.303in machine gun installation on a Mosquito NF II. *(BAE Systems/RTP10782)*

RIGHT AI Mk VIIIB indicator and receiver in the operating position as seen from the observer's seat of a Mosquito NF XIII night-fighter. The visor has been removed from the screen on the indicator unit (top). The receiver unit (bottom) was hinged to allow it to be stored in the space below the indicator to enable the crew to enter and exit the cockpit via the door at the front right. *(Crown Copyright/ RAF Air Historical Branch)*

RIGHT This is the helical scanning parabolic dish of the AI Mk X/SCR 720 radar as used in the Mosquito NF 30, seen here in Brussels at the Belgian Royal Army Museum inside the nose of NF 30, RK952. After the war the AI Mk X installation was used in the Gloster Meteor. *(Copyright unknown)*

MOSQUITOES AND THE WAR OF THE ETHER

In the 21st century, radar and electronic countermeasures (ECM) have become two highly developed facets of the air combat environment. The Second World War acted as a catalyst in many fields of technology, not least that of applied electronics, and it was during the 1940s that electronic warfare came of age.

Mosquito fighter, bomber and intruder squadrons were almost unique in the inventory of the Allied air forces for the diversity of cutting edge radar and electronic equipment they carried in pursuit of the Luftwaffe, and for bombing the Reich. These devices were operated by the navigator and can be divided into airborne interception (AI) radars, homing and warning devices, navigational and blind bombing aids, and jamming equipment. Their bulky cathode ray tubes and bundles of power leads added to what was already a snug cockpit environment.

AIRBORNE INTERCEPTION (AI) RADARS

AI Mk IV – This was the first mass-produced AI radar of the war until it was phased out in late 1944. AI Mk IV was a metric radar operating on a wavelength of 1.5m and a frequency of 190–195MHz. The set's optimum operating height was at about 18,000ft where a target aircraft could be picked up at a range of 3½ miles and followed in to a range of 400ft. The technical limitations of the metric wavelength meant it was a far from perfect device until the arrival of centimetric radar (AI Mk VII/VIII).

AI Mk VIII – This 9cm wavelength radar was an important development in that it became the British standard centimetric AI radar set. Under optimum conditions the AI Mk VIII had a range of between 6½ and 5½ miles dead ahead.

AI Mk X – This American-designed device was the second centimetric AI radar to see RAF service, partially replacing the home-developed AI Mk VIII. At heights above 5,000ft it had a range of between 6 and 10 miles. Both the AI Mk VIII and Mk X were weak at low altitudes where they suffered from a fall-off in range.

AI MK XV – Also American-designed, AI MK XV (also known as ASH) was originally developed as a maritime Air to Surface Vessel (ASV) radar.

It was trialled by 100 Group, which urgently needed a centimetric set to augment limited supplies of the AI Mk X. The scanner was housed in a distinctive 5ft-long torpedo-shaped fairing protruding from the nose of the aircraft. It was a fair performer at low level with a range of 3¾ miles, and with its relatively slow scan speed it could also be used as a navigational aid in the same way as the H2S device.

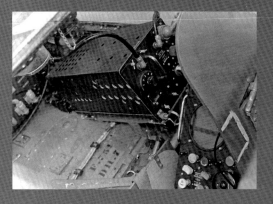

HOMING AND WARNING DEVICES

Fighter Command/Air Defence of Great Britain Mosquito fighters and 100 (Bomber Support) Group night intruder Mosquitoes were fitted with two types of homers – 'Serrate' and 'Perfectos' – designed to give bearings on the transmissions from enemy IFF sets and AI radars, and the 'Monica' family of active tail-warning radars.

NAVIGATIONAL AND BLIND BOMBING AIDS

Gee – Virtually all of the RAF's Mosquitoes were fitted with this highly accurate passive radio navigational aid, which used three ground transmitters in southern England, an airborne receiver and a cathode ray tube display in the aircraft, with which to pinpoint its position. Because Gee depended on transmissions from ground stations its effective range was limited by the curvature of the earth to about 350 miles (for the bomber Mossies, Germany's industrial Ruhr valley was just within this range limitation). However, the device eventually became compromised by German jamming east of the Dutch coast.

Oboe – Only two RAF squadrons (both Mosquito units – 105 and 109 Squadrons in Bomber Command's 8 (Pathfinder) Group) – used Oboe for bombing and primary marking of targets with coloured pyrotechnic target indicators. Oboe was similar to Gee in that it was a hyperbolic navigation system that depended on transmissions from a pair of ground stations in England. Its accuracy was such that an Oboe-equipped aircraft flying at 28,000ft over the Ruhr could release its bombs within 120yd of the selected target. Initially only one aircraft at a time could be controlled by a pair of Oboe transmitters every ten minutes, but this was partly solved later in the war. Like Gee, Oboe's range was limited by the curvature of the earth. The Mosquito's

high-altitude performance meant it was better suited to Oboe than contemporaries such as the Lancaster and Halifax.

Rebecca – A handful of 100 Group's Mosquito FB VIs were fitted with the 'Rebecca' airborne direction-finding device, which comprised a ground-based transmitter beacon and an airborne interrogator.

H2S –Transmissions from a downward-looking, rotating, ground-mapping radar scanner fitted in the bomb-aimer's compartment scanned the terrain below. The echoes that bounced back to receiving equipment in the aircraft were displayed on a television-type screen, painting a radar impression of the ground over which the aircraft was flying. RAF Pathfinder Mosquito B XVIs of 8 (PFF) Group were equipped with H2S to assist with navigation to the target and for blind target marking duties. It was first used operationally in Mosquitoes by 139 Squadron on 1 February 1944 against Berlin. H2S was the only one of the three wartime navigational aids that was self-contained inside the aircraft and not limited in any way by range or altitude.

H2X – This was an American development of the British H2S radar and used a shorter 3cm (10GHz) wavelength than H2S, giving a sharper picture. It was used in very small numbers by the USAAF's Mosquito PR XVI aircraft of the 25th Bomb Group (Reconnaissance) from May 1944 until February 1945 on radar mapping night missions.

JAMMING EQUIPMENT

American-designed 'Dina II' and 'Piperack' electronic devices were intended to jam enemy ground radars and AI radars respectively. When the device was used against the German FuG 220 AI radar it was known as 'Piperack'.

ABOVE The Mosquito F II was a day- and night-fighter and intruder variant, armed with four 20mm Hispano cannon and four 0.303in machine guns. These F IIs belong to 456 (RAAF) Squadron and are pictured at Middle Wallop on 5 June 1943 where groundcrew are hard at work replenishing fuel and other consumables. *(IWM CH10317)*

151's score mounted it wasn't until the latter part of August that 157 claimed its first 'definite' when Gordon Slade shot down a Do 217. The crew baled out safely and said they had no idea the Mosquito was there until the bullets ripped in.

As more units were equipped with Mosquito night-fighters, an experimental finish was applied to some early NF IIs to alleviate glistening in searchlights or moonlight. Looking like black suede, it cut down the glistening – but it also cut down the top speed. Then it was found that black of any type was not the ideal answer to night operations, as it could give too much of a silhouette effect. The solution was to use the night-fighter scheme of medium sea grey overall with dark green disruptive camouflage on the upper surfaces.

Dream team

The most famous night-fighter crew of the war was John Cunningham and Jimmy Rawnsley, who worked together as the perfect team. Before the war Cunningham was a junior test pilot at de Havilland, working under Geoffrey Jr, but with the outbreak of war he was posted to 604 Squadron, which operated Blenheims from Middle Wallop in Hampshire. The Blenheim wasn't really up to the job, and although it had a new lease of life when fitted with airborne interception radar, the Bristol Beaufighter was much better, and it was in this machine that Cunningham and Rawnsley honed their skills – skills that were to be fully realised when they went into battle with the Mosquito NF II with 85 Squadron, which Cunningham commanded.

Chalking up a total of 20 kills during the war, most of them at night but not all on Mosquitoes, this success rate was due to Cunningham's skill as a pilot and Rawnsley's use of AI radar, backed up by ground control radar and searchlights, all working as a team. It had nothing to do with eating carrots – an amusing bit of British propaganda aimed at covering up the use of airborne radar. Unfortunately for the self-effacing Cunningham, it led to him being known as 'Cat's Eyes' for the rest of his life.

Throughout the war the Mosquito was constantly developed to stretch its performance, and by 1943 there was a need for steeper climbing ability plus more speed at 20,000ft for the night-fighters. Two Mosquitoes were fitted out at Farnborough with a nitrous oxide injection system for trials by 85 Squadron. This gave a very useful extra 47mph at 28,000ft with enough capacity for six minutes' operation, so 50 NF XIIIs for 96 and 410 (RCAF) Squadrons were equipped with it by Heston Aircraft.

LEFT Wg Cdr John Cunningham was probably the most famous RAF night-fighter pilot of the war. He is seen here with his navigator, Flt Lt Jimmy Rawnsley (left). The pair joined 85 Squadron in January 1943. *(Andy Thomas)*

How some came back

Burning petrol and oil from an exploding German Dornier Do 217 badly damaged its assailant, 410 (RCAF) Squadron's Mosquito NF II, DZ757, 'RA-Q'. On the night of 27 September 1943 Flt Lt Martin 'Cy' Cybulski, RCAF, (pilot) and Flg Off Harold Ladbrook (navigator) destroyed the Dornier east of the Zuider Zee. Cybulski was temporarily blinded in the ensuing violent explosion and flames engulfed the Mosquito, sending it into a steep dive from which Ladbrook only managed to recover after losing some 4,000ft. Although the dive extinguished the flames, the port engine stopped and the aircraft became extremely difficult to control because of damage to the rudder. Nevertheless Cybulski and Ladbrook managed to steer DZ757 back on one engine over 200 miles to Coleby Grange, for which both men were awarded immediate DFCs. *(BAE Systems/DH1963L)*

Heroism on the ground

Tales of selfless heroism in the war are legion, when ordinary men and women caught up in extraordinary events displayed complete disregard for their own lives by plunging into burning wrecks to save stricken airmen.

This dramatic rescue from a Mosquito of 157 Squadron, which crashed at Predannack on 26 February 1944, is typical of the courage to which so many aircrews owed their lives.

Piloted by Flg Off John L. Clifton of the RAFVR, with Flg Off Scobie in the observer's seat, Mosquito NF II (DZ707) was on a practice flight when it stalled at 200ft on the landing approach, dived to the left and crashed on to the airfield. A fierce fire broke out and rescuers raced to the scene, desperately trying to reach the cockpit amid the intense heat, exploding ammunition and Verey cartridges going off in all directions, and huge quantities of foam being sprayed over the burning wreck from the fire tenders.

The pilot was dead, but Scobie was alive, trapped by his legs after being thrown across Clifton's body and unable to escape. Team after

team of rescuers, including the station padre, made frantic efforts to reach him, but each attempt became more difficult than the last as the inferno intensified. It looked as though Scobie was doomed, but then a final desperate effort was launched by Cpl George Greenwood, NCO in charge of the crash tender, and Sqn Ldr Ernest Brown, station medical officer.

At this point the fire tenders had temporarily run out of foam and for several minutes the blaze grew even fiercer, yet the two men fought their way to the cockpit, knowing they may never get out alive. They were faced with a terrible situation: if they couldn't free Scobie they would have to amputate his leg on the spot or let him burn to death. With what was described as 'great courage and determination', the two men made calm and skilful use of axes and other tools to free Scobie's leg from the twisted wreckage, and were finally able to drag him clear.

As the rescued man was given first aid, Brown then scrambled back through the flames to make absolutely certain that there were no signs of life from Clifton. Scobie was taken to hospital where he was expected to make a full recovery, owing his life to the outstanding bravery of two men who would not give up.

Their courage did not go unrecognised: Greenwood was awarded the BEM, while Brown was made an MBE. *(IWM CH18732)*

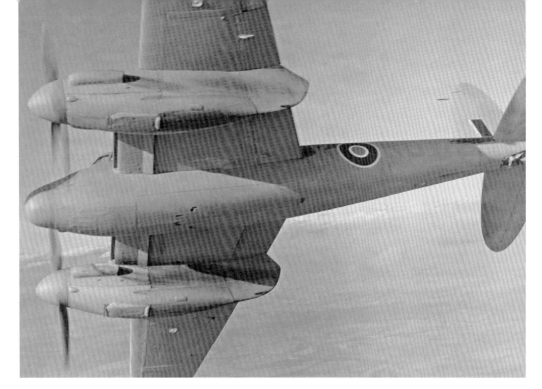

Women in a man's sky

Overcoming the blatant sexist attitudes of the time, women pilots of the Air Transport Auxiliary proved they could fly every bit as well as men, and did outstanding work on ferry duties during the war. Shown here at Hatfield in November 1942 with a Mosquito NF II are Mrs Winifred Crossley (left) and Miss Mabel Glass. One of Pauline Gower's 'first eight' to be accepted into ATA service, Winifred was highly skilled, having flown as a stunt pilot in an air circus before the war, as well as towing banners for aerial advertising.

A couple of months before this picture was taken, Mabel had a narrow escape when a Mosquito B IV she was piloting crashed during take-off at Hatfield on 14 September. The aircraft, DZ311, was repaired and later joined 105 Squadron, only to be lost over the North Sea on 23 January 1943 while on a mission to bomb rail targets between Oldenburg and Osnabrück. Pilot Leonard Skinner and navigator Frederick Saunders, both of the RAFVR, were killed.

Women had a tough time convincing the Air Ministry that they should be allowed to fly military aircraft, the attitude being that it was a man's job. The official view was that aviation was an unsuitable profession for a woman, and that women pilots would be taking flying jobs away from men.

Charles G. Grey, editor of *Aeroplane*, Fascist sympathiser and never one to mince words, took the sentiment to an unashamedly new level of sexism – even for those days: 'We quite agree', he wrote in an editorial, 'that there are millions of women in the country who could do useful jobs in war. But the trouble is that so many of them insist on wanting to do jobs which they are quite incapable of doing. The menace is the woman who thinks that she ought to be flying in a high-speed bomber when she really has not the intelligence to scrub the floor of a hospital properly, or who wants to nose around as an Air Raid Warden and yet can't cook her husband's dinner.'

But the Ministry was soon forced to recognise the sterling work done by women pilots, and – surprisingly for the time – eventually awarded them the same pay as men. *(BAE Systems/DH817)*

Pilot	Victories	Unit	Nationality	Nav/Radar Op
Burbridge, Bransome Arthur (DSO*, DFC*)	21 (+3 V1)	85	English	Skelton, F.S. (DSO*, DFC*)
Scherf, Charles Curnow (DSO, DFC*)	14 [13+1]	418	Australian	Brown, A; Finlayson, C. (DFC*); Caine, J. (DFC**); Stewart, W. (DFC); Gurnett, R.
Green, Wilfrith Peter (DSO, DFC)	14 (+13 V1)	85, 410, 96, 219	English	Grimstone, Arthur (DFM); Oxby, Dougie (DSO, DFC, DFM*)
Allan, John Watson (DSO, DFC)	14	256	Scottish	Davidson, H.J. (DFC*)
Doleman, Robert Daniel (DSO, DFC)	12 [10+2] (+3 V1)	157	English	Bunch, D.C. (DSO, DFC*)
Kipp, Robert Allan (DSO, DFC)	11 [10+1]	418	Canadian	Hulctsky, Peter (DFC*)
White, Harold Edward (DFC**)	9	141, BSDU	English	Allan, Mike
Parker, Gartrell Richard Ian (DFC, DFM)	9 (+6 V1)	219	English	Godfrey, Donald Ling (BEM, DFC*, DSM)
Owen, Alan Joseph (DFC*, DFM)	9 (+1 V1)	85	English	McAllister, James Samuel Victor (DFC*, DFM)
Bannock, Russell (DSO, DFC*)	9 (+18½ V1)	418/406	Canadian	Bruce, Robert (DFC*)

Note: eg: [10+2] = 10 + 2 enemy aircraft shared
eg: (+3 V1) = flying bombs destroyed
DSO* = DSO and Bar   DFC* = DFC and Bar   ** = two bars

LEFT The 85 Squadron night-fighting team of Sqn Ldr Bill Skelton (navigator, on the left) and Wg Cdr Branse Burbridge (pilot). Burbridge flew Havocs with 85 Squadron before it converted to Mosquitoes. Between February 1944 and January 1945 he was credited with 21 enemy aircraft and 3 V1 flying bombs destroyed, making him the top-scoring Mosquito night-fighter pilot of the war. Skelton and Burbridge became lifelong friends. *(Branse Burbridge via Andy Thomas)*

LEFT Sqn Ldr Russ Bannock (left) and Flg Off Robert Bruce of 418 (RCAF) Squadron were one of the most successful Mosquito intruder crews of the war. They are seen at Middle Wallop in August 1944 with their FB VI (HR147) *Hairless Joe*. *(Andy Thomas)*

The V1 menace

In terms of weapons development the Germans were ahead of Britain, a classic example being the V1 flying bomb, which became known as the Doodlebug. First evidence that this new menace was being used in anger was on 14 June 1944 when the crew of a Mosquito returning from intruder patrol saw 'a rocket projectile heading northwards and leaving a red trail'. Not much happened then, but on the following night 244 V1s were launched, 73 reaching Greater London. It was the start of a concentrated offensive and Mosquitoes played a major role in shooting them down or sending them off course, the latter being achieved by overtaking a V1 and upsetting it with wake turbulence.

The Mosquito FB VI just had the edge in speed over the Doodlebug, thanks largely to the single-stage Merlin 25 on 150-grade fuel, which gave some extra urge. Firing on these small craft was not easy by day, but by night the flame from its power unit made judging distances very tricky. There were many frightening moments, as attacking one from behind – the most successful method – could result in the Mosquito flying through an inferno of exploding debris with severe risk to the radiators and, in some instances, the whole airframe being severely scorched and blistered. Nevertheless, by the end of hostilities Mosquitoes had destroyed a total of 486 V1s.

During that summer the Mosquito NF 30 was entering service with 219 Squadron, but there were some early problems. Although there had been 100 hours of testing at Hatfield, the exhaust system was useless once in service and all of the aircraft were grounded following 50 exhaust shroud failures within 40 days. The trouble went on well into November before louvred shrouds were retro-fitted. Before the end of the year seven night-fighter squadrons had the NF 30.

In November 1943, with the approach of the invasion of Europe by Allied forces, RAF Fighter Command had been split into two elements – one for defence, the other for tactical operations. Under the command of Air Marshal Roderic Hill, Air Defence of Great Britain (ADGB – originally formed in 1925 and then disbanded in 1936) was resurrected for defence against an expected offensive on London. It controlled ten Mosquito squadrons, while other squadrons came under the control of 85 Group, Allied Expeditionary Air Force (2nd Tactical Air Force), in preparation for the assault on occupied Europe.

In January 1944 the raids that had been expected on London happened with Operation Steinbock, when Germany launched 447 sorties against the capital, mainly made up of Ju 88s and Do 217s. The operation, which lasted until May, was hardly a resounding success: on the first raid the total bomb load was around 500 tons, but only about 30 fell on London, and half of it didn't even fall on land, while a large number of bombers never crossed the coast. Mosquitoes were on a constant offensive against the raiders, and the net result for Germany was that Steinbock greatly reduced the effectiveness of their bomber fleet due to heavy losses. It was the last major bombing offensive against Britain.

Fighter-bombers

The Mosquito's performance and versatility made it ideally suited as a fighter-bomber, and the decision to produce this variant was taken in July 1941. But in May the following year the FB VI prototype, DZ434, renumbered HJ662/G for flight trials at Boscombe Down, was destroyed on 13 June after an engine failed on take-off. When about 10ft off the ground the aircraft swung to the left, slicing into two

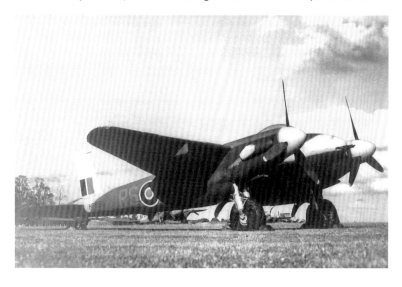

BELOW Some Mosquito night-fighter squadrons used the FB VI on intruder Ranger flights and one such unit was 157 Squadron. FB VI, HP850, flew several Rangers with 157 before it was transferred to 464 (RAAF) Squadron, with whom it was shot down near Metz–Woippy on 3 October 1943. *(F.P. Bodey via Andy Thomas)*

RIGHT In the heat of the Mediterranean sun 23 Squadron's CO, Wg Cdr John Selby, DSO, DFC, and his navigator, contemplate their Mosquito NF II, 'P–Peter', as other squadron members look on from the top of the dispersal pen blast wall at Luqa, Malta, on 27 June 1943. The Mossie's tatty paintwork suggests heavy use; the barrels of its four 0.303in machine guns are plugged to prevent damage from dirt. Selby, who had learned to fly privately at Redhill before the war, interrupted a career in broadcasting to take a commission in the RAF in December 1940. He enjoyed rapid promotion and commanded 73 Squadron in the desert during 1942–43. In April 1943 Selby was promoted to wing commander and given command of 23 Squadron in Malta, which at the time was the only Mosquito-equipped intruder squadron in the Mediterranean. He remained with 23 until September, when he became air liaison officer to Brigadier Fitzroy Maclean in Yugoslavia, working with Tito's partisans. Selby scored five kills during his operational flying and survived the war. *(IWM TR1076)*

stationary Beaufighters, but miraculously the pilot escaped unhurt and the observer was only slightly injured.

This caused a long delay and it wasn't until February 1943 that the first production machine flew, although had it not been for the constantly changing numbers and requirements from the Ministry, it might have flown rather earlier. By May, 410 (RCAF) Squadron received their first FB VIs, which were powered by the Merlin 25 with 18lb of boost to maximise low-level performance, and two months later 23 Squadron in Malta took their Mk VI deliveries. These were both intruder squadrons.

The FB VI Series 1 carried two 250lb bombs in the bomb-bay and a further two under the wings, but the Series 2 had a much greater capacity and could take two 500lb bombs in the fuselage and two more under the wings. Both versions could carry 50gal underwing drop-tanks or two extra tanks housed in the bomb-bay. On intruder missions, a smaller tank would be fitted in the bomb-bay along with a pair of 250lb bombs.

The FB VI with guns and bombs was a force to be reckoned with, but carrying rocket

BELOW Grp Capt P.C. 'Pick' Pickard, DSO and two Bars, DFC (centre), commander of 140 Wing, 2 Group, is flanked by Wg Cdr I.G.E. 'Daddy' Dale, CO of 21 Squadron (to Pickard's right), and Wg Cdr A.G. 'Willie' Wilson, DFC, CO of 487 (RNZAF) Squadron, during a visit to 464 (RAAF) Squadron at Hunsdon, Hertfordshire, in February 1944, prior to a daylight raid against flying-bomb sites in the Pas-de-Calais. No 464's Mosquito FB VIs have been loaded with 250lb MC bombs for the operation. HX913, 'N', which can be seen in the background, was destroyed in a flying accident when it flew into the ground on Portland Bill during a night navigation exercise on 21 July 1944. *(IWM HU81335)*

MOSQUITO BITE

With its ability to carry a variety of weapons that included 0.303in machine guns, 30mm and 57mm cannon, unguided rocket projectiles, bombs ranging from 250lb to 4,000lb, and air-dropped sea mines, in the Second World War the Mosquito came second to none as a multi-role combat aircraft.

LEFT The Mosquito fighter-bomber variant's main armament of four 20mm cannon and four 0.303in machine guns could pack a deadly punch. *(BAE Systems/DH9856)*

ABOVE No 105 Squadron's B IV, DZ367, 'GB-J', is loaded with four 500lb bombs during 1942. On the first daylight raid on Berlin, 30 January 1943, the aircraft was being flown by a 139 Squadron crew when it was brought down over the German capital by flak, claiming the lives of its crew, Sqn Ldr Donald Darling, DFC, and Flg Off William Wright. Darling's first tour had been on Defiant night-fighters with 151 Squadron. *(TopFoto)*

ABOVE A rocket projectile (RP) comprised of a 55in-long light metal tube, 3in in diameter, packed with quick-burning rocket propellant, which was fired electrically. When used against U-boats an RP was fitted with a 25lb solid shot armour-piercing (AP) warhead; for general purpose use a 60lb HE head was fitted. Mossie crews found the best results were obtained if they aimed their

ABOVE Armourers winch a 4,000lb 'Cookie' into the bulged bomb-bay of Mosquito B IV, DZ637, 'X', of 692 Squadron in April 1944. *(IWM CH12622)*

RIGHT The 57mm Molins gun replaced the four 20mm cannons beneath the nose of specially modified Mosquito FB VIs, which were designated Mk XVIII. Firing 6lb shells at the rate of about 60 shells per minute from a magazine containing 25 rounds, the appropriately nicknamed 'Tsetse' Mosquito (after the large biting fly found in central Africa) could pack a devastating punch against shipping and U-boats running on the surface. *Oberleutnant zur See* Günther Heinrich, commander of U-960, recalled that 'the shells of the 5.7cm gun caused remarkable damage to our boats'. *(BAE Systems/DH1690E)*

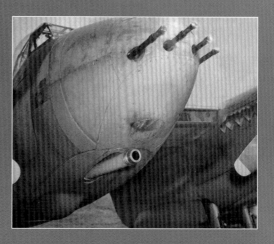

rocket salvoes to strike the sea at an angle of about 15 degrees to the surface and 20yd short of the U-boat, they continuing downwards for some 10ft before turning upwards to strike the hull below the waterline. This is 47 Squadron's FB VI, RF942, pictured in Java soon after the war's end. *(IWM)*

projectiles under the wings moved it into a different league. The main rockets used were the 60lb or 25lb armour-piercing types with high-explosive warheads, and four of these were mounted under each wing. Lethal for anti-shipping strikes and ground attacks, a single Mosquito had the firepower of a broadside from a cruiser when all eight rockets were unleashed.

In August 1943, two squadrons from 140 Wing of the RAF's 2nd Tactical Air Force – 464 (RAAF) and 487 (RNZAF) – took delivery of their first FB VIs, and were later joined at Sculthorpe by 21 Squadron. Their station commander was Grp Capt Charles 'Pick' Pickard, DSO, DFC, already known to the public from his part in the famous Government propaganda film *Target for Tonight*. He was keen to learn about the Mosquito so that he could fly as wing leader, so on a three-day visit to Hatfield he put in a total of ten hours, much of it at low level. Two months later, on 2 October, he was leading a dozen aircraft from 487 (RNZAF) Squadron after refuelling at Exeter, followed by 12 more from 464. Each aircraft carried four 500lb bombs, the targets being power stations at Pont-Chateau and Guerleden.

Streaking in at tree-top level, the leaders dropped their 11sec-delay bombs, followed by the rest who dived in from 2,000ft to release their bombs at 800ft. These had only ¼sec-delay. For good measure, a train was shot up on the way home and Typhoons demolished a pair of Focke Wulf Fw 190s. Pickard struggled back on one engine after flak hit a radiator. Another aircraft had part of its cockpit canopy blown away by a shell and four other machines were damaged.

Precision bombing

Squadrons equipped with the versatile Mosquito found they could extend their repertoire of operations very considerably, and pilots appreciated its speed and manoeuvrability, coupled with its light and responsive controls. Many precision low-level bombing raids were carried out by 464 (RAAF) Squadron, and in its three-year history of going into battle had attacked 2,353 targets, its operations covering Flowers, Ranger, Intruder, and Noball patrols.

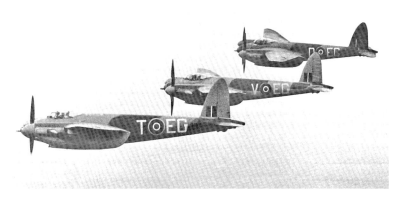

Flowers was the name given to patrols engaging and destroying German night-fighters, Intruder was for patrols operating just after sunset or before dawn aimed mainly at German bombers, Ranger referred to aircraft roaming over enemy territory picking on targets of opportunity, while Noball were strikes against the assembly and launching sites for the V1.

The squadron's most famous operation, in which it took part with 487 (RNZAF) and 21 Squadrons, was the epic raid on Amiens prison on 18 February 1944. Known as Operation Jericho – but never officially called that – it was a raid carried out with an accuracy worthy of today's smart bombs and is generally viewed as the first-ever precision bombing raid.

The story at the time was that more than 100 French patriots in Amiens jail were awaiting execution, some of them for helping Allied airmen to escape, so the French had asked the RAF to bomb the prison walls. The request was accepted and Air Vice-Marshal Basil Embry was put in charge. He would have led the attack, but was forbidden to fly because he was involved in D-Day planning. And so the task fell to the charismatic Pickard. This was going to be a very low-level mission, and he'd had only a few hours of that sort of flying, but everyone was raring to go: this was a mission with a difference.

The weather on the morning of 18 February was foul as the crews from 464, 487 and 21 Squadrons assembled on a misty and snowy Hunsdon airfield in Hertfordshire. Supported by Typhoons from 198 Squadron, 18 Mosquitoes took off, and many of the airmen reckoned the weather conditions were the worst in which they had ever flown. One RNZAF pilot later said that

ABOVE Mosquitoes of 487 (RNZAF) Squadron led the daring low-level raid on Amiens prison on 18 February 1944. This three-ship of FB VIs was photographed a few weeks later with the unit's CO, Wg Cdr 'Blackie' Smith at its head in MM417, 'EG-T'. *(Andy Thomas)*

ABOVE To emphasise just how low the Mosquito could be flown in combat by a skilled pilot, these Mossies of 487 (RNZAF) Squadron thunder over Amiens jail at extremely low level as their 500lb bombs detonate near the south wall of the prison. This precision daylight raid on 18 February 1944 by 18 Mosquito FB VIs of 140 Wing, 2 Group, was led by Grp Capt 'Pick' Pickard. The 'official' reason for the attack was to free Resistance members awaiting execution, but subsequent research has suggested a plausible alternative explanation. *(IWM C4732)*

RIGHT Casualties of the Amiens raid, Sqn Ldr A.I. McRitchie, DFC (left) and his navigator Flt Lt R.W. Sampson, of 464 (RAAF) Squadron, were shot down by flak near Amiens in FB VI, MM404, 'SB-T'. Sampson was killed outright, but McRitchie survived the 200mph crash-landing to become a prisoner of war. *(Copyright unknown)*

when the order came to take off he thought it was either some form of practice or a practical joke. It was certainly no joke, and the crews experienced some strange emotions, for this time they were bombing to save rather than end lives.

Four Mosquitoes lost contact in the weather and had to turn back, landing in a blizzard. The rest pushed on at extremely low level across the Channel. Over France the weather was better, the sun shining on a snow-covered landscape. The attack force, led by 487 on the toss of a coin, snarled low and fast down a long, straight, poplar-lined Roman road that led to the prison. The leading section dropped their 500lb bombs just after midday.

There were two objectives: to pierce the prison walls, which were 3ft thick and 20ft high, and to attack the guards' quarters at a time when they were likely to be sitting down for lunch. Both parts of the mission were accomplished with spectacular success, Wg Cdr I.S. Smith's bombs breaching the wall, while others fell nearby. The two remaining Mosquitoes from 487 attacked the northern wall, just managing to clear it after releasing their bombs.

The accuracy of the bombing was astonishing, and as Pickard circled the target at 500ft in HX922, Typhoons took on some Fw 190s that had raced to the scene. Meanwhile, Mosquitoes from 464 met some light flak, which claimed one aircraft, but the pilot of another, temporarily blinded and his right arm paralysed, managed a skilful landing in the snow.

The mission completed, Pickard headed for home fast and low at 50ft – and then his luck ran out. His aircraft was probably damaged by ground fire before a pair of 190s swooped on him and shot his tail off. He and his navigator, Flt Lt John Broadley, stood no chance; the aircraft piled into the ground. The two airmen were buried next day near the prison. Pickard was 28 years old.

Typhoon pilots, who had been flying higher than the Mosquitoes, later said they were overwhelmed by the incredible skill of the Mosquito pilots.

By the time German soldiers reached the prison 258 prisoners had escaped, including 79 Resistance members, but 155 were recaptured and 102 prisoners had been killed in the bombing raid.

The story of how we liberated Resistance fighters awaiting execution has long been popular, but doubt has been cast on the official version of events, particularly by the French historian Jean-Pierre Ducellier. He even goes so far as to say that the RAF version was 'sheer lies', for it appeared that no executions were planned at the time of the raid and the mission was not in fact requested by the Resistance.

Whatever the truth, the fact remains that it was a stunning example of what bravery, a cool head and skill could achieve from the cockpit of the Mosquito.

For the rest of February the squadrons concentrated on bombing V1 sites, many of which had been discovered by the PR Mosquitoes. They made 16 attacks, but on 1 March a new technique was introduced when two Mosquitoes from 109 PFF Squadron led a Noball raid by 21 Squadron and marked the target using Oboe, with the actual bombing being done from above the clouds. This system enabled Mosquitoes to carry out raids with virtually no response from the enemy, even in the dangerous phase of approaching the target.

The daylight low-level precision bombing of the Amiens raid was repeated on 11 April 1944 in one of several attacks on Gestapo headquarters. The target in the Hague was just one house: it was 95ft high, had five storeys and contained Gestapo records of the Dutch Resistance movement. Six FB VIs from 613 Squadron crossed the North Sea at 50ft to maximise surprise, climbed to 4,000ft over the Dutch coast and then swooped down to very low level, encountering some map-reading problems due to flood water. Two Mosquitoes led the attack, planting their 500lb delayed-fuse bombs right on to the building, while two more dropped incendiaries through the thick smoke. All returned to base safely, just one being slightly damaged by flak.

A similar attack was made on 31 October that year when the Jericho squadrons bombed the Gestapo headquarters in Jutland, again to help the Dutch Resistance, and on 21 March 1945 carried out the famous Operation Carthage raid on the Gestapo HQ at the Shellhaus building in Copenhagen. This was a very important mission, as Danish Resistance leaders feared that Gestapo records kept there would lead to mass arrests in a bid to eliminate the movement. Sweeping low over the Danish capital, the Mosquitoes released their bombs with unerring accuracy, one bomb

ABOVE The Dutch Population Central Registry in Scheveningsche Wegg, The Hague, which held Gestapo documentation on Dutch Resistance members, was the target of a precision daylight attack on 11 April 1944 by six Mosquitoes of 613 Squadron. Led by the squadron CO, Wg Cdr Robert Bateson, DSO, DFC, the raid succeeded in destroying the building without the loss of any Dutch lives. In this photograph the target area is obscured by smoke and sparks from 500lb delayed-action HE and incendiary bombs. In the right distance can be seen the tower of the Peace Palace, which suffered only a broken window during the raid. Today it is home to the United Nations' International Court of Justice. *(IWM C4320)*

LEFT Photographed from a Mosquito of the RAF Film Production Unit (RAFFPU) using a rear-facing mirror camera, this is the precision attack under way on the Gestapo headquarters in Jutland at the University of Aarhus in Denmark by Mosquito FB VIs of 140 Wing, 2 Group. Two Mosquitoes can be seen dropping their 500lb delayed-action bombs over the already damaged halls of residence. *(Jonathan Falconer collection)*

going into the building between the first and second storeys. Soon the whole building was ablaze and many Gestapo officials were killed, with most of the records destroyed. But this operation had a tragic outcome, as one FB VI crashed into a nearby school, killing many children, while four other aircraft were lost.

With their attacks on V-weapon sites, precision bombing of specific buildings, elimination of various key communication networks, and a number of other spectacular operations, the effect of the Mosquito is incalculable – and all for a low attrition rate. For example, in almost 1,000 sorties by 2 Group's Mosquitoes only 136 failed to return, while 57 were damaged beyond repair.

Day-bombers and night-bombers

Until it had proved its worth, scepticism about the unarmed bomber still lingered within the Ministry, and because of this it was the last version to be ordered. It would fall to 105 Squadron to see just what the Wooden Wonder would do in the role for which it had originally been conceived.

Although policy decisions resulted in the role of daylight bombing being handled by the Americans with their B-17 Flying Fortress, for a year the Mosquito demonstrated its potency in the most dramatic way. And one thing it could do was carry the same bomb load as the B-17, only faster and with far less potential loss of life.

The first B IV Series 1 (W4064) was delivered to 105 Squadron at Swanton Morley in Norfolk by Geoffrey de Havilland Jr on 15 November 1941. There was much rumour and excitement among the crews, who had been operating with their vulnerable old Blenheim IVs, but they could never have guessed just what they were in for. For their benefit, Geoffrey gave one of his no-holds-barred displays with his repertoire of loops, rolls and high-speed runs at practically daisy-cutting level. It was enough to impress even the Spitfire pilots from 152 Squadron who had been watching with interest, and when their CO was taken for a flight he was somewhat shaken by the Mosquito's performance. As for the 105 Squadron crews, they couldn't wait to fly it in anger.

During working up with their new arrival, they engaged a Spitfire in mock combat – and considered they had beaten it. After some mock bombing attacks, the squadron was ready for operations by May, the crews raving about the Mosquito's abilities. Still the Ministry weren't sure: they felt that its performance would soon be eclipsed by the enemy unless more power could be provided, and low-level bombing was not seen then as the most effective role for the Mosquito, much of the practice being done from around 20,000ft.

Initial deliveries were fairly slow, as by the end of May 1942 there were only eight B IVs with 105 Squadron, and their first mission from their base at Horsham was to Cologne, immediately after the 1,000-bomber raid. Not surprisingly, they found the city completely obscured by smoke rising to 14,000ft and their bombs had to be dropped by dead-reckoning.

Within the next week a second Mosquito squadron, 139, was formed at Horsham, initially using 105's aircraft. Their first mission was a raid on an airfield at Stade, Wilhelmshaven, returning in darkness, which virtually marked the start of round-the-clock bombing sorties.

During early missions the loss rates were as high as 16%, but as experience was gained and new tactics developed, the figure fell considerably and the Mosquito's destructive power was soon evident – even to the Air Ministry.

As raids increased, the Mosquito demonstrated time and again its ability to outrun enemy fighters. On 29 August

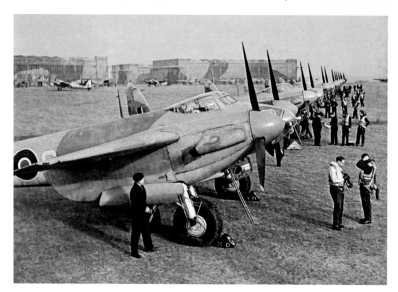

BELOW **This rare colour photograph of 139 Squadron Mosquito B IVs was taken at their base at Marham during the spring of 1943. In the foreground, in shirtsleeves and Mae West, is Wg Cdr Peter Shand, DFC, the squadron CO, who is standing in front of DZ421, 'XD-G'. Shand and his navigator, Plt Off Christopher Handley, DFM, were killed when their Mosquito was shot down over the IJsselmeer in the early hours of 21 April, returning from the first high-level night nuisance raid by Mosquitoes to Berlin to 'celebrate' Hitler's birthday.** *(Copyright unknown)*

105 Squadron went on a low-level daylight sortie to Pont-a-Vendin in northern France. They were met head-on by two Fw 190s that opened fire and then turned to attack from the rear, but they were unable to keep up.

The first daylight raid on Berlin was launched by six Mosquitoes from Horsham on 19 September, but a cloud-covered city and a fierce response from enemy fighters thwarted the attack. Flt Lt George Parry's Mosquito was attacked four times and, with the aircraft damaged, he got rid of his bombs over Hamburg – also cloud covered. Only one Mosquito reached the target and dead reckoning was used to drop the bombs. But a few days later Parry and three other Mosquitoes launched a successful low-level attack on the Gestapo HQ in Oslo, lobbing their bombs on to the building with an accuracy that astounded the public. Three Fw 190s attacked from above, and one Mosquito that fell behind was damaged and crashed into a lake. But it had been a very successful operation and it was at this point that the existence of the Mosquito was announced to Britain over the radio on the six o'clock news.

The most gleeful operation carried out by 105 Squadron was resoundingly scuppering a major rally aimed at demonstrating Nazi domination. Important speeches were to be delivered by Göring and Goebbels, starting with Göring at 11am on 30 January 1943, so three Mosquitoes set off with the aim of disrupting this. They succeeded, arriving just before Göring was about to deliver his address, and delayed proceedings for about an hour by dropping their bombs at a railway junction to the north of the city.

MOSQUITO CENTENARIANS

It depended upon the type of operation that Mosquitoes were called upon to fly that determined whether they would survive to score a high number of sorties. Among the Mossie's heavy-bomber stable-mates a goodly number of Lancasters (35 in fact) defied the odds to enable their groundcrews to paint 100 or more bomb symbols on their fuselage flanks. Only four Halifaxes exceeded 100 ops (LV907 *Friday the 13th* achieved the most at 128 ops), and not one Stirling came close to this magical number. The Mosquito was different, however, and in a league of its own when it came to survivability and the potential for scoring a century, maybe more.

Individual night-bomber Mosquitoes recorded the greatest number of sorties flown among all Allied aircraft of the war, of which the RAF's Pathfinder Force can lay claim to the biggest scorer in 109 Squadron's Oboe-equipped Mosquito B IX (LR503), which racked up an incredible 213 ops.

Total sorties for Mosquito fighter-bombers were never going to be as high as this, given the risky nature of their daylight low-level operations against heavily defended targets; the same was true of their day-bomber counterparts. The only known fighter-bomber centenarian is FB VI (LR385) at 104 ops, although most fighter-bomber Mossies achieved considerably less than this; the highest number of ops flown by a Mosquito day-bomber is thought to be in the upper 20s.

RAF photo-reconnaissance squadrons were credited with a number of successful PR Mosquitoes, but none is known to have surpassed the magical 100 ops. No 540 Squadron's PR IX, LR422, is believed to be the top-scorer with 69 sorties to its credit. Here are the ten top scorers:

ABOVE High-scoring Mosquito B IX, LR503, 'F for Freddie', was flown across the Atlantic to Canada on 5 May 1945 where its crew were to take the aircraft on a tour in support of a Victory War Bond drive and to mark the end of the European war. *(All photos Glenbow Museum Archive, Calgary)*

Serial	Mark	Squadron/unit	Ops
LR503	B IX	109/105 Sqn	213
LR504	B IX	109/105/109 Sqn	200
ML897	PR IX	1409 Met Flt	161
LR507	B IX	109/105 Sqn	148
ML914	B IX	105 Sqn	148
ML922	B IX	105 Sqn	111
LR385	FB VI	21/487/16/268/487/268	104
DZ319	B IV	109 Sqn/MTU	102
ML907	B IX	109 Sqn	100
DK331	B IV	109 Sqn	100

RIGHT Soon after landing at Calgary on 9 May 1945, Flt Lt Maurice Briggs, DSO, DFC, DFM (left), with Flg Off John Baker, DFC and Bar and ground engineer Edward Jack, pose for a photograph beside 'F for Freddie'.

BELOW Briggs and Baker beat up the tower at Calgary airport on 9 May. Twenty-four hours later they made an almost identical low pass but collided with the anemometer pole atop the control tower, shearing off the Mossie's port wing, which caused the aircraft to crash and burn more than half a mile away, killing its crew.

RIGHT Calgarians flocked in their hundreds to the airport to welcome Briggs and Baker.

They all returned safely to base, having met surprisingly little resistance from fighters or ground fire. Göring was one of the few Nazi leaders who could take a joke about himself, but humiliation was another matter – and the Mosquito, which he so admired, had seriously humiliated and embarrassed him. The raid was publicised in Britain as thumbing your nose at the school bully, and was a great morale-booster. A follow-up raid later that day by Mosquitoes from 139 Squadron messed up Goebbels's address as well.

But soon afterwards, on 26 February 105 suffered a terrible blow when their leader, Wg Cdr Geoffrey Longfield, was killed in a collision with another Mosquito during a successful raid on the naval stores serving U-boats at Rennes. Command of the squadron was taken over by Wg Cdr John Wooldridge, DSO, DFC and Bar, DFM, who had already flown more than 70 missions. Affectionately known as 'Dim', Wooldridge was unusual in that as well as being a courageous and skilled pilot he was also a talented composer and academic, having studied under Lukno, a disciple of Sibelius, and was a friend of William Walton. He was anything but dim.

He led 105 on low-level raids and was greatly impressed by the Mosquito – so much so, that he wrote a glowing letter to de Havilland, describing how it could absorb huge punishment and concluding that it was 'a sturdy, pugnacious little brute, but thoroughly friendly to its pilot'.

Pathfinders and Light Night Striking Force

The successful use of 109 Squadron's Oboe-equipped Mosquitoes as target marking aircraft in the night offensive against the Ruhr in early 1943, led Air Chief Marshal Sir Arthur 'Bomber' Harris, Commander-in-Chief, RAF Bomber Command, to conclude that the Mosquito was now 'indispensable' in the pathfinding role. No 109 Squadron had been one of the founder units of the newly formed Pathfinder Force in August 1942 (renamed 8 (Pathfinder) Group in January 1943) and used Oboe for the first time in December. It was soon joined in

the pathfinding role by two more Mossie squadrons, 105 and 139.

The principle of pathfinding was simple but effective: a small force of aircraft would locate the target and drop coloured marker flares for the following Main Force of heavy bombers to aim at. This technique was not suitable for precision bombing because the parachute flares were prone to drift on the wind, but it was ideal for the massed area bombing of German cities. At first pathfinder Mosquitoes were used only to target-mark for the Main Force 'heavies' like the Lancaster and Halifax, but later they combined marking duties with their own nuisance raids or 'spoofs' to divert attention away from the Main Force targets.

'Spoofing' was aimed at fooling the enemy with diversionary raids, and jamming their ground-

based radar system by dropping clouds of chaff made from thin strips of aluminised paper, which fogged enemy radar screens. Known as 'Window', it was first used by Mosquitoes of 139 Squadron on 18–19 November 1943, four months after its initial use over Hamburg. The idea was that enemy fighters would be directed on to the 'spoof' bomber formation, leaving the real one to get on with its business.

The Oboe-equipped Mosquitoes, mainly B IXs and B XVIs, played a vital role in pathfinding, and use was made later of H2S ground-mapping radar, but inaccurate marking was worse than none at all, as 617 Squadron found during raids on smaller targets. Their bombing was spot-on, landing right in the marked zone, but the markers dropped from high altitude had often drifted away from the intended target, leading to a wasted mission.

Commanding officer of 617, the legendary Wg Cdr Leonard Cheshire, pioneered a new and accurate, but extremely dangerous, method of marking by approaching the target at very low level before releasing the marker. However, it caused some political rumblings: Air Vice-Marshal Sir Ralph Cochrane, 5 Group commander, was all for it, but AVM Don Bennett felt it encroached on operating methods by 8 (PFF) Group, of which he was the Air Officer Commanding.

Cheshire always put himself in the most dangerous position, never leaving it to anyone else. A classic example was when he used his marking procedure during an attack on Munich on 24 April 1944, and he chose this

target because of its formidable battery of searchlights and anti-aircraft weaponry so that his method could be tested to the full. The weather was bad and his Mosquito was under continuous fire on the approach to the city. Flares dropped above by other aircraft on the mission lit him up from above, while searchlights picked him out from below.

Almost blinded by their intensity, he nearly lost control but succeeded in dropping his markers with great precision from 700ft altitude. He then circled the area from 1,000ft to assess his accuracy, and even though his aircraft was hit by shell fragments, he stayed at the scene to direct other aircraft until the mission was complete. Turning for home, he was continually under what his Victoria Cross citation described as 'withering fire' for 12 minutes.

In early 1944 the Light Night Striking Force (LNSF) was formed in 8 (PFF) Group, initially with 139, 627 and 692 Squadrons, although 627 soon left to join 5 Group's marker force. Later, 128, 571 and 608 Squadrons joined the LNSF and took part in the all-Mosquito force's frequent 'spoofing' missions over Germany, guided to their targets by Oboe-equipped PFF Mosquitoes.

In the closing months of the war, the Light Night Striking Force launched relentless attacks on Berlin, carrying out sorties on 27 nights in March 1945. It became known as 'the milk run' among Mosquito crews, and 'the Berlin Express' by the Germans. The pilot of a Canadian-built B XXV of 142 Squadron claimed in his log book to have done the *Daily Telegraph* crossword on the way home from a raid. By this time the Third Reich was crumbling and the end was near.

The Mosquitoes of 8 (PFF) Group had performed exceptionally well and, since its formation, they had flown 28,215 sorties with the loss of just 100 aircraft (0.4%). Approximately 26,000 tons of bombs, of which nearly 10,000 of them were Cookies, were dropped on Germany.

Bomber support

Mosquitoes served in greater numbers than any other type used by 100 (Bomber Support) Group, with which its primary role was to destroy the Luftwaffe's night-fighter force,

BELOW Preparing to bomb-up 692 Squadron's B IV, DZ637, 'P3-X', at Graveley, with a 4,000lb 'Cookie' in April 1944. This particular aircraft was the third RAF Mossie to drop a Cookie. Ten months later DZ637 was serving with 627 Squadron at Woodhall Spa when she was hit by flak on ops to Siegen on 1–2 February 1945, forcing her pilot Flt Lt Ronald Baker to crash-land on a road in Germany, killing him and his navigator Sgt Douglas Betts. *(Copyright unknown)*

and so protect Bomber Command's Main Force heavies and pathfinders. In its role of Bomber Support, the Mosquito struck real fear into German pilots – and they had a name for it: '*Moskitoschreck*' – Mosquito terror.

Night-fighter Mossies (NF XIXs and NF 30s) mingled with the bomber stream, while F IIs and FB VIs headed straight for German night-fighter assembly beacons, or flew low-level airfield intruder sorties where they lurked in the circuit waiting for 'custom'.

'Flower' operations saw Mossies patrol enemy night-fighter airfields while overhead the main bomber force flew through the night-fighter belt. Usually operated in two phases, bomb-carrying Mosquitoes flew ahead of the Main Force to bomb airfields and keep enemy fighters on the ground, while long-range Mosquito fighters attacked night-fighters coming in to land.

Mossies were also engaged in 'Mahmoud' sorties, which were carried out independently of Bomber Command operations, and consisted of homing in on German night-fighter assembly points and attacking any aircraft they found before they could intercept the bombers.

Mosquito B IVs and PR XVIs of 100 Group were fitted with specialised electronic equipment to jam German radar and radio, and for electronic intelligence (ELINT) gathering.

Luftwaffe crews became very wary of the constant and potent presence of the Mosquito, never knowing where or when they might come under attack, and this fear alone accounted for a number of aircraft lost as pilots made hurried landings in a bid to escape actual or imagined attacks. The combined Bomber Support operations claimed 249 enemy aircraft destroyed in flight for the loss of 69 Mosquitoes.

Coastal strike

On a bitterly cold November morning in 1943 a U-boat was nosing its way silently towards the calm waters south of Brest. Its crew were tired after weeks at sea, constantly on the alert for attacks from Coastal Command aircraft or naval warships. But they had got through unscathed, and now they were nearing base. Soon they could get cleaned up, eat some

ABOVE '**Are ops scrubbed?**' '**No, you're "Dicing" tonight boys!**' **Inside the officers' mess at Little Snoring in north Norfolk, intruder Mosquito crews of 100 Group behold the simple contraption of a scrubbing brush and a dice tied to a piece of string, suspended from a ceiling beam, which reveals what's in store for the night ahead. Between November 1943 and May 1945 the Mossie equipped all eight of 100 Group's fighter squadrons and flew nearly 8,000 offensive sorties, claiming a total of 267 enemy aircraft destroyed for a loss of 69.** (*BAE Systems/DH1692B*)

BELOW **German Type XXI electro-boat, U-2502, comes under cannon fire from a Mosquito FB VI during an attack on four surfaced U-boats and an M-class minesweeper escort south of Göteborg in the Kattegat by 22 Mosquitoes of the Banff Strike Wing on 19 April 1945. U-2502 received only slight damage, but the Type VIIC U-boat, U-251 (*Oblt Franz Säck*), was sunk. A Type XXIII was seriously damaged and the minesweeper was left burning.** (*IWM C5338*)

decent food, get some good sleep and relax, for they were in safe waters – or so they thought.

As the cold fingers of early light stole across the sky and the sun began to rise over the horizon, lookouts on the conning tower suddenly spotted a Mosquito diving towards them. They sounded the alarm: 'Enemy aircraft approaching!' Moments later they saw a red flash and then there was a tremendous crash as the sub was hit by a large shell which penetrated the hull, killing several members of the crew who, only seconds earlier, had been looking forward to shore leave.

They had been on the receiving end of a devastatingly powerful field gun installed under the nose of an FB XVIII from 248 Squadron based at Predannack in Cornwall. This howitzer,

known as the Molins after the cigarette machine company that designed the feed mechanism, could fire 57mm shells at the rate of 60 per minute, and was not fitted to many Mosquitoes but proved a highly effective weapon in Coastal Command's arsenal. Although U-boats were its intended target, it was also used against enemy aircraft with success.

Greater punch

With their terrific performance and ability to carry a wide variety of armament, Mosquitoes were the ideal choice to join the Strike Wings of Coastal Command, offering greater punch than the slower Beaufighters. Operating to the extreme north and south of the

BELOW Mosquito FB XVIII, NT225, 'O', of 248 Squadron Special Detachment at Portreath in Cornwall, banks away from the camera on 5 August 1944 to reveal the 57mm Molins gun in its installation beneath the nose. The 'Tsetse' was among the few Allied fighter-bombers to carry armour protection in the nose section and around the engines, which undoubtedly saved a number of its crews from serious injury or worse. 'Tsetse' navigator Des Curtis from 618 Squadron remembers the experience of firing the 57mm round: '... with a blinding flash and a bang its tracer tip sped towards the waterline ... that noise was backed up by the clang as the heavy brass shell case was ejected from the breach'. *(IWM CH14114)*

BELOW On 12 December 1944 23 Mosquitoes of 143, 235, 248 and 333 Squadrons from the Banff Strike Wing attacked an enemy convoy off Eid Fjord in Norway. In this remarkable photograph a 57mm Molins gun shell streaks towards its target, fired from a 248 Squadron 'Tsetse' Mosquito. The *Wartheland* (3,678 tons) was sunk and the 815-ton *Molla* was badly damaged in the attack. Note the two Mosquitoes just visible above the mast-tops. *(Jonathan Falconer collection)*

United Kingdom, they were targeting three main types of shipping: merchant vessels between Norway and Germany supplying iron-ore for the German war effort, the much more dangerous capital ships in the northern fjords, and U-boats in the Bay of Biscay and Western Approaches leaving or returning to their French bases.

These would usually be on the surface and presented theoretically easy targets, but the subs could put up some lethal return fire from their deck-mounted guns. However, it was not enough, and after strikes in what were considered friendly waters off the French coast, the German Admiralty were forced to provide an escort of surface ships and fighters to protect their U-boats.

In spite of this umbrella of protection, Mosquitoes continued to press home attacks on the U-boats with success. Information on their movements was often provided by code-breakers, and the usual method of assault was to dive at the target, open fire on the way down, and then break away to leave other Mosquitoes to strafe escorting ships.

Coastal Command had seven squadrons equipped with Mosquitoes, mostly the FB VI but also some FB XVIIIs, and they were employed mainly on patrolling the Norwegian coast and Biscay areas, often mixing with Beaufighters on sorties – not too popular with Mosquito pilots,

who had to throttle back to match the Beau's 180mph cruising speed.

The effectiveness of the Molins gun was demonstrated on 10 March 1944 when FB XVIIIs from 248 Squadron, escorted by four FB VIs, came upon a German force of one U-boat and four destroyers, with considerable air support from ten Ju 88s. The FB VIs attacked the Ju 88s and shot down three of them, one being destroyed by four shells and falling in flames with one engine shot clean away by the big cannon, while the XVIIIs concentrated on the shipping, scoring hits on the U-boat and damaging a destroyer.

Two weeks later a pair of Molins Mosquitoes destroyed submarine U-976, and on 10 June the crew of U-821 abandoned ship in the face of fierce attacks by similarly armed aircraft from 248 Squadron. The submarine was finished off by a Liberator.

The Banff Strike Wing

Shortly after D-Day Germany withdrew its U-boats from the west coast of France to bases in Germany and Scandinavia, so Coastal Command made plans in mid-1944 to transfer its Mosquito and Beaufighter squadrons to the north-east of Scotland on the coast of the

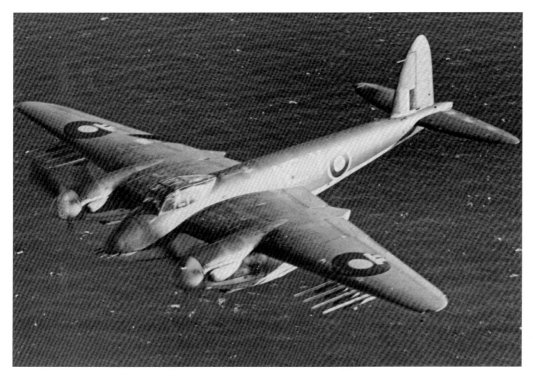

LEFT Fully armed and ready for action, 143 Squadron's Mosquito FB VI, 'NE-Y', photographed at low level over the sea. *(Jonathan Falconer collection)*

RIGHT Mosquito FB VI, PZ446, of 143 Squadron, is serviced and re-armed with 60lb rocket projectiles at Banff, Aberdeenshire, for an anti-shipping strike off Norway in December 1944. PZ446 survived the war. *(IWM HU1626)*

BELOW The Banff Strike Wing fought a fierce and bloody war at close quarters against Axis shipping. A Mosquito FB VI of 143 Squadron pulls away over the German-controlled Norwegian vessel *Lysaker*, after pulverising it with a barrage of rocket projectiles in the little harbour of Tetgenaes near Stadlandet in Dalsfjord, Norway. A strike force of 42 Mosquitoes from the Banff Strike Wing escorted by 12 Mustangs were involved in the attack on 23 March 1945, which left a large German merchant vessel on fire and the 910-ton *Lysaker* seriously damaged. The return fire from convoys and U-boats was usually fierce and few Mossies returned from an op without sustaining some sort of damage. Three Mosquitoes were lost on this operation. *(Jonathan Falconer collection)*

Moray Firth. It was here in September that the famous Banff Strike Wing was formed, led by the charismatic Grp Capt Max Aitken, DSO, DFC, son of Lord Beaverbrook, the Minister of Aircraft Production, and made up of Mosquitoes from 235 and 248 Squadrons from Cornwall, while 333 Squadron, which was crewed by Norwegians, concentrated on reconnaissance sorties along the Norwegian coast and acted as pathfinders for the strike force. Later the wing was joined by 143 Squadron, which had just been equipped with Mosquitoes, followed by 144 and 404 Squadrons.

Aitken was a man to be reckoned with: legend has it that when told very firmly that station commanders were not to fly on operations, he replied with just two words, the second of which was 'you'. He was just the kind of leader that crews needed on these missions. Operating only a few months before the end of the war, the Wing's life was brief but its success was spectacular.

Mosquitoes were being equipped with rocket projectiles – four under each wing – which wreaked havoc on surface shipping. With a full complement of rockets and under-wing drop-tanks, the wings would waggle noticeably on take-off and low-speed handling was affected. The method of attack was to start a 45° dive from 2,000ft, opening with the machine guns as sighters at between 1,500 and 1,000ft, then unleash the rockets at about 500ft.

These were set to form a pattern spread, so that if aimed correctly half would hit a ship above the waterline with the rest undershooting slightly and doing damage below the waterline. Some would pass right through the ship, while others would cause mayhem as they ricocheted around inside.

Attacking ships in the Norwegian fjords had obvious hazards such as sheer rock faces, which enemy vessels would use as shelter. The Germans added one more in the form of wires strung across the cliffs. These could not be seen from the cockpit until it was too late, and 235 Squadron's commanding officer, Wg Cdr Richard Atkinson, DSO, DFC, fell victim to this ruse. A wing of his Mosquito was sliced clean off, and both he and navigator Flg Off Valentine Upton were killed.

Aided by 333 Squadron's skill in locating enemy shipping in the mountain-fringed fjords, Mosquitoes were able to inflict massive damage on surface vessels and U-boats, thus seriously disrupting vital supplies to Germany. Sometimes missions were carried out with a mixed strike force of Mosquitoes, Beaufighters from RAF Dallachy and Mustangs from the Polish 315 Squadron based at RAF Peterhead.

The climax to attacks on shipping came in the spring of 1945, when on 5 April Mosquitoes with Molins cannon attacked five German surface ships in the Kattegat and soon had them all ablaze and foundering. A total of some 900 Germans died in this raid.

Then, four days later, 37 Mosquitoes from 143, 235 and 248 Squadrons armed with under-wing rockets attacked three U-boats heading for Norway – U804, U843 and U1065. Rocket after rocket hurtled on to the subs, causing one to sink and another to blow up, while the third was set on fire. But the U-boat gunners fought back hard, resulting in three Mosquitoes having to land in Sweden and a fourth to crash into the sea.

Coastal Mosquitoes were not only dealing with shipping, for on 19 April 12 of them armed with rockets came across 18 Ju 88 torpedo bombers 150 miles off the Scottish coast. The Mosquitoes pounced and before long the sea was a mass of blazing and wrecked Junkers aircraft. The whole episode was over very quickly.

Banff Strike Wing's final attack of the war on shipping was on 4 May in the Kiel and Kattegat areas. This was a massed operation by five squadrons and involved 40 Mosquitoes, 18 Mustangs for fighter cover, and 3 air-sea rescue Vickers Warwicks ready to drop lifeboats to ditched crews. As the Mosquitoes dived in to attack a convoy they were met by a hail of flak, but they sank the German merchant ship *Wolfgang L.M. Russ* and inflicted serious damage on the *Gunther Russ* and the Danish merchant vessel *Angamos*.

One Mosquito came back with a souvenir from this mission: as Flt Lt Gerry Yates pulled out at the last moment after launching his rockets he felt an impact and knew he had clipped the mast of his target. When he landed back at Banff the top of the mast was embedded under the nose, complete with German ensign. Four days later the war in Europe was over.

Meteorological reconnaissance

Another very important operation performed by Mosquitoes was weather reconnaissance over hostile territory to forecast conditions for coming raids. Code-named PAMPA (Photorecce And Meteorological Photography Aircraft), these were first carried out by Spitfires of 1401 Flight at Bircham Newton and later by Mosquito B IVs fitted with meteorological equipment. By 1944 the PR XVI was being used for most of these flights, often in conditions so appalling that most other operations had to be aborted.

It was dangerous work, and devious courses had to be devised to mislead the enemy, as flying direct to a planned target would have given the game away. Crews were specially trained to bring back accurate and useful information, and some weather sorties were carried out at night, flares being used to illuminate cloud formations. Unlike bomber squadrons, the Mosquito weather crews were on constant call night and day, and security was of great importance. On average, each Meteorological Flight member carried out 87 sorties, flying around 25 missions per month.

ABOVE A BOAC Mosquito comes in to land at Leuchars in Scotland. BOAC operated a fleet of Mosquitoes aircraft between 1943 and 1945 on regular 'ball-bearing runs' between Leuchars and Stockholm, Satenas and Göteborg in Sweden, a round trip of about 1,600 miles. The Mossies made 520 return trips to Sweden for the loss of four aircraft with eight crew and two passengers. Churchill also relied on the Mossie for long-range courier mail services during some of his overseas conferences. *(Jonathan Falconer collection)*

BELOW It was certainly not an ideal way to travel for anyone with claustrophobia, but a single VIP passenger or a courier could be carried lying flat inside the converted cannon/bomb-bay of a BOAC Mosquito. The bomb-bay was lined with felt and fitted with an oxygen supply, intercom, ventilation controls, and a reading lamp. The passenger was provided with a flask of coffee, sandwiches and reading material for the three-hour journey. *(IWM CH14389)*

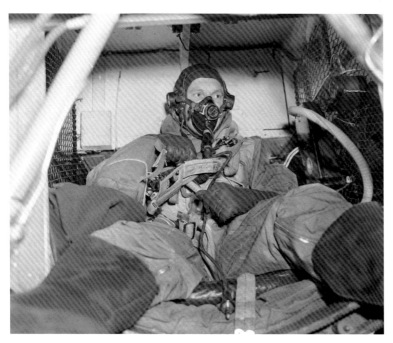

BOAC Mosquitoes

Perhaps the most unlikely role for the Mosquito was as an airliner, albeit one in which space was restricted and hardly in the luxury travel category. But the main purpose was to ensure the air link to Sweden was kept open for the continuous supply of high-quality engineering and electrical products, especially ball bearings, as well as mail and other light freight.

Sweden was a neutral country and supplied both Britain and Germany, but their products were vital to us. The air service between Leuchars and Stockholm had been provided by BOAC since 1942 with Lockheed Hudsons and Lodestars, but these were slow and becoming very vulnerable, especially in light summer evenings, or when silhouetted against the Northern Lights. Something faster was needed, something that could outrun enemy fighters, something that could fly higher than the 20,000ft of these older machines.

The obvious answer was the Mosquito. BOAC received its first one, a PR IV, in mid-December 1942. Its military serial DZ411 was changed to G-AGFV, and it began operating on 4 February. The Germans immediately stepped up their offensive and an Fw 190 opened fire on it as it crossed the Skagerrak in April. Battered and bruised, it belly-landed near Stockholm and operations were stopped until FB VIs were ready, and these managed to sail through unhindered.

Then came a potential problem caused by a major raid on the Schweinfurt ball-bearing factories by B-17s from the US Eighth Air Force: the Germans planned to source their ball bearings from Sweden until the works were up and running again. Something had to be done, and thanks to the BOAC Mosquitoes it was. Two were converted in a few hours to carry a passenger in the bomb-bay, and each immediately set off to Stockholm with a British negotiator on board. The speed of the Mosquito ensured they arrived just an hour or so before a team from Germany on a similar mission, and they managed to secure for Britain Sweden's entire ball-bearing export.

Other passengers on various tasks began to be carried, but there was only space for two, and tight space at that. Comfort was not the name of the game: he would lie on a mattress above the former cannon-bay access doors and would wear a flying suit, flying boots and a Mae West. There was a reading light, temperature control, and an intercom to the pilot, who could give instructions on how to adjust the oxygen setting, or perhaps warn of an impending attack – an event which required some reassuring words.

BOAC operated a total of 13 civilian Mosquitoes for 27 months. By the time the service ended on 17 May 1945, they had flown 520 round trips at an average of around 9 trips each week – some crews making as many as 3 trips in one night. Out of all those flights only 8 crew members and 2 passengers lost their lives.

Middle East

Operations in the Middle East got off to a tentative start, with the first Mosquitoes flying over from British bases and then returning after a few hours. However, this gave them time to assess fuel consumption over these long flights, and also an opportunity to photograph parts of Italy.

The first squadron to use them in the Mediterranean was No 23. After several months of productive intruder flights over Europe, they were unexpectedly posted to Malta in December 1942. Fighter Command told de Havilland that 18 Mosquitoes would be

needed and would require long-range fuel tanks before they went. Once set up in Malta, the squadron carried out similar duties over Sicily, Italy and Tunisia, but conditions there were something of a shock after England, the word 'primitive' hardly doing them justice. Looking for a squadron HQ, Intelligence room, briefing room and pilots' locker room was fruitless: all they had was a 12ft-square stone-walled room with a bit of corrugated iron loosely fixed on top as a roof. Aircraft went to their dispersals down a country lane and through a herd of goats.

Then there was the problem of spares: none had arrived, and after damage received in low-level attacks they were urgently needed. But in the true British spirit of improvisation, repairs were done with cigar box wood, old tea chests and parts from bomb-bay doors. The most skilled repairs were carried out by the local coffin-maker – although his presence cast a slight feeling of foreboding over the crews.

Yet in spite of these makeshift repairs, the aircraft remained serviceable, and gradually operations in the Med and Middle East expanded as 256 Squadron moved to Malta in July 1943 in preparation for the invasion of Sicily, known as Operation Husky, which went on for more than a month in the summer of 1943. Mosquitoes also had the better of the enemy's air bases in the battle for Africa, often shooting up bombers after they had landed –

BELOW Mosquito II, DZ231, 'YP-R', of 23 Squadron, pictured over Malta on 27 June 1943. Under the command of Wg Cdr John Selby, DSO, DFC, (see also page 67), the squadron's main task was long-range intruder missions to Sicily, Italy, Tunisia and southern France, which caused havoc particularly among enemy transport aircraft and helped establish the squadron's reputation as 'The Flying Pirates'. *(IWM TR1075)*

even, in some cases, as they were about to enter the safety of their hangar.

Other squadrons using the Mosquito in the Middle East theatre were 108, based at Shandur near the Suez Canal, which was engaged in intruder operations, and No 46, which used a small number of the aircraft in the eastern Mediterranean from July 1944.

In 1945 two other squadrons converted to Mosquitoes: 255 who were conducting intruder sorties over the Balkans, and 600 Squadron, which carried out night-fighter defensive and offensive operations until the end of the war. In the summer of 1945, Mosquito B 25 pathfinders arrived for 614 Squadron, but the war was over before they could be put to any real use.

Far East

There were concerns about the effect on the Mosquito airframe from climatic conditions in the Far East, and of four F IIs shipped to India for weathering trials in May 1943, two had formaldehyde glue, which was thought to give some protection against attacks on the woodwork by insects. Two more

arrived on 9 August, and the crews of 681 PR Squadron were so impressed with them that reconnaissance flights were under way before the end of the month.

By the close of the year Mosquitoes were withdrawn from 681 and passed to 684 (later 81 Squadron), which operated over Rangoon, the Andaman Islands, Thailand, the Shan States, Akyab and other targets in the area. From February to May the following year they took delivery of PR IX and PR XVI Mosquitoes. The first squadron fully to convert to the Mosquito was 45 Squadron, which took delivery of the FB VI in February 1944, but it would not fly its first Mosquito missions until October.

Back at Hatfield there was surprise that things were going so well, as aircraft were being kept outside in temperatures of up to 130°F and 88% humidity, with very heavy rainfall at Calcutta between April and August. But such was the success even in these conditions that it was decided to equip more squadrons in the Far East with Mosquitoes.

Reconnaissance and mapping flights extended further as the aircraft did what it had done everywhere else: excelled in whatever role was chosen for it. Then came trouble.

ABOVE **Mosquito PR 34, RG203, 'E', of 684 Squadron detachment is towed into position for take-off at Brown's West Island, Cocos Islands, during July–August 1945. South East Asia Command (SEAC) planned to use the Cocos Islands as a forward operating base to retake Malaya, Singapore and the Dutch East Indies from the Japanese. In June 1945 a detachment of Mosquitoes from 684 Squadron and a squadron of Spitfires arrived, followed by five squadrons of Liberators and Catalinas, but the unexpectedly sudden collapse of Japan prevented their full deployment.** *(IWM CI1544)*

Just as a major operation to retake Burma was about to begin, which would have involved disabling the rail network to Mandalay and Rangoon, and in which Mosquitoes would have played a vital role, one fell apart in mid-air. An aircraft from 82 Squadron was making a practice bombing attack on 20 October, when the starboard wing outboard of the engine crumpled during a shallow dive. The crew were killed, victims of the weather conditions that had finally caused the glue to fail and the skin to lift.

Operations over Burma were suspended while all Mosquitoes were grounded and checked. Those using Casein glue were found to be problematic – but in some instances the faults originated in the construction at Hatfield and Leavesden rather than the glue itself, so it wasn't all down to the climate.

This caused a delay, but early in November Mosquitoes that had been cleared were back in the air and began bombing attacks and intruder operations.

Two more squadrons would go operational with the Mosquito from bases in India, bringing the total up to four. No 82 Squadron received its Mosquitoes from July 1944, beginning operations

in December 1944. No 110 Squadron's Mosquitoes arrived in November, finally going operational in March the following year.

The four squadrons made repeated and effective attacks on Japanese ground targets in Burma, such as Japanese air bases and the communication system – especially the railways, where bridge-busting operations became legendary. Towards the end of the war some of the units were withdrawn to prepare for the expected invasion of Malaya, but the sudden surrender by the Japanese meant that this operation never happened.

Mosquitoes of 110 Squadron dropped the last bombs of the Second World War on 20 August 1945, against a group of Japanese holding out to the bitter end in Burma.

'Everybody wanted Mossies, because the Mossie was the Rolls-Royce of the air'

W/O R.G. Browne

Chapter Four

Mosquito at peace

After hostilities ended, the Mosquito's versatility diversified from striking a blow at the enemy. Its photo-reconnaissance and high-altitude capabilities found many peacetime applications and it was in demand with a number of air forces overseas. It also became something of a celebrity on the big screen, and was even chosen for an attempt at a round-the-world speed record.

OPPOSITE Mosquito T 3s TV959 (foreground) and RR299 are pictured during service with the Home Command Examining Unit (White Waltham) during the 1950s before joining their first units, which were 13 and 51 OTUs respectively. (See pages 158–9 and 167 for further information about these aircraft.)
(Jonathan Falconer collection)

ABOVE Celebrate! The war is over. The date is Sunday 1 July 1945 and Danish civilians gather to watch a flypast by 21 Mosquitoes of 125 Wing from the RAF's 2 Group at Copenhagen airport, during an air display given by the RAF in aid of the liberated countries. Bad weather reduced the number of aircraft participating but the day was still a tremendous success. The roar of 42 Merlin engines passing low overhead must have been thrilling, as well as deafening. *(IWM CL2965)*

BELOW LEFT A Canadian-built Mosquito B XXV with its crew. This aircraft, KB637, was a late production example that arrived in the UK in April 1945 and was stored until issued to RNAS Middle Wallop in February 1946 for service with the Naval Air Radio Installation Unit (NARIU). It was returned to the RAF in March 1947 (with which it is seen here in the Middle East) and struck off charge a year later. *(Jonathan Falconer collection)*

BELOW RIGHT Wearing the post-war Bomber Command colour scheme of black-painted fuselage sides and large serial code, this is 139 Squadron's B 35, TK648, in 1951. *(T.W. Cooper via Andy Thomas collection)*

The Mosquito story did not end when the war was over. From 1945 until the last aircraft rolled off the production line in November 1950, several new variants were introduced and the Mosquito continued to serve in numerous roles both at home and abroad, from photographing devastating floods in Britain to reconnaissance missions in the jungles of Malaya – and also performed as mini-airliners carrying diplomatic mail and newspapers.

The major RAF versions were the PR 34, B 35 and NF 36, which had actually flown during the war, but most of their service was in peacetime. The PR 34 was a development of the PR XVI for operation over very long distances in the Far East, and for this role it could carry the maximum fuel load of 1,268 gallons, giving it a 3,600-mile capability at a cruising speed of

ABOVE After Britain threw away any chance of being the first to crack the sound barrier with the sudden and unexpected cancellation of the Miles M52 project, followed by the handing of all its data to America, attention was switched to supersonic research being conducted with rocket-powered models. These were safer – but, with 24 being built, hardly less expensive than the real thing – and scored zero in terms of national prestige.

With the aid of a Mosquito B XVI (PF604) to carry them aloft, the three-tenth-scale models, fitted with autopilot and telemetry equipment, were dropped from about 35,000ft. The picture shows one being loaded into the bomb-bay, but the whole exercise was fraught with failure. The first launch was on 8 October 1947, but the model was lost in turbulence before flight – and then a few days later on 14 October, as though to rub salt in the M52 wounds, Chuck Yeager made his

famous Mach 1 flight in the Bell X-1, thus making America the first through the so-called sound barrier.

The Labour Government faced a storm of protest over the M52 cancellation, and it wasn't until 10 October 1948, after numerous other failures, that an M52 model, again launched from the Mosquito, reached Mach 1.38 in level flight, thus vindicating the basic design of the M52. However, it failed to respond to radio commands and carried on out over the Atlantic – but by then Britain already had a manned supersonic aircraft when the swept-wing tailless de Havilland DH108 achieved Mach 1.0 in a dive on 6 September piloted by John Derry – albeit a dive that was wildly out of control.

The Government and the aviation industry have never been the happiest of bedfellows, but the M52 fiasco highlighted the relationship at its bumbling worst. *(Copyright unknown)*

LEFT The ultimate development of the Mosquito was the blisteringly fast de Havilland DH103 Hornet. It was overpowered and therefore sensational to fly, sporting a pair of the most highly developed Merlin 130/131 engines housed in clean, low-slung nacelles driving huge four-bladed propellers. Although it came too late to see active service in the war, it was a further example of the collective genius of the DH design team, and came to represent their defining statement of what was possible from a propeller-driven aircraft. The prototype touched 485mph, and even production models could exceed 470mph. Several versions of the Hornet and Sea Hornet were produced, including fighter, photo-reconnaissance and fighter-reconnaissance. *(Jonathan Falconer collection)*

LEFT Flg Off 'Collie' Knox (pilot, on the right) and Flg Off 'Tommy' Thompson (navigator) with Sqn Ldr Stan McCreith (81 Squadron CO) with 81 Squadron's PR 34A, RG314, at RAF Seletar in Singapore after flying the last operational sortie by an RAF Mosquito on 15 December 1955, just over 15 years after the prototype Mosquito (W4050) first flew. *(Copyright unknown)*

BELOW LEFT The wing structure of the Mosquito was complex from the start, and introducing folding wings for carrier operation was another challenge to test the genius of senior designer Bill Tamblin. The picture shows TR 33 (LR387), the first Sea Mosquito prototype, at Hatfield in June 1945. Both aircraft were converted FB VIs, but the first did not have folding wings. Slung under the fuselage is an 18in torpedo. *(BAE Systems/ DH1922)*

BELOW How to spoil a beautiful aircraft. The TT 39 target tug, with its huge, bulbous, multi-faceted glazed nose for camera operator and equipment. The nose conversion was carried out by General Aircraft Ltd, and there was also a dorsal observation dome. Three Fleet Air Arm squadrons used the TT 39 until May 1952. *(Copyright unknown)*

300mph. It was powered by the latest Merlin 113 and 114 engines. A total of 118 were built and they had carried out 38 operations before Japan surrendered in August 1945.

But peace is a relative word, and in 1948 PR 34s of 81 Squadron found themselves taking part in their most important post-war operation. A state of emergency was declared in Malaya on 17 June and a campaign was launched against Communist-backed insurgents, with Mosquitoes providing photo coverage of ground forces. The final combat sortie by an RAF Mosquito was on 15 December 1955 when a PR 34A from RAF Seletar flew a reconnaissance mission over suspected Communist strongholds in the Malayan jungle.

A small number of Mosquitoes also saw action with the Israeli Air Force during the Suez Crisis of 1956. At the time they were being taken out of service, but 13 aircraft of various marks were brought out of storage and made operational, with an additional 13 ex-Fleet Air Arm TR 33s being purchased from a British scrap dealer in 1954 and flown out from Blackbushe Airport.

At home, 58 and 540 Squadrons received PR 34s and one of their major peacetime operations was to photograph the severe floods on Britain's east coast in 1953, their comprehensive surveys with around 100,000 images being invaluable for rescue and repair work. Other variants used after the war were the T III trainer and TT 35 target tugs.

Away from home, the Dominican Air Force obtained six ex-RAF FB 6s in 1948, and in the same year the Royal Swedish Air Force

purchased 45 ex-RAF NF XIX Mosquitoes to be used as night-fighters under the J 30 designation. These had been overhauled before purchase and were fitted with four-bladed propellers. It was the first and only dedicated night-fighter unit of the Swedish Air Force. There were a significant number of failures and crashes during service, and the Swedish Air Force's General Björn Bjuggren wrote in his memoirs that mechanical problems in the swivelling nose-mounted radar antenna caused destructive vibrations that broke apart one or two J 30s in the air.

ABOVE The dual-control trainer version of the Mosquito was the T 3. This is TV959, which is now the subject of a major restoration to flying condition by Avspecs in New Zealand on behalf of its owner, Microsoft co-founder Paul G. Allen. *(Jonathan Falconer collection)*

BELOW TT 35, TA724, serving with 3 Civilian Anti-Aircraft Cooperation Unit (CAACU) at Exeter in the late 1950s. Between 1951 and 1954 more than 140 surplus B 35s were converted into target tugs by Brooklands Aviation at Sywell, Notts. This Mossie is fitted with a wind-driven ML Type G (Mk 2) winch mounted in the ventral bay. *(Jonathan Falconer collection)*

RIGHT CF-HMS was built as a B 35 (RS700) by Airspeed in 1946 and then converted to a PR 35 before service with 58 Squadron RAF between 1952 and 1954. In 1954 RS700 and nine other B 35 Mosquitoes were sold to Spartan Air Services in Canada for $1,500 each. RS700 was given the Canadian civil registration CF-HMS and for ten years she flew aerial survey work over northern Canada before her retirement from flying in 1964. She is now owned by the City of Calgary and is currently under restoration at the Bomber Command Museum of Canada in Nanton, Alberta.
(Calgary Mosquito Society)

The Belgian Air Force operated 24 Mosquito NF 30s between 1949 and 1956. They were flown by 10 Smaldeel of 1 Wing based at Beauvechain Air Base in Belgium, and in 1954 Belgium also received three Mosquito FB 6s which had been converted to target tugs.

In Canada, Spartan Air Services of Ottawa purchased 15 ex-RAF Mosquitoes, mostly B 35s, from the Air Ministry in 1955. Of these, ten were modified by Derby Aviation at Burnaston Airport for high-altitude aerial survey work.

After a complete overhaul, all military equipment was removed, Bendix ADF and HF/RT equipment installed, and long-range fuel tanks were fitted into the bomb-bay. Each aircraft was finished in eye-catching silver with arctic markings of red tips on the wings and tailplane.

Before purchasing the Mosquitoes, Spartan

had used P-38 Lightnings for photographic work, but found they did not have the altitude and load-carrying capability needed, and if they took on enough fuel for the required endurance they could not reach the target altitude. The Mosquito fulfilled all Spartan's needs.

On the other side of the world, Mosquitoes from the Royal Australian Air Force carried out extensive photographic sorties over India, Cambodia and Australia.

The last of the 7,781 Mosquitoes to be built, an NF 38, was completed on 15 November 1950 at de Havilland's Chester factory, and on Thursday 9 May 1963 the last Mosquitoes in service, six TT 35 target tugs operated by No 3 Civilian Anti-Aircraft Co-operation Unit, made a farewell flypast at Exeter Airport before being retired.

RIGHT The end of the line. Canadian-built Mosquito FB 26s KA273 and KA286 succumb to the flames at RAF Ismailia, Egypt, in November 1946, where dozens of surplus Mossies were stripped of engines and other useful parts by RAF salvage teams and the redundant fuselages burned.
(Jonathan Falconer collection)

MOSSIES ON THE BIG SCREEN

The Mosquito featured in any number of wartime newsreel and documentary films, but it achieved lasting fame in the 1950s and '60s with its lead roles in three big screen productions. It also had a 'walk-on part' in *The Dam Busters* (1955).

The Purple Plain (1954, Two Cities (Rank), directed by Robert Parrish)

Based on the novel by H.E. Bates, the film starred Gregory Peck and was made on location in Ceylon. Set in Burma during the war, Peck plays the part of an emotionally scarred Canadian pilot who is forced to make a crash-landing in the jungle. The film features ground and take-off shots of two PR 34 Mosquitoes, RG238 (which had set a London to Cape Town record in 1947), and RG177, both of which were modified to represent Mosquito FB VIs of South East Asia Command.

633 Squadron (1964, Mirisch (UA), directed by Walter E. Grauman)

Ron Goodwin's rousing film score and the breathtaking low-level flying sequences stick in the minds of all who have ever seen *633 Squadron*. Based on Frederick E. Smith's best-selling novel of the same name, the film tells the story of a fictitious RAF Mosquito squadron tasked with bombing a vital German-run fuel plant for Nazi V2 rockets at the head of a Norwegian fjord in the summer of 1944.

The cast was led by Cliff Robertson as Wg Cdr Roy Grant, supported by performances from George Chakiris, Erik Bergman and Maria Perschy. *633 Squadron* was one of the first British war films to be made in colour and in Panavision, and following its release in August 1964 the film quickly became a box office hit.

Grp Capt Hamish Mahaddie, a former RAF Pathfinder and 'Mr Fixit' to the film world, was hired by the Mirisch Corporation to buy a number of Mosquitoes on their behalf, and to secure the hire of several others from the RAF, the Imperial War Museum and the Skyfame Museum. Many were obtained direct from No 3 Civil Anti-Aircraft Co-operation Unit (CAACU)

THE GREATEST ADVENTURE SINCE MEN FOUGHT ON EARTH...OR FLEW OVER IT!

CLIFF **ROBERTSON** GEORGE **CHAKIRIS** **633 SQUADRON** *The Winged Legend Of World War II*

CO-STARRING MARIA PERSCHY HARRY ANDREWS DONALD HOUSTON DIRECTED BY WALTER E. GRAUMAN SCREENPLAY BY JAMES CLAVELL and HOWARD KOCH EXECUTIVE PRODUCER LEWIS J. RACHMIL PRODUCED BY CECIL F. FORD RELEASED THRU UNITED ARTISTS COLOR by DE LUXE PANAVISION

LEFT The movie *633 Squadron* (1963) starred Cliff Robertson, George Chakiris and Maria Perschy in the big-screen adaptation of Frederick E. Smith's best-selling novel of the same name. *(Jonathan Falconer collection)*

BELOW Owing to a lack of surviving Mosquito fighter-bombers, film maker the Mirisch Corporation was forced to modify TT 35s to represent FB VIs. This involved over-painting the Perspex nose and fitting dummy machine guns. The result was a hybrid Mossie whose appearance was not much like an FB VI, but it was the best compromise available in the circumstances. *(Jonathan Falconer collection)*

BELOW In this engine start-up scene, Bovingdon's control tower makes an authentic Second World War backdrop. During the war the airfield was home to B-17 Flying Fortresses of the US 8th AF. *(Jonathan Falconer collection)*

ABOVE Formation flying in the film was on occasions very close indeed. Here are TT 35 (TA719) alias HT-G (HJ898) in the foreground, with T 3 (TW117) alias HT-M (HR155) behind, and an unidentified Mossie in the background. *(Jonathan Falconer collection)*

ABOVE An unidentified Mosquito TT 35 pictured over the sea during filming. *(Jonathan Falconer collection)*

ABOVE Non-airworthy TT 35 (RS718) was used on 9 August 1963 for the dramatic undercarriage collapse sequence. Capt John Crewdson taxied the Mossie and then veered off Bovingdon's runway on to the grass at high speed with smoke billowing from canisters attached to the fuselage underside. At the required moment he selected undercarriage 'up' and the aircraft collapsed on to its belly before slewing to a stop in front of the cameras. *(Jonathan Falconer collection)*

at Exeter where they had just been retired from service. Eventually seven Mosquito TT 35s were acquired: four for flying sequences (RS709, RS712, TA719 and TA639); and three for ground sequences (TA642, TA724 and RS718). In addition, two T 3s were acquired: TW117 for flying sequences and to convert pilots on to type for the film; and TV959 for cockpit shots. A further two TT 35 fuselages (RS715 and TJ118) were dismantled and their forward fuselages used for the cockpit scenes.

The aircraft obtained from No 3 CAACU were stripped of their target-towing equipment and repainted in grey-green camouflage to replace their overall silver and yellow paint scheme. The bomb-aimer's glazed position in all the aircraft was over-painted and dummy gun barrels were fitted. For reasons best known to the film production team the modified aircraft bore little resemblance to the wartime B IV or FB VI.

Filming began in late July 1963 and lasted until early September with most of the airfield scenes and ground crash sequences filmed at Bovingdon, Hertfordshire, and the flying sequences shot over Scotland, the Wash and the Norfolk coast, and at Elstree Studios. The crash sequences led to the intentional destruction of TA724, TA642 and RS718 which, in today's climate of aircraft preservation, has led to the film acquiring a bad name with enthusiasts.

The aircrew for the film were supplied by John Crewdson of Film Aviation Services, who was also responsible for co-ordinating the flying sequences. The pilots were Capt John Crewdson, Flt Lt 'Jeff' Hawke, Sqn Ldr 'Taffy' Rich, Capt Peter Warden and Flt Lt 'Chick' Kirkham.

For all of the low-level flying sequences, TA719 was borrowed from the Skyfame Museum and re-engined with two zero-time Rolls-Royce Merlin engines to give it the required technical performance and reliability

LEFT A fire crew attends to RS718 during the undercarriage collapse scene at Bovingdon. *(Jonathan Falconer collection)*

to carry out the dramatic near-vertical passes of the cliff face in the fjord, as demanded by director Walter E. Grauman. The action in the Norwegian fjord was actually filmed at Loch Morar on the west coast of Scotland and is among the best war film flying sequences ever shot.

Mosquito Squadron (1969, Oakmont (UA), directed by Boris Sagal)

Screenwriters Donald Sandford and Joyce Perry based their storyline for *Mosquito Squadron* on the Amiens prison raid of 1944, although in their film the prisoners were British and their prison was the secondary target. The real purpose of the mission for the fictitious 641 Squadron was to destroy a German underground factory where a deadly new V-weapon was being made, adjacent to the Chateau Charlon where British prisoners were being held. No 641 Squadron's task was to use 'Highball'-type bouncing bombs to accomplish their mission, led by Squadron Leader Quint Monroe who was played by David McCallum. The story was interwoven with a slightly uncomfortable love affair between Monroe and Beth Scott, played by the lovely Suzanne Neve – uncomfortable because Beth's husband was one of the prisoners in the chateau, but she didn't know that.

Director Boris Sagal was handicapped with a far smaller budget than *633 Squadron* enjoyed and there were no established stars involved in the production. For the same cost reasons Oakmont (United Artists) were also compelled to cut down on flying time for filming the aerial sequences. Further economies were made by reusing footage of the crash sequence from *633 Squadron* involving RS718, together with a number of other short clips including the airfield raid. (This is why the aircraft in *Mosquito Squadron* wear the 'HT' squadron codes, the same as those used in *633 Squadron*.) It will come as no surprise to learn that *Mosquito Squadron* was not a hit with movie-goers and was often screened as part of a double-bill or as a supporting feature.

Much of the film was made in the summer of 1968 at Bovingdon in Hertfordshire and

BOMB IT, BUT DON'T BLOW IT! The bombing raid and the prison break were each impossible... the Mosquito Squadron did them both at once!

OAKMONT PRODUCTIONS presents

"MOSQUITO SQUADRON"

DAVID McCALLUM · Music by FRANK CORDELL · Written by DONALD S. SANFORD and JOYCE PERRY
Produced by LEWIS J. RACHMIL · Directed by BORIS SAGAL · COLOR by DeLuxe · United Artists

LEFT *Mosquito Squadron* (1969) starred David McCallum and is popularly regarded as a poor sequel to *633 Squadron*. *(Jonathan Falconer collection)*

used four airworthy Mosquitoes, one static example, and a cockpit section. The airworthy aircraft included two of the Mosquito TT 35s that had flown in *633 Squadron*: RS709 (owner Skyfame Museum), and RS712 (owner Hamish Mahaddie); plus one other TT 35 (TA634) owned by Liverpool Corporation, and a T 3 (RR299) owned by Hawker Siddeley. TT 35, TA719, which played the star role in *633 Squadron*, had been badly damaged in a flying accident at Skyfame's Staverton airfield, so it was used for the crash scene involving McCallum and filmed in the fields behind the MGM Studio at Borehamwood.

Four experienced pilots were selected for the flying sequences – Sqn Ldr 'Taffy' Rich, Neil Williams (ex-RAF test pilot and aerobatics pilot), and civilian test pilots Dizzy Addicot and Pat Fillingham.

The opening scene where four Mosquitoes approach a coastline was filmed near Scarborough. 'Chateau Charlon' where the British PoWs were incarcerated was portrayed in the film by Minley Manor near Blackbushe, Surrey, then in use as an annexe of the Army Staff College, Camberley.

The Mosquito has also appeared in written works of fiction, most notably in Frederick Forsyth's delightful novella *The Shepherd,* in which a ghostly Mosquito and its pilot escort a stricken Vampire to safety. Mosquitoes play a major role in the *Tintin* comic album *The Red Sea Sharks* and in the Marvel Comics *X-Men*, where brothers Scott and Alex Summers are orphaned after parachuting out of their father's Mosquito when it is set on fire in an alien attack. They have also appeared in the *Commando* comics, which were published from 1961 until 1993.

Mosquito record-breakers

Royal Air Force

The Mosquito's superlative performance enabled it to smash many existing time, speed and distance records. On the transatlantic route over which thousands of different aircraft were ferried during the Second World War from the factories of North America to the airfields of Britain, Mosquitoes kept on setting new records – only to break them.

On 13 May 1944 two Canadian-built Mosquitoes were flown across the North Atlantic in non-stop flights that broke all existing transatlantic records. The first aircraft was flown by Wg Cdr John Wooldridge, DFC and Bar, DFM, who crossed from Labrador, Newfoundland, to Prestwick, Scotland, coast to coast in 5hr 40min, take-off to landing 6hr 40min (which was 2hr 10min faster than the previous record set by an RAF B-24 Liberator).

The second Mosquito was piloted by 26-year-old Kirk Kerkorian, an American commercial pilot, who completed the flight in 7hr 9min. (After the war Kerkorian became a successful businessman and a billionaire who was responsible for developing America's gaming capital, Las Vegas.)

More time was shaved off the transatlantic record less than 12 months later on 1 April 1945 when a Mosquito flown by Flt Lt M.C. Graham crossed the Atlantic on a routine delivery flight in 5hr 38min.

Late in 1944 the RAF used a Mosquito to test the practicability of the type for a fast freight service between Britain and India. A PR XVI (NS688) piloted by Flt Lt James Linton with W/O Edwin Goudie as his navigator, flew from Britain to Karachi with a time of 16hr 46min (with stops at El Adem, Libya and Shaibah, Iraq).

Sqn Ldr John Merifield, a highly experienced RAF photo-reconnaissance pilot who had flown dozens of daring long-range sorties during the war, set a new westward transatlantic record of 6hr 58min in a Mosquito PR 34 on 6 September 1945 with navigator, Flt Lt John Spires.

Almost two years were to pass before a

RIGHT Warrant Officer Edwin Goudie, navigator (left), and Flt Lt James Linton, pilot, pictured on their arrival at Karachi just as dawn was breaking. Their record-breaking flight from England clipped 5hr and 27min off the record set ten years earlier in 1934 by Jim and Amy Mollison in their de Havilland DH88 Comet Racer on the MacRobertson Air Race. *(Copyright unknown)*

Mosquito again made the front pages of the national press, this time with a record-breaking flight from London to Cape Town. With former Dam Buster Sqn Ldr Mickey Martin, triple DSO, DFC, at the controls of Mosquito PR 34 (RG238) and Sqn Ldr Ted Sismore, DSO, DFC and two Bars (the RAF's finest low-level navigator of the Second World War) in the navigator's seat, the pair took off from London Airport at 8.04pm GMT on 30 April 1947. Martin and Sismore made only two stops for fuel, at El Adem and Kisumu, Kenya.

At 3.35pm GMT on 1 May, RG238 touched down at Brooklyn Airport, Cape Town, completing an officially timed point-to-point flight of 6,717 miles in 21hr 31min, thus lowering by 10hr 50min the unofficial record set up by the RAF Lancaster *Aries I* on 17 January 1946 and breaking the DH 88 Comet's pre-war record by 23hr 36min.

Dianna Bixby – Mosquito aviatrix

One of the most interesting civilian Mosquitoes was the B 25 purchased by Dianna Converse Cyrus Bixby, a skilled and courageous American aviatrix with a burning ambition to be the first woman to fly solo around the world and set a new speed record. Had she succeeded, it would have placed her as one of the all-time greats in aviation history, and earned the Mosquito a unique entry in the record books.

But it was not to be: a frustrating series of mechanical and weather-related issues caused

RIGHT Dianna Bixby chats with technicians as they examine a carburettor from the Mosquito in which she hoped to fly solo around the world in 1954. This is a Bendix-Stromberg PD18 twin-choke updraft unit from one of the Packard Merlin V-1650-9 engines fitted to her aircraft.
(Robert Converse)

three attempts to be aborted, and Dianna's life ended in tragedy before a fourth attempt could be made.

Born in 1922, she grew up in California and, like many girls, worshipped Amelia Earhart. In 1943 she married pilot John Cyrus – on condition that he taught her to fly, which he did. But after less than two years of marriage, Cyrus was killed when his Douglas A-20 bomber was shot down on a mission over France in January 1945.

In her grief she set her sights on the ultimate: to do what Earhart had died trying to accomplish before the war – be the first woman to circle the globe.

In June 1947 the petite 24-year-old set a new speed record between Burbank and Denver in a Douglas A-26 Invader, and later was responsible for resurrecting the famous all-women's air race, the Powder Puff Derby. Dianna was also a very keen and skilled horsewoman.

She made her living by flying for Eagle Air Freight and in 1948 had saved enough money to buy the aircraft of her dreams, a Mosquito. This was a Downsview-built B 25 (KA997), originally purchased from surplus production stock by Robert Swanson, who sold it on to her. That year she met and married pilot Bob Bixby, who became the guiding force in her ambition.

Her Mosquito was overhauled at Lockheed

Burbank and sported an eye-catching paint job of maroon and light grey, with its name *The Huntress* painted on the nose and bearing the US registration N1203V. But after meticulous preparations by the couple to cover every conceivable emergency, the flight was called off due to mechanical problems. Meanwhile, working for the Flying Tiger Line air freight company, she made history by becoming the first woman to fly as a commercial airline captain, echoing the achievements of her grandmother, Mary Parker Converse, who was the first woman to captain a merchant ship.

Two years later she was ready for another round-the-world attempt, but after the autopilot developed a fault her husband insisted on accompanying her. They set off on 1 April, and all looked promising until they reached Calcutta where a blown head gasket put paid to any chance of a record trip. The couple eventually completed the journey, arriving home exhausted and dispirited and later sold *The Huntress* to the Flying Tiger Line – but at least they had the distinction of being the first husband and wife team to circle the globe.

They then turned their attention to setting up a small air cargo company, Bixby Airborne Products, operating out of Long Beach Municipal Airport. By 1954 they were the parents of two young children – but Dianna's dream would not let go, especially in a moment of nostalgia when she came across her old Mosquito at the Flying Tiger Line.

The company agreed to loan it to her for the flight if she would cover the costs. This time the aircraft showed off an even more spectacular finish, with prominent shark's teeth on the nose and drop-tanks in addition to the maroon and grey paintwork. It was named *Miss Flying Tiger* and, unlike the previous attempts, featured a pressurised cockpit.

This work had been carried out by the Aviation Export Company under Clair M. Waterbury so that the freight line could carry out high-altitude survey flights. It was a radical conversion, with the whole of the fuselage forward of the wing leading edge being sawn off and replaced with a metal section which was designed to operate at a much higher pressure differential than de Havilland's wartime conversions – although due to problems with the blower, the high pressures designed for were not obtained. The only way in and out of N1203V was through a hatch on top of the reinforced cockpit, and because of this some pilots refused to fly it. It was a tricky machine to handle.

Dianna planned to do the 20,525-mile journey in just over 60 hours, which would have beaten Bill Odum's history-making flight of 73 hours. Take-off was scheduled for 3 April 1954, and Dianna was feeling confident: 'It should be a cinch!' she told reporters – but, as before, fate intervened with engine problems and unfavourable weather. The trip was abandoned. Yet again, Dianna's dream lay in ruins.

Still she would not give up, and planned to make yet another attempt the following year. But before she even had a chance, fate dealt its cruellest card. On 2 January 1955 Dianna took off in a Douglas A-20 Havoc from Long Beach for a routine 600-mile trip to the ranch that she and Bob leased in La Paz, Mexico. She was followed by Bob in a much slower DC-3.

As Dianna neared the ranch she encountered bad weather for the first time in the five years they had operated there, and decided to divert to a landing strip 150 miles to the north at Baja in California. As she got very near she radioed Bob that she was running low on fuel and was going to put down on the beach. Breaking through a 200ft cloud base into very poor visibility, she decided to go round again – but as she banked, one engine may have cut out, starved of fuel, and the port wingtip clipped the sea. She died instantly. It was thought that another ten gallons of fuel would have got her safely to the landing strip.

So ended the life of a brave and determined woman, gone before her time, her dream unfulfilled. By a strange quirk of fate, her death came ten years to the day from that of her first husband, also flying an A-20. Dianna was buried at her childhood home in Santa Paula. The wreck of her A-20 still lies in about 20ft of water.

As for N1203V, it too was wrecked the following year after breaking in half in a ground loop accident while landing at Haiti.

BELOW Clair Waterbury pictured at his home in Virginia Water, Surrey, at the age of 93 in May 2013 with a scale model of *Miss Flying Tiger*. This model was used by Dianna Bixby in 1954 to promote her proposed record-breaking flight. *(Brian Rivas)*

'The Mosquito proved that metal is not the only material for high performance aircraft.'

Mike Ramsden, de Havilland

Chapter Five

Anatomy of the Mosquito

The Mosquito has been likened to a full-size model aircraft, with its wooden formers, stringers and doped finish. But there the similarity ends, for with the Mosquito there were more than 10,000 drawings, and the many complex electrical, pneumatic and hydraulic systems that all added up to make it the superb multi-role warbird that it became.

OPPOSITE The fighter-bomber variant of the Mosquito. This is FB 26, KA114, a Canadian-built version of the FB VI, under restoration at Avspecs Ltd in New Zealand. The FB 26 was fitted with American-built Packard Merlin 225 engines, but in most other respects it was almost identical to its English-built cousin. *(Avspecs)*

Fuselage

Being built in two sections split vertically and skinned with a very strong ply–balsa–ply sandwich over the seven bulkheads, as much fitting-out as possible on the fuselage was done on the individual halves before they were bonded together. Control runs were installed in the port half, with hydraulic piping in the starboard side. Rudder and elevator linkage was mounted in the cockpit floor, and connections were made to the control column and rudder bar before the halves were joined.

The photo-reconnaissance and bomber versions, which were unarmed, had a glazed nose for the bomb-aimer or camera operator, while the fighters had a solid nose to accommodate the four .303 Browning machine guns and four 20mm Hispano cannon. The ammunition boxes and belt feeds for the cannons were housed in the forward section of the ventral bay and accessible via the ventral bay doors. The latter also featured chutes for the empty shell cases.

The crew entry hatch on bombers was on the underside at the front of the fuselage. On fighters, where this space would be taken up with the cannons and associated equipment, the entry was on the starboard side beneath the cockpit canopy. A further hatch was behind the wing aft of bulkhead number four on all variants.

Among the equipment in the nose of unarmed Mosquitoes were the bomb-aimer's elbow pad and writing tablet, stowage pouch for camera leads, fireman's axe, fire extinguisher and portable oxygen bottles. The glazed area had a heated flat transparent section with an external de-icing jet to ensure that the bomb-aimer always had the clearest view, whatever the weather.

Immediately to the rear of the cockpit in front of bulkhead number two was the voltage regulator, and behind that were the high-tension power unit, oxygen bottles, hydraulic reservoir and stowage for the dinghy. By

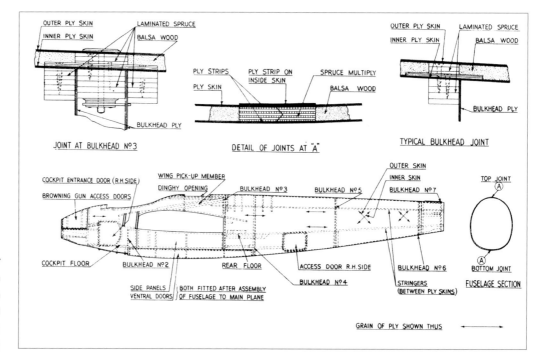

bulkhead number three, over the rear of the wing, were four metal oxygen bottles, accumulators, bomb winch and the pneumatic gear hydraulic control panel. Just in front of bulkhead four on the port side of the fuselage skin, was the ground starter socket.

The two fuselage fuel tanks, each with a 68gal capacity (B IV), were in the centre section between bulkheads two and three, while underneath was the bomb-bay with bomb rack, bomb winch and bomb-rack carriers.

In the forward space between bulkheads four and five were the aneroid switch for the supercharger, cabin lamp above the rear entry hatch, compressed air container, de-icing fluid tank and – near to bulkhead five – camera stowage and mounting boxes.

The rearmost bulkheads, six and seven, carried the front and rear fin attachment posts. This area was particularly busy, being taken up with the rudder spring-loaded rod, rudder mass balance and linkage, support rods for the tailplane rear spar, elevator mass balance and the jack for retracting the tailwheel.

Cockpit

Mosquito crews enjoyed a superb all-round view from the framed cockpit, with a 'teardrop' bulge either side for keeping an eye on what was happening behind. The pilot's seat was on the port side, angled slightly inwards, and the navigator sat next to and slightly behind him.

Bombers and PR variants had a V-shaped windscreen with centre bracing, but fighters had a flat bulletproof screen. A windscreen de-icing jet protruded from the fuselage immediately in front of the screen.

A thick steel armoured plate provided protection at the back of each seat, and housed in the rear section of the cockpit behind the crew were the transmitter, receiver and upward-facing navigation lamp.

ABOVE The basic structure of the Mosquito before anything is hung on it, in this case B 35, VR796, which is seen in April 2009 while under restoration to flying condition by Victoria Air Maintenance in Canada on behalf of its owner, Bob Jens. *(Victoria Air Maintenance)*

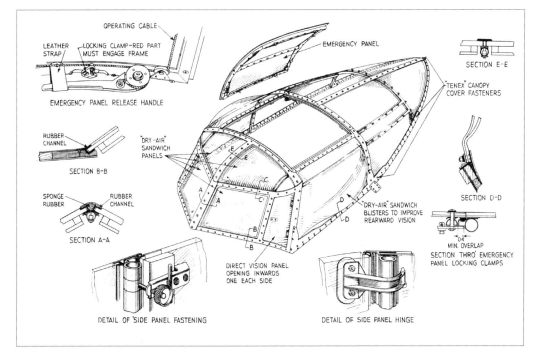

LEFT Cockpit canopy assembly – bomber version. The Mosquito canopy is a welded steel tube structure bolted and screwed to the fuselage skin. *(Crown Copyright)*

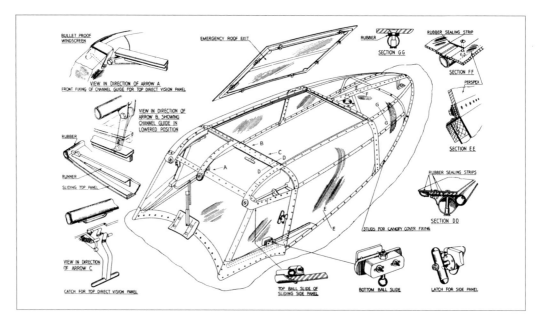

Converting Mosquitoes for extreme high-altitude work presented some special challenges for the backroom boys in terms of pressurising and adapting the cabin.

Double-glazing the canopy

The front panels, pilot's direct vision panel, the upper front panels, the bulged sides of the cockpit canopy and the bomb-aimer's elliptical panel in the nose were made up of double layers of Perspex to avoid misting and frosting at altitude, at least up to 35,000ft. The air supply to these 'Perspex sandwich' interspaces was dried by passing it through a single large reservoir of silica gel located in the nose of the aircraft before being circulated between the layers of glazing. The remainder of the canopy was made up of single-layer Perspex, which was still prone to misting and frosting above 23,000ft, but which was easily cleared with a manually directed stream of warm air from the flexible air supply tube.

Pressure cabin

Sealing the fuselage

The Mosquito pressure cabin extended from behind the cockpit forward, to include the bomb-aimer's compartment in the nose. In order to make the forward fuselage airtight for pressurising, no fewer than 36 apertures in the cabin needed to be sealed – doors, hatches, windows, joints, cables and control tubes.

This was achieved by various means that included glanding with rubber washers and plastic seals. The wing-to-fuselage joint was sealed with felt strips soaked in a sealing compound. A release valve was fitted to allow equalisation of cabin pressure so the aircraft could be abandoned if necessary.

Pressurisation

The cabin was pressurised by a single Marshall supercharger (or blower) mounted on top of the port Merlin 73 engine. Air for pressurising the cabin was drawn in by the blower from the underside of the port wing leading edge, outboard of the airscrew disc, and passed through a filter in the suction duct. From the blower it was fed through the cabin heater where it was warmed, then via a felt-lined duct and a non-return valve to the cabin. It entered through two fish-tailed tubes, one of which was fixed, the other flexible (see drawing opposite).

The air pressure inside the cabin, in relation to the external air pressure, was controlled automatically by a Westland valve that acted like a leak in the cabin, and was fully open at any height below 15,000ft. As the aircraft climbed above this level the valve gradually closed so that at heights above 30,000ft there was a differential pressure in the cabin of 2psi above the external atmosphere (the equivalent of 10,000ft). An altimeter and pressure gauge indicated the cabin 'height' and pressure.

Incorporated in the Westland valve was a

safety valve, which blew off at 2½psi pressure should the normal controlling mechanism develop a fault. However, if the pressure fell as low as ½psi, then a warning light appeared on a panel in the cockpit and the crew knew that they had to adjust their oxygen supply to the actual, as distinct from the equivalent, height.

One of the main reasons for setting the Mosquito's differential cabin pressure to the equivalent of 10,000ft below the actual operating height was to mitigate the effects of explosive decompression on the crew and the aircraft structure in the event of a hit from flak or a fighter puncturing the pressure cabin.

During night operations Mosquito crews always wore their oxygen masks with the oxygen supply turned on from take-off to landing.

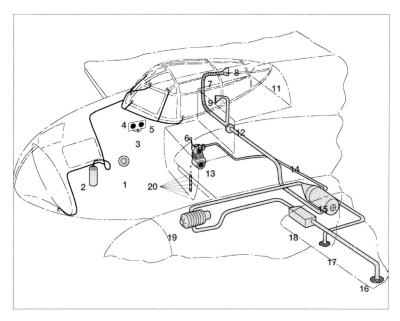

Wing

The wing was built in one piece and attached to the fuselage by five pick-up points – two on the top wing surface and three on the rear spar. Radiators and engine mountings were carried in the centre section.

The two full-span 50ft spruce spars had top and bottom booms of laminated spruce boxed with plywood webs. Construction of the ribs depended on the loading, the strongest being rib one nearest the centre line. This had a top boom of five spruce laminations and a bottom boom of Douglas fir and three-ply webbing.

ABOVE Cabin pressurisation schematic.

(Matthew Marke)

1 Ground testing point
2 Silica gel drying tube feeding dry air to double-glazed windows
3 Warning light for cabin pressure
4 Cabin pressure indicator
5 Cabin altitude indicator
6 Cabin air off/cold/ warm
7 Flexible tubing
8 Pressure inlet
9 Pressure inlet
10 Emergency cabin pressure release valve
11 Cabin bulkhead
12 Non-return valve
13 Westland valve blowing at 2½lb/sq in
14 Teleflex control
15 Heater (heated by glycol from engine)
16 Intake on underside of mainplane
17 Spill from heater
18 Air filter
19 Marshall-type cabin blower
20 Flying controls

LEFT Removal of the fuselage from the wing. *(Crown Copyright)*

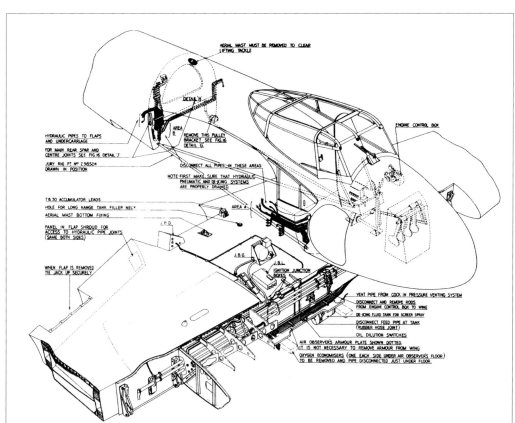

Ribs three and four carried fittings for the tubular welded engine mounting frame and metal parts for the undercarriage installation, while the remaining outboard ribs were of lighter half-box construction.

The underside of the wing was skinned with a single layer of ply glued to the ribs and stringers, but to handle the high compression loads the top surface was double-skinned, with each layer separated by span-wise stringers – spruce inboard, Douglas fir towards the tip. The wingtips themselves were detachable.

ABOVE Reminiscent of a giant Airfix kit, the fuselage is gently lowered on to the single-piece wing. In the foreground, note the hole in the upper surface of the wing for the fuel tank filler cap, and the engine bulkhead that has yet to be fitted out to receive engine bearers and firewall. *(Avspecs)*

RIGHT Port mainplane showing the principal structural features. *(Crown Copyright)*

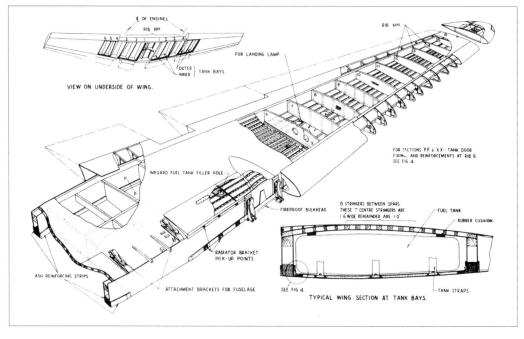

BELOW Awaiting the separate wingtip section, this is KA114 with engine nacelle, engine and undercarriage attached to the wing structure. *(Avspecs)*

BELOW Inboard upper wing surfaces of B 35, VR796, showing the wing root joint with the fuselage that awaits sealing with fabric strip and dope. Note also the open dinghy access panel, unglazed cockpit canopy, and radiator top cover awaiting its installation. *(Victoria Air Maintenance)*

The inboard and outboard sections of the slotted wooden flaps, which operated simultaneously on both sides of the engine nacelle rear extension, were linked by a torque tube with a jack-operated crank. Ailerons were made of metal, were aluminium skinned and spanned 12ft 5in.

Each half of the wing outboard of the centre section contained four fuel tanks sited between the front and rear spars. The two outboard units had capacities of 24 and 32gal, while the pair inboard of the engine held 65 and 79gal (B IV).

The leading edge inboard of each engine contained the coolant and oil radiators, and behind those on the underside of the wing were the controllable radiator shutters. When opened these would allow a free flow of air. The starboard radiator installation also supplied air for heating the guns, while the port unit provided air for cabin heating.

Tailplane and fin

Like the wing, the tailplane was built in one piece, each half comprising a front and rear spar and 11 ribs. Upper and lower surfaces were skinned with a single-ply panel, and on production aircraft the metal elevators were also metal-skinned to cure early aero-elastic problems.

The fin, set slightly forward of the tailplane,

was of conventional wooden spar and rib construction, but the rudder had metal ribs and was fabric-covered.

Undercarriage

The undercarriage assembly was simple and did not require any precision machining. Each unit consisted of two legs containing compression rubber blocks supporting a single large Dunlop wheel with pneumatically operated brakes and block-tread tyre. There were no

LEFT Tail fin and rudder on VR796, showing the wooden laminated fin and metal framework for the rudder, both ready to receive their fabric skin. *(Victoria Air Maintenance)*

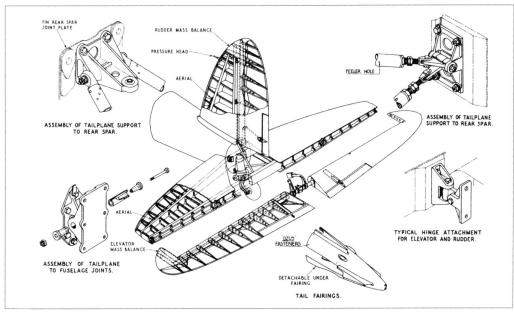

LEFT Tail unit structure showing the various assembly attachments and the detachable tail fairing. *(Crown Copyright)*

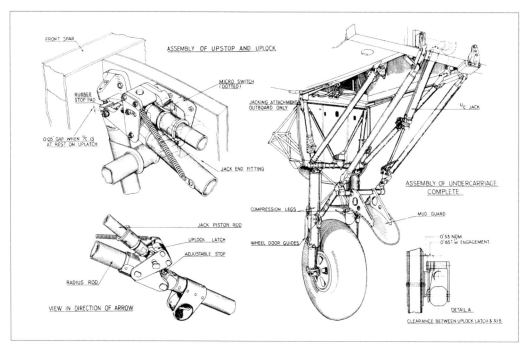

LEFT The port undercarriage installation on
VR796, showing its method of attachment to the
wing structure, the wheel and tyre, compression
legs, wheel door guides, radius rods and jack.
(Victoria Air Maintenance)

BELOW LEFT Rubber compression block shock
absorber segments sit one on top of the other
inside the compression leg metal casing.

BELOW An undercarriage retraction test on
KA114. The Dunlop 5in AH.10.191 wheel was
fitted with a Dunlop 1.G.11 tyre inflated to an
operating pressure of 40psi. *(Avspecs)*

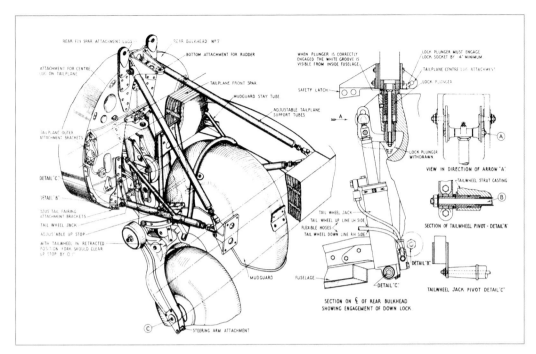

LEFT Tailwheel assembly inside the rear fuselage. *(Crown Copyright)*

fluid-filled dampers to cause any troublesome leaks, and rebound was handled by a special rubber block on the piston tube. The assembly was operated hydraulically and retracted backwards into the engine nacelle, and the doors were closed by a cable and pulley system.

The castoring tail wheel, which also retracted rearwards, was fitted with a single Dunlop-Marstrand tyre that had a double contact area to prevent shimmy.

Bomb-bay

The bomber version of the Mosquito had a pair of hydraulically operated doors enclosing the bomb-bay that ran the length of the fuselage beneath bulkheads 2 and 4. The top (inner) skin of the bomb doors was dished at the rear to clear the tail ends of 500lb bombs by ½in.

For the fighter-bomber version of the Mosquito, the pair of full-length bomb doors were divided to give two sets of ventral bay

FAR LEFT Tailwheel. *(Avspecs)*

LEFT The view looking through bulkhead number six towards the tailwheel installation and its retraction mechanism. Also seen are the rudder control linkage (at top), with elevator and rudder trimming cables (below). *(Victoria Air Maintenance)*

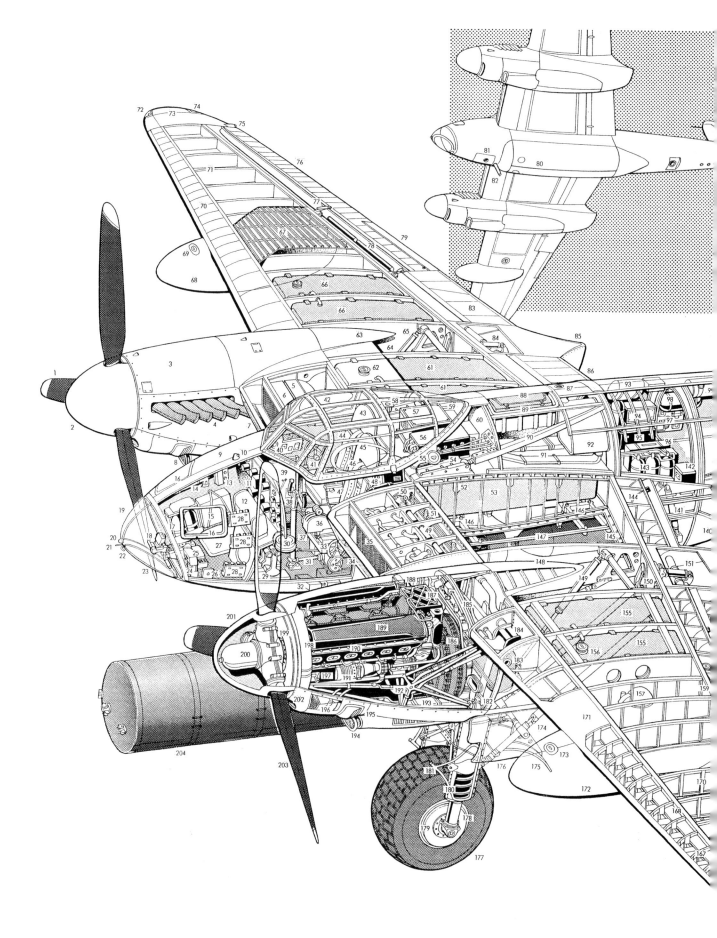

De Havilland Mosquito B XVI cutaway.

(Mike Badrocke)

1 Three-bladed de Havilland Type 5000 hydromatic propeller
2 Spinner
3 Starboard engine cowling panels, Merlin 73 engine
4 Exhaust stubs
5 Starboard oil radiator
6 Coolant radiator
7 Radiator air intake
8 Carburettor air intake and guard
9 Fuselage nose skinning
10 Windscreen de-icing fluid nozzle
11 Instrument panel
12 Parachute stowage
13 Junction box
14 Fire axe
15 SYKO apparatus stowage
16 Nose compartment side windows
17 Portable oxygen bottles
18 Mk XIV bomb sight
19 Nose glazing
20 Forward navigation/ identification light
21 Temperature probe
22 Windscreen de-icing fluid nozzle
23 Optically flat bomb-aiming window
24 Bomb sight mounting

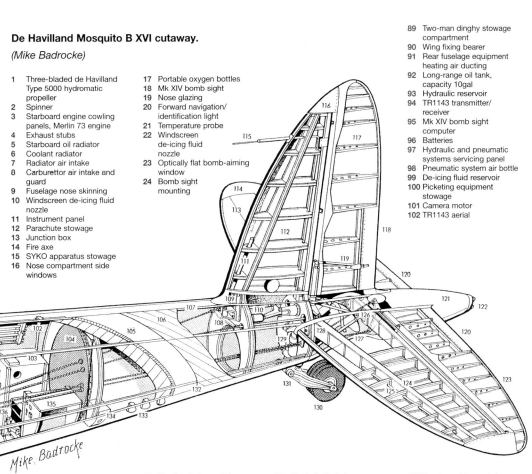

Mike Badrocke

25 Bomb selector switches
26 Camera remote control box
27 Bomb-aimer's kneeling cushion
28 Signal pistol cartridge racks
29 Rudder pedals
30 Compass
31 Control linkages
32 Oxygen system economiser units
33 Elevator trim hand wheel
34 Port radiator ram air intake
35 Oil and coolant radiators
36 Engine throttle levers
37 Ventral entry hatch
38 Control column hand wheel
39 Folding chart table
40 Windscreen panels
41 Trailing aerial winch
42 Cockpit roof escape hatch
43 Seat back armour plate
44 Navigator/bombardier's seat
45 Bulged 'sandwich' side panel
46 Pilot's seat
47 Intercom socket
48 Portable fire extinguisher
49 Cabin pressurisation and heating air ducts
50 Non-return air valve
51 Engine control runs
52 Wing root rib
53 Centre section fuel tanks (x 2), capacity 68gal each (restricted to 46gal port and 47½gal starboard, with 4,000lb bomb load)
54 Wing upper surface attachment joint
55 Centre fuel tank filler cap
56 ARI-5083 receiver
57 IFF transmitter/receiver
58 Signal pistol aperture

59 Cockpit aft glazing
60 Rear pressure bulkhead
61 Starboard inboard fuel tanks, capacity 78gal inner and 65½gal outer
62 Fuel filler cap
63 Nacelle fairing
64 Starboard main undercarriage bay
65 Hydraulic retraction jack
66 Outboard fuel tanks, capacity 34gal inner and 24gal outer
67 Wing stringers
68 Starboard auxiliary fuel tank, capacity 50gal
69 Fuel filler cap
70 Plywood leading edge skinning
71 Wing top skin panelling, double-plywood sandwich construction
72 Starboard navigation light
73 Wingtip fairing
74 Formation light
75 Resin light
76 Starboard aileron
77 Aileron hinge control
78 Mass balance weights
79 Aileron tab
80 Underside view showing bulged (increased volume) bomb-bay doors
81 Ventral entry hatch with drift sight aperture
82 Trailing aerial fairing
83 Starboard outer plain flap segment
84 Flap hydraulic jack
85 Nacelle tail fairing
86 Flap inboard segment
87 Oil filler cap
88 Dinghy access panel

89 Two-man dinghy stowage compartment
90 Wing fixing bearer
91 Rear fuselage equipment heating air ducting
92 Long-range oil tank, capacity 10gal
93 Hydraulic reservoir
94 TR1143 transmitter/ receiver
95 Mk XIV bomb sight computer
96 Batteries
97 Hydraulic and pneumatic systems servicing panel
98 Pneumatic system air bottle
99 De-icing fluid reservoir
100 Picketing equipment stowage
101 Camera motor
102 TR1143 aerial
103 Fuselage stringers between inner and outer skin laminations
104 Heat conserving canvas bulkhead cover
105 Fuselage half-shell sandwich skin construction (plywood/balsa/plywood)
106 Diagonal graining pattern
107 Centre line fuselage half-shell joint strip
108 Rudder control linkage
109 Fin attachment bulkhead
110 Rudder mass balance weight
111 Ferrite aerial rod
112 Tail fin construction
113 Starboard tailplane
114 Elevator horn balance
115 Pitot tube
116 Rudder horn balance
117 Fabric-covered rudder construction
118 Rudder tab
119 Tab operating rod
120 Elevator tabs
121 Tail cone
122 Tail navigation lights
123 Metal-skinned elevator construction
124 Tailplane construction
125 Ferrite aerial rod
126 Elevator operating linkage
127 Tailwheel housing
128 Tailplane spar attachment joint
129 Tailwheel leg strut
130 Retracting tailwheel
131 Levered suspension tailwheel forks
132 Fuselage skin fabric covering
133 Identification code lights – white, amber, green

134 Beam approach aerial
135 Camera mounting
136 F24 camera
137 Tailplane control cables
138 Rear fuselage entry hatch
139 Crew equipment stowage bag
140 Bulged bomb-bay tail fairing
141 Bomb door hydraulic jacks
142 Beam approach receiver
143 Oxygen bottles
144 Flap shroud ribs
145 Inboard fuel tank bay ventral access panel
146 Bomb carriers
147 500lb short finned HE bombs (x 4)
148 Port engine nacelle top fairing
149 Main undercarriage hydraulic retraction jack
150 Undercarriage leg rear strut mounting
151 Flap hydraulic jack
152 Nacelle tail fairing
153 Port plain flap segments
154 All-wooden flap construction
155 Port outer fuel tanks
156 Fuel filler cap
157 Retractable landing lamp
158 Aileron tab control linkage
159 Rear spar
160 Aileron hinge control
161 Aileron tab
162 Aluminium aileron construction
163 Resin lamp
164 Port formation lamp
165 Detachable wingtip fairing
166 Port navigation light
167 Leading edge nose ribs
168 Front spar, box beam construction
169 Wing lower surface single skin/stringer panel
170 Wing rib construction
171 Plywood leading edge skinning, fabric-covered
172 Port auxiliary fuel tank, capacity 50gal
173 Fuel filler cap
174 Main undercarriage rear strut
175 Mudguard
176 Main wheel doors
177 Port main wheel
178 Main wheel leg strut
179 Pneumatic brake disc
180 Rubber compression block shock absorber
181 Spring-loaded door guides
182 Main undercarriage pivot fixing
183 Engine oil tank, capacity 16gal
184 Cabin heater
185 Fireproof bulkhead
186 Two-stage supercharger
187 Intercooler
188 Heywood compressor
189 Rolls-Royce Merlin 72, V12 engine
190 Exhaust ports
191 Alternator
192 Engine bearers
193 Carburettor air intake duct
194 Intake guard
195 Intercooler radiator exhaust
196 Intercooler radiator
197 Engine mounting block
198 Coolant header tank
199 Spinner armoured back plate
200 Propeller hub pitch change mechanism
201 Spinner
202 Intercooler radiator intake
203 Port three-bladed de Havilland hydromatic propeller
204 4,000lb HC bomb

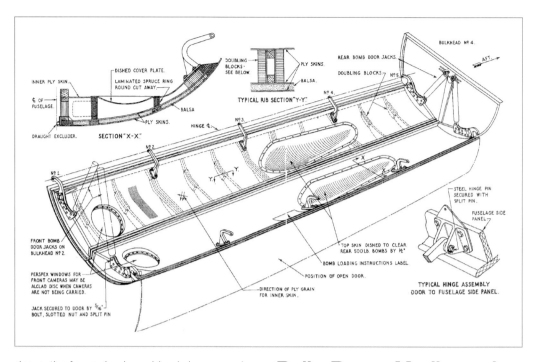

doors: the forward pair could only be opened manually when the aircraft was on the ground and provided access to the cannon bay; the rear pair were hydraulically operated and functioned as doors for the rear bomb-bay as well as providing access to long-range fuel tanks inside the fuselage.

The Mk XVIII 'Tsetse' Mosquito featured a modified starboard gun bay door to accommodate the rear of the 57mm cannon and shell case ejection chute.

Rolls-Royce Merlin engine

At the heart of the Mosquito was the most famous aero engine of the war – the Rolls-Royce Merlin, a 60-degree V12 with liquid cooling, which also powered the Spitfire and Lancaster as well as many other military and, later, civil aircraft. There were some 50 variants of the Merlin, so de Havilland were able to select the most suitable for any mark of Mosquito, whether it be for optimum performance at high altitude or response and power at low level.

Cylinder block and heads

Although there were many variants, with the engine being under constant development, the basic unit had twelve cylinders in two banks of six at 60° to each other. Detachable high-carbon wet steel liners were installed in engine blocks of cast RR50 high-strength aluminium alloy with separate heads and skirts. A bore of 5.4in and a stroke of 6in gave a capacity of 1,649cu in – approximately 27 litres. The cylinder heads were fitted with cast-iron inlet valve guides, phosphor bronze exhaust valve guides and replaceable steel-alloy valve seats.

Valves

Each hemispherical combustion chamber had four trumpet-type valves – two inlet, two exhaust – and two Lodge or KLG spark plugs.

The valves were of KE965 steel with Stellited ends to resist wear, while the exhaust valves also had sodium-cooled stems and heads protected with a nickel-chromium coating known as 'Brightray'. Each valve was kept closed by a pair of concentric coil springs.

Camshafts

The valves were actuated by a single overhead seven-bearing camshaft in each cylinder block, mounted in pedestal brackets and driven from the wheelcase by inclined shafts terminating in bevel pinions which meshed with bevel wheels at the end of the camshafts. Each camshaft operated 24 steel rockers, 12 pivoting from a rocker shaft on the intake side of the block to work the exhaust valves, the others pivoting on a shaft on the exhaust side to operate the inlet valves. Earlier versions of the engine had valve timing of 43° overlap and 263° duration, while later generations had 70° overlap and 288° duration.

Pistons

Pistons were machined from RR59 alloy forgings and the fully floating hollow gudgeon pins were of hardened nickel-chrome steel and retained in the piston with steel wire circlips. Above the gudgeon pin were three compression and one oil-control rings, with a further oil-control ring beneath it. A pair of oilways were drilled obliquely upwards towards the centre of

the piston to meet just above the gudgeon pin, and these helped to cool the piston.

Connecting rods

The H-section connecting rods were machined from nickel-steel forgings, the 'big end' being

BELOW **The 1,690hp Merlin 114 engine (which drove a Marshall cabin supercharger to pressurise the cockpit on later marks of Mosquito) installed on the port wing on VR796, but still far from being ready. Note the silver-coloured coolant header tank, propeller shaft, and the six blank exhaust ports awaiting their stubs.** (*Victoria Air Maintenance*)

RIGHT Reduction gear. *(Jonathan Falconer)*

fitted with steel-backed lead-bronze-alloy bearing shells, while the 'small end' carried a floating phosphor bronze bush for the gudgeon pin.

RIGHT Main coolant pump is situated underneath the wheelcase. *(Jonathan Falconer)*

RIGHT The wheelcase (front face) for a two-stage Merlin. From the top: inclined drives for the two cams; magneto skew gear; input shaft connected to the crank; lower (idler) gear for driving the oil pumps; at the bottom is the tower to which the main coolant pump is attached. The 'wing' on the right houses the generator layshaft gear. *(Jonathan Falconer)*

FAR RIGHT The fuel pump is situated on the port side of the wheelcase. *(Jonathan Falconer)*

Crankshaft

The crankshaft was machined in one piece from a nitrided nickel-chrome molybdenum steel forging, statically and dynamically balanced, and carried in seven main bearings.

Crankcase

The crankcase consisted of two aluminium-alloy castings bolted together horizontally. The upper part carried the crankshaft main bearing housings, wheelcase, supercharger and accessories, and part of the propeller reduction gear, which on the Mosquito operated at 0.4471 times engine speed. The lower section was the sump containing oil pump and filters.

Wheelcase

The wheelcase, an aluminium casting bolted to the rear of the crankcase, housed drives to the camshafts, magnetos, supercharger, starters, generator, and pumps for fuel, oil and coolant. The fuel pump, mounted on the port side of the wheelcase, consisted of two separate pumps working in parallel – but each pump could work independently and had enough capacity to supply more than the maximum amount of fuel needed. The bottom-fed centrifugal coolant

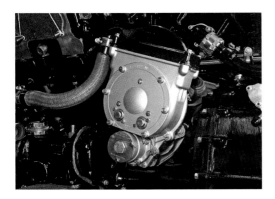

pump served each cylinder block through a separate outlet.

Ignition system

Two magnetos bolted to the wheelcase fed the high-tension leads for the spark plugs. The leads were shrouded in a metal-screened harness that served as a collector for the induced field around the HT leads and also earthed the resulting electrical current, thus preventing radio interference. One magneto supplied plugs on the inlet side, the other the exhaust side, so that if one magneto failed the engine would still function with the other.

Supercharger

The key to the Merlin's outstanding performance was the supercharger, which provided excellent torque and power – but it also put heavy demands upon the engine in terms of cooling, freedom from detonation, and the capability of withstanding high gas and inertia loads. As research progressed, it was realised that a two-stage supercharger would have to be developed to increase performance of the Merlin at high altitude, and this paid dividends for the Mosquito in the constant struggle to achieve ever greater altitude yet maintain performance.

There were three basic types of Merlin supercharger:

- Single-stage, single-speed gearbox on Merlin I to III, XII, 30, 40 and 50 Series.
- Single-stage, two-speed gearbox on experimental Merlin X and production Merlin XX.
- Two-stage, two-speed gearbox with inter-cooler used mainly on Merlin 60, 70 and 80 Series.

The unit was driven by the crankshaft, and because it was sited at the rear of the engine the intake duct was small, with the result that the original unit was designed

ABOVE First- and second-stage supercharger rotor assemblies. *(Jonathan Falconer)*

LEFT Lower rear view of the engine showing the location of the carburettor (bottom), the snail shell-shaped supercharger casing with its inlet elbow (top right) and automatic boost control unit (top left). *(Jonathan Falconer)*

to develop maximum power at only about 16,000ft altitude. However, by the time the first Mosquito flew in November 1940 the new central-entry supercharger designed by Sir Stanley Hooker and Geoffrey Wild was in production, and this allowed more advantage to be taken of 100 octane fuel. The two-speed drive was designed by the French company Farman, and although there were some initial problems it represented a significant advance in supercharger performance.

The Packard-built Merlins used an epicyclic drive, as the Americans were not too keen on the numerous hand-fitting operations required for the Farman – but the epicyclic drive put a large load on to the planet gear bearings, so neither type was perfect. In the constant quest for more performance, Rolls-Royce continued to develop Hooker's two-stage supercharger and, following the success of this on a Spitfire Mk XI, Mosquito MP469 with two Merlin 61s reached an altitude of 42,000ft and was still climbing at 500ft a minute.

Nitrous oxide injection

Experiments were also made at RAE Farnborough with power-boosting systems, and 50 Mosquito NF XIIIs were fitted with nitrous oxide injection, which gave a substantial performance enhancement at high altitude. An extra 300hp at 18,000ft was available on a Merlin 23 with this system, while at 30,000ft a total of nearly 1,000hp would be available. John Cunningham was impressed with this extra performance – but it came with the penalties of extra weight and space and the short time for which it could be used.

Further developments

Chief development engineer Cyril Lovesey preferred getting higher power from a supercharger with petrol, rather than fitting separate power-boosting systems – but the Merlin had shown it was tough and dependable enough to run at high boost pressures. Cunningham found it could hold 23–24lb of boost for as long as he wanted without showing any signs of distress, and the Merlin 66 was cleared for 25lb boost, which gave an output of 2,250hp – double that of the Merlin III used in the Battle of Britain.

The final Merlin version used in the Mosquito was the 113/114, which represented a major redesign based on experience in combat conditions and produced on the assumption that the war would go on much longer than it did. Among the new features were a redesigned crankcase with strengthening at the major stud locations and an end-to-end lubrication system for the crankshaft. The supercharger for this series, with its new rotor arrangement, was also a departure from previous generations. An inter-stage roller bearing to give better supercharger intake replaced the old plain tail bearing that had concentric floating bushes, and also used was a single-point SU injection carburettor that fed fuel directly into the supercharger using a pump driven as a function of crankshaft speed and engine pressures.

The Tilly Orifice

Unlike the Messerschmitt Bf 109E, which had fuel injection, the Merlin used carburettors, as these were calculated to give higher output due to lower temperature and thus greater density of the fuel–air mixture. But there was one embarrassing shortcoming with the float-controlled SU carburettor of the Merlin: negative g would cause the engine to lose power, so putting the nose down to pursue or elude an enemy fighter was out of the question: a half-roll before diving was the only answer. But it wasn't a very satisfactory answer, as having to concentrate on avoiding negative g manoeuvres at a time when you most needed them was hardly ideal. It took the ingenuity of RAE scientist Beatrice 'Tilly' Shilling to find a solution.

Under negative g, all the fuel in the float chamber would rise, causing the engine to run momentarily lean, the float would lose control and then there was an enormous squirt of fuel from the two pumps giving about twice as much as the engine needed. This caused it to fluff and splutter, and it was some moments before power was regained.

As well as being an aeronautical engineer, Tilly Shilling was one feisty lady who raced motorcycles in the 1930s, beating professionals such as Noel Pope, and was awarded the Gold Star for lapping Brooklands at 106mph on her Norton M30. Described by a colleague as 'a flaming pathfinder for women's lib', she was contemptuous of bureaucracy and had a brusque manner – but also a talent for getting to the nub of a problem. And this she did with the Merlin's carburettor.

First she devised what was called the RAE Restrictor, which limited flow through the carburettor to just over the maximum needed for take-off. This resulted in considerable improvement, but she followed up with an anti-g version of the SU by formulating a float control setting which limited the amount the needle valve came up when the float lost control, and fitting an excrescence on the tip of the needle that cut off the flow under negative g. There were two versions – one for engines with 12psi manifold pressure, and another for boosted engines with 15psi. The device solved the problem and became affectionately known as 'Miss Shilling's Orifice', or simply 'The Tilly Orifice'. She and a team of fitters travelled around the country in 1941 fitting these restrictors, with priority given to front-line units.

In 1943 the Bendix-Stromberg carburettor was introduced, which injected fuel at 5psi directly into the supercharger, and from then on the Merlin suffered no cutting-out under negative g. This carburettor was fitted to the Merlin 66, 70, 76, 77 and 85.

Propellers

The Mosquito was fitted with three-blade de Havilland Hydromatic constant-speed, variable-pitch, propellers. These were originally developed by Frank W. Caldwell of the Hamilton Standard Division of the United Aircraft Company in America, and de Havilland bought the rights to produce the propellers in the UK. Four-blade Rotol propellers were fitted to the Sea Mosquito and 25 Mosquito B IVs for the proposed carrier-based Highball operations, and these had narrower blades than the standard three-blade units so that they would rev up faster and give the more immediate response needed for the limited length of take-off run. Paddle-bladed propellers were fitted to some photo-reconnaissance versions in the successful quest for higher altitude.

LEFT Rolls-Royce Bendix 8D44 was a pressure- or direct injection-type carburettor. This is the top showing the butterflies in a semi-open position. *(Jonathan Falconer)*

BELOW The de Havilland three-blade hydromatic Type 5000 propeller. This is the paddle-blade type seen fitted here to a Mosquito PR IX, minus its spinner. *(BAE Systems/DH1437)*

LEFT The view inside the propeller hub showing the propeller shaft (centre) and the bevel gears that turn the blades to the desired position. *(Paul Blackah)*

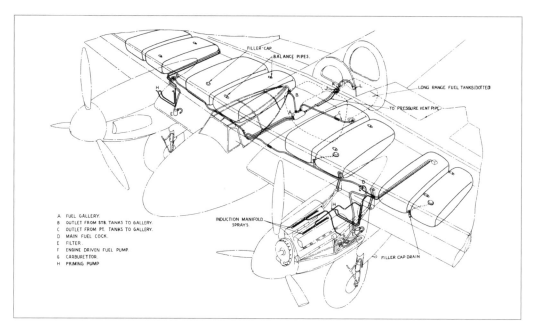

RIGHT **A pair of CIMA-protected self-sealing aluminium-alloy wing fuel tanks and a green-coloured long-range ventral tank, waiting to be fitted inside VR796.** (*Victoria Air Maintenance*)

Systems

Fuel

The long range and endurance demanded of the Mosquito, particularly in the Far East using the PR 34, required a heavy fuel load. High-performance engines such as the Merlin 72/73 and 76/77 for example, as used in the PR IX and PR XVI, could burn up to 158gal of fuel an hour.

BELOW **The port outer fuel tank bays with their dangling straps are ready to receive the fuel tanks (No 4, 34gal; No 5, 24gal). Pilots were advised not to rely on the outer tanks when flying at low level because their capacity was small and the gauges diminished in accuracy as the fuel level fell.**

(*Victoria Air Maintenance*)

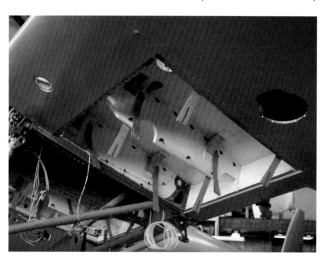

BELOW **VR796's port inner fuel tanks (No 2, 78gal; No 3, 65½gal), in place and secured by their white tank straps. Note the vent pipe connection between tanks. Engine controls, hydraulic and pneumatic pipelines can be seen running along the leading edge of the front spar above.**

(*Victoria Air Maintenance*)

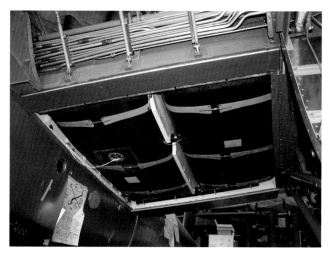

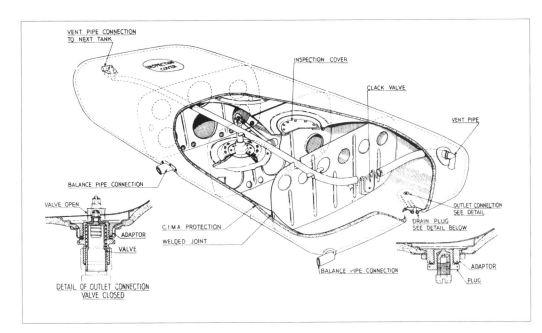

Fuel was carried in eight wing tanks – two inner and two outer on each wing, making four tanks per wing – 1 x 24gal and 1 x 34gal in the outer tanks (total = 116gal), and 1 x 65½gal and 1 x 78gal in the inner tanks (total = 287gal). Inside the centre fuselage were twin 25gal tanks mounted behind the cockpit between bulkheads two and three. The inner wing and centre tanks were designated as the main fuel tanks. The basic total internal fuel load was 453gal, although this figure could increase significantly depending on the mark of Mosquito.

For example, the FB VI could carry larger centre tanks, increasing the overall fuel capacity by 63gal. The NF XII carried an extra 144gal in twin centre tanks, while the total fuel capacity for the long-range PR 34 more than doubled that of the standard fighter-bomber, at 1,267gal.

An additional fuselage (long-range) tank could be carried in the bomb-bay/equipment bay, as well as twin drop-tanks beneath each wing.

The inner wing tanks supplied both engines through a fuel collector box, when the two fuel cocks behind the pilot's seat were set to MAIN SUPPLY. If long-range fuel tanks were carried, these also supplied both engines through the fuel collector box with the fuel cocks at MAIN SUPPLY and the immersed fuel pump switch ON. When the fuel cocks were set to OUTER TANKS the port outer wing tanks supplied the port engine and the starboard outer wing tanks

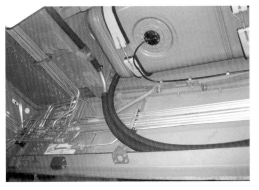

LEFT Long-range fuel tank inside the bomb-bay of VR796. (*Victoria Air Maintenance*)

fed the starboard engine. It was not possible to cross-feed from the outer tanks.

To reduce the loss of fuel through vaporisation, which was a phenomenon experienced by Mosquito PR variants at their high operating altitudes, the central and inner

BELOW The fuel gallery is located inside the equipment/bomb-bay on the starboard side. (*Victoria Air Maintenance*)

developed for the Mosquito. These were available in 50gal and 100gal versions, and the 200gal drop-tank, developed especially for the long-range PR 34. The tanks were fitted in pairs, one tank beneath each wing outboard of the engine nacelle, attached to under-wing pylons at rib 8. They were filled through the filler caps at the top of the tanks, forward of the wing leading edge. The contents of a drop-tank were transferred via a fuel transfer pipe to an outer wing tank (numbers 5 and 6), delivered under pressure by an engine-driven vacuum pump. Fuel-tank jettison was achieved from the cockpit by electromagnetic slip release gear.

PR 34 additional fuel tanks

The PR 34 was developed from the PR XVI for ultra long-range photo-reconnaissance. It featured enlarged ventral bay doors (similar to the bulged bomb-bay doors of the B XVI) to accommodate two large fuel tanks mounted in tandem beneath the centre section tanks. The forward tank was a short type containing 100gal, while the rear tank held 152gal. This extra capacity, combined with the twin 200gal wing drop-tanks, raised the PR 34's fuel load to 1,267gal, endowing the aircraft with a range of 3,340 miles at 300mph and 25,000ft.

All this extra weight could create handling problems and was not ideal for operational flying as it increased the maximum all-up weight from around 19,000–20,000lb to about 25,000lb. But the additional fuel gave much needed extra range, which was essential for the long-distance PR operations in the Far East flown by Mosquito PR 34s from bases in India across the Bay of Bengal and into Burma, Thailand and Singapore.

Oil

Two 15¾gal self-sealing oil tanks were provided, one in each engine nacelle above and between the undercarriage legs. The lubrication system had four circuits: main pressure feed, low pressure feed, front pump scavenge circuit and rear pump scavenge circuit. The main and lower circuits were operated by a single pump and relief valves, while the two scavenge circuits had individual pumps. Oil was drawn from a tank through a filter by the engine pressure pump and was returned after circulation by two

ABOVE Mosquito PR 34 with 200gal drop-tanks, designed especially for the PR 34 and the largest that operational Mosquitoes were cleared to carry. It was advised that the contents of the wing drop-tanks should be transferred as early as possible to avoid loss of fuel if they had to be jettisoned. (BAE Systems/DH1752)

wing tanks were pressurised. The system was controlled by a pressure venting cock located behind the pilot's seat, which operated a pressure valve. As the altitude increased the valve boosted the volume inside the tank by means of a pump.

A positive supply of fuel to the carburettor or fuel injection pump, irrespective of the relative position of the fuel tanks, was ensured by a gear-type fuel pump mounted on the port side of the engine wheelcase.

Wing drop-tanks

To improve range and endurance, three different sizes of wing drop-tank were

RIGHT A long-range PR 34 showing the two additional fuel tanks fitted inside the Mosquito's equipment bay. (BAE Systems)

scavenge pumps through an oil cooler situated adjacent to the main coolant radiator. Oil consumption at maximum cruising speed was between 6 and 20pt/hr.

Coolant

Engine

The main engine cooling radiators were fitted inside the inboard leading edges of the wings, one radiator per wing. The coolant radiator shutters in the forward part of the inner wing, between the engine nacelle and the fuselage, directed and controlled the airflow to the radiators. On fighter variants the shutters were electro-pneumatically operated, while those on bomber and PR variants were cable-operated by hand controls. The radiators were divided into three discrete sections: the outboard part was the oil cooler on single-stage Merlin Mosquitoes only; two-stage Merlin Mosquitoes featured the oil coolant radiator running span-wise behind the main coolant radiator. The middle component was for engine coolant; the inboard section on the port unit served the cabin heating, while air from the starboard side heated the guns.

Normally a centrifugal vane-type pump delivered the coolant, consisting of a mixture of 70% pure water plus 30% ethylene glycol, at a rate of about 125gal a minute through the cylinder blocks to the coolant header tank behind the propeller, from which it flowed to the coolant radiator and back to the pump.

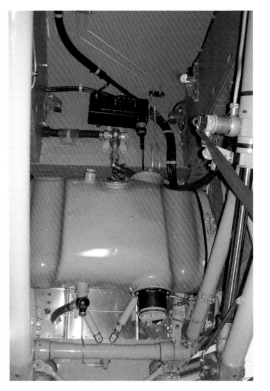

LEFT An oil tank was mounted inside each wheel well on the forward bulkhead. (Victoria Air Maintenance)

LEFT Location of the starboard coolant radiator housing before installation. (Victoria Air Maintenance)

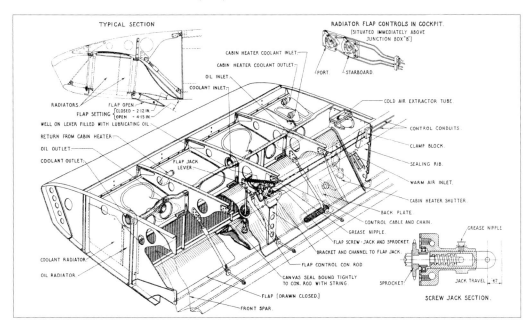

LEFT Radiator installation for a two-stage Merlin. The oil radiator is located at the rear of the coolant radiator block. (Crown Copyright)

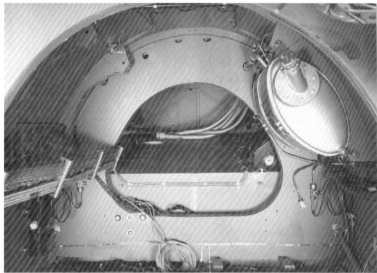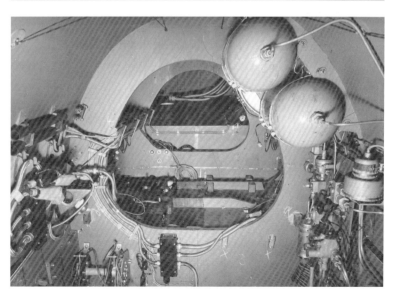

RIGHT Intercooler housing. *(Jonathan Falconer)*

BELOW Hydraulic fluid reservoir inside the fuselage against bulkhead number three. *(BAE Systems)*

BOTTOM Pneumatic panel with twin air bottles. *(BAE Systems)*

This was known as 'normal flow', but on the Mosquito, with its high-set radiators, coolant was instead drawn from the header tank by the pump and fed to the radiators through the pump outlets that normally supplied the cylinders, and it was then fed back via a split connection to the cylinder blocks. This was known as 'reverse flow', and it was the changes needed to the coolant pipes that led to Mosquito engines having a different identity from other similar engines.

The total coolant capacity per engine, including the pipe system, was 15½ to 16gal.

Supercharger intercooler

In order to reduce the high mixture temperature resulting from the two stages of supercharging, the system employed a similar type of pressure liquid cooling to that used in the main cooling system, with its own integral header tank, using 70% pure water plus 30% ethylene glycol.

Hydraulic system

Two engine-driven pumps, one on each engine, supplied hydraulic pressure for the operation of the undercarriage, tailwheel, flaps and bomb doors. The system could function on one pump, but only at a reduced rate.

A hand-pump for operating all the services through the normal system, when the engine pumps were not running, was mounted in a socket beneath the pilot's seat and the detachable handle was stowed on the cockpit door. Lowering the undercarriage by hand-pump took about four minutes.

This pump could also be used to operate the separate emergency undercarriage lowering system, when the emergency selector valve on the right of the pilot's seat was pushed down.

Pneumatic system

An air compressor on the port engine charged an air bottle for the operation of the brakes and guns, the electro-pneumatic rams for the radiator shutters, automatic supercharger gear change and carburettor air-intake filter control.

The available pressure was shown on the gauge for the pneumatic system and brakes, triple pressure and should have read 200psi in flight. All services except the brakes were cut off by a pressure maintaining valve if the supply fell below 150psi.

Two vacuum pumps, one driven by each engine, operated the flight instruments. If either pump failed it was automatically isolated from the suction system. Each pump could be tested on the ground by alternatively starting the port and starboard engines and checking that the artificial horizon erected properly.

Electrical

Depending on the mark of Mosquito aircraft concerned, electrical power was derived from either a single generator on the starboard engine, or a generator on the starboard engine and a tandem generator fitted to the port engine, and a battery, which supplied electrical power at 24 volts for:

- Carburettor air intake filters
- Undercarriage warning lights and horn
- Fuel pressure warning lights
- Oil dilution valves
- Engine starters and booster coils
- Fire extinguishers
- Radio (Gee, GP HF communications set, VHF, IFF)
- Pitot head heater
- Air recognition, identification, navigation and landing lights
- Instrument panel and cockpit lighting
- Feathering pump motors
- Windscreen wiper
- Controls operating radiator shutters
- Automatic superchargers, tropical air filters
- .303in machine guns and 20mm cannon (where fitted)
- Reflector gun sight (where fitted)
- Camera gun (where fitted)
- Bomb selection, fusing and release gear for fuselage and wing bombs (where fitted)
- Rocket projectile release (where fitted).

Electrical wiring in the fuselage was mainly contained in protected and screened flexible conduits, or in short lengths of open-ended light alloy ducts. Engine services were wired via a cable loom assembly, fed from two plugs on the bulkhead. Pipes, metal-braided cables, fuel tanks and oil tanks etc were earth-bonded to

the main structure, while the tailwheel was fitted with a conducting tyre.

Oxygen

The crew's oxygen supply was contained in four metal cylinders, two on each side of the interior fuselage in front of bulkhead number three, connected via a series of three-way pieces and non-return valves to a crew-operated master control valve in the cockpit. Oxygen pressure regulators were located inside the cockpit on the front instrument panel (pilot) and starboard sidewall (observer) adjacent to the high-pressure oxygen control valve, which controlled the oxygen supply to both pilot and observer via two economiser units.

Pressure filling of the oxygen bottles was through the HP valve positioned on the hydraulic-pneumatic panel in the rear compartment behind bulkhead number four, near the rear fuselage door.

Flying controls

All the flying controls were conventional and operated cable and pulley systems to the control surfaces. The control column on bomber variants had a wheel-type control, while fighters used a plain stick. Some pilots, including night-fighter Cunningham, preferred the simple stick arrangement.

The elevator trimming tab control was to the left of the pilot's seat, with the indicator on the port cockpit wall. On fighter variants the rudder trim tab control and indicator were on the front

ABOVE Trolley accumulator connected to the ground starter socket on a Mosquito NF XIII of 604 Squadron on 31 December 1943. Flg Offs R.G.A. Beaumont and D. Ruddiman pose for the photographer. *(Copyright unknown)*

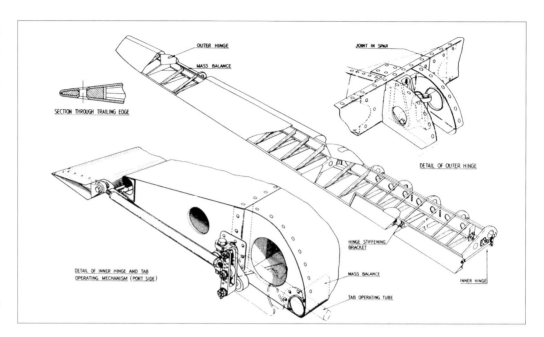

CENTRE Wing flap
with detail of jack and
torque tube. (Crown
Copyright)

BELOW Port wing
trailing edge showing
the attachment points
for the flaps. (Victoria
Air Maintenance)

BELOW RIGHT
Starboard nacelle
aft fairing with flap
jack inspection door,
inboard and outboard
flaps, aileron servo
and aileron centre
hinge inspection
panels. (Victoria Air
Maintenance)

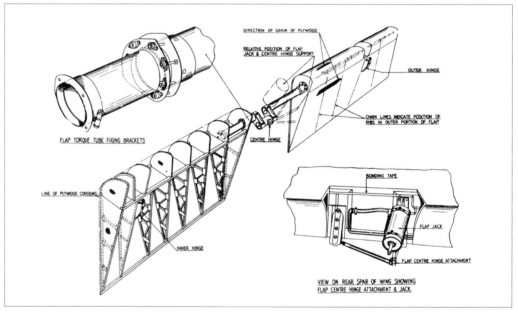

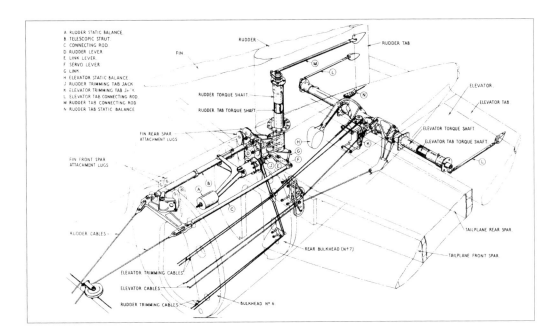

A RUDDER STATIC BALANCE
B TELESCOPIC STRUT
C CONNECTING ROD
D RUDDER LEVER
E LINK LEVER
F SERVO LEVER
G LINK
H ELEVATOR STATIC BALANCE
J RUDDER TRIMMING TAB JACK
K ELEVATOR TRIMMING TAB JACK
L ELEVATOR TAB CONNECTING ROD
M RUDDER TAB CONNECTING ROD
N RUDDER TAB STATIC BALANCE

RUDDER
RUDDER TAB
FIN
ELEVATOR
ELEVATOR TAB
RUDDER TORQUE SHAFT
RUDDER TAB TORQUE SHAFT
ELEVATOR TORQUE SHAFT
ELEVATOR TAB TORQUE SHAFT
FIN REAR SPAR ATTACHMENT LUGS
FIN FRONT SPAR ATTACHMENT LUGS
TAILPLANE REAR SPAR
TAILPLANE FRONT SPAR
RUDDER CABLES
REAR BULKHEAD (N°7)
ELEVATOR TRIMMING CABLES
ELEVATOR CABLES
RUDDER TRIMMING CABLES
BULKHEAD N° 6

LEFT Flying surface control mechanisms in the rear fuselage. *(Crown Copyright)*

BELOW Fuselage bulkhead number five looking aft, showing control cable runs. *(Victoria Air Maintenance)*

cockpit coaming; on bomber and PR variants the rudder trim control was mounted centrally above the v-shaped windscreens; the aileron trimmer control and indicator were on the lower right side of the instrument panel.

To the centre of the instrument panel were the flap and undercarriage controls, the propeller feathering buttons were in front of the navigator's seat, and to the left of the pilot were the throttle and pitch levers.

The flaps were controlled by a lever marked 'F' to the right of the undercarriage selector, and a safety catch had to be pushed to the right before 'Flaps Down' could be selected. Maximum flap angle was 45°, although the gauge was marked up to 70°.

The undercarriage selector lever always had to be moved quickly to the 'Up' or 'Down' positions, as it could become locked if moved slowly. In cold weather the undercarriage system had to be exercised by selecting 'Up' and 'Down' a few times, as fluid congealing in the lines could cause the selector to return to the neutral position before hydraulic pressure had reached the tailwheel.

A warning horn would sound if the main wheels were not locked down and with throttles less than a quarter open.

Control levers to vary the governed pitch of the propellers from 1,800 to 3,000rpm were on the side of the engine controls box. The feathering push-buttons were on the right-hand front panel.

The bomb door selector marked 'B' was to the left of the undercarriage lever, and was designed to return automatically after operation. A warning light showed if the doors remained open. A panel on the right of the instrument fascia contained switching for the fuselage bombs, wing bombs and wing drop-tanks. A switch on this panel allowed a push-button on the control column to operate either the bomb release or cine camera – but bombs could not be selected or fused until the switch had been moved to 'Bombs' or 'Tanks'.

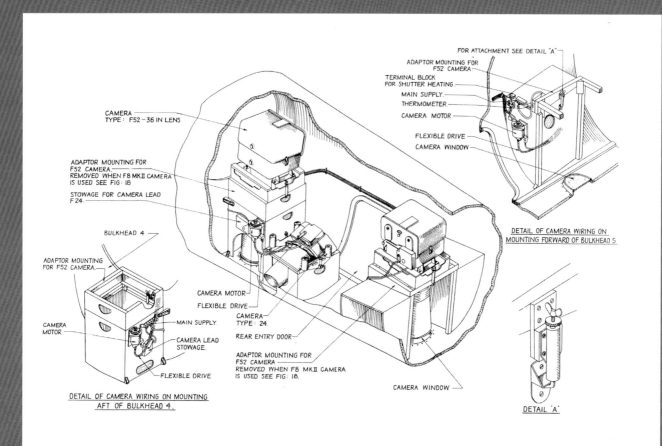

CAMERA
TYPE: F52 – 36 IN LENS

ADAPTOR MOUNTING FOR
F52 CAMERA.
REMOVED WHEN F8 MK.II CAMERA
IS USED SEE FIG: 18

STOWAGE FOR CAMERA LEAD
F 24.

BULKHEAD 4

ADAPTOR MOUNTING
FOR F52 CAMERA.

CAMERA
MOTOR

MAIN SUPPLY

CAMERA LEAD
STOWAGE.

FLEXIBLE DRIVE

**DETAIL OF CAMERA WIRING ON MOUNTING
AFT OF BULKHEAD 4.**

CAMERA MOTOR
FLEXIBLE DRIVE
CAMERA
TYPE: 24.
REAR ENTRY DOOR
ADAPTOR MOUNTING FOR
F52 CAMERA
REMOVED WHEN F8 MK.II CAMERA
IS USED SEE FIG: 18.

CAMERA WINDOW

FOR ATTACHMENT SEE DETAIL "A"
ADAPTOR MOUNTING FOR
F52 CAMERA
TERMINAL BLOCK
FOR SHUTTER HEATING
MAIN SUPPLY
THERMOMETER
CAMERA MOTOR

FLEXIBLE DRIVE
CAMERA WINDOW

**DETAIL OF CAMERA WIRING ON
MOUNTING FORWARD OF BULKHEAD 5**

DETAIL "A"

ABOVE Rear fuselage camera installation common to the PR XVI and PR 34. *(Crown Copyright via airrecce.co.uk)*

RIGHT Camera equipment for a PR 34 (RG176). Left to right: F52 camera with magazine and Type 39 mounting; K17 camera, magazine and mounting; K17 magazine and mounting; F24 camera and magazine. In the background three adaptor mountings can be seen. *(BAE Systems/DH1731)*

LEFT PR 34 (VL619) banks away to reveal her camera ports and bulged belly for accommodating twin long-range fuel tanks. An ultra long-range development of the PR XVI, the PR 34 was powered by Merlin 113 and 114 engines and achieved a maximum speed of 422mph, making it fastest of all the Mosquitoes. VL619 served with 13 Squadron (motto: *Adjuvamus Tuendo* – 'We assist by watching') after the war, carrying out photo-reconnaissance and photo-survey duties in the Mediterranean from its base at Fayid in the Suez Canal Zone. *(Crown Copyright/AHB)*

1 Clear unframed Perspex nose cone.
2 F52 36in split pair vertical cameras.
3 Under-wing 200gal drop tanks.
4 Bulged equipment bay doors to accommodate long-range fuel tanks.
5 2 x F52 20in or 36in vertical cameras.
6 K17 6in or 12in or F24 vertical camera.
7 F24 14in oblique camera (on fuselage side).
8 Identification code lights – white, amber, green.

BELOW LEFT Rear fuselage camera stations inside the PR 34, looking forward. The adaptor mounting in the mid-position bears the legends: 'Spacer position F52 camera split 14, 20 & 36" lens' and 'Spacer position K.17 12" lens'. *(BAE Systems)*

BELOW CENTRE F52 36in vertical camera with adaptor mountings and in the foreground a port-facing oblique F24 14in camera. *(BAE Systems)*

BELOW RIGHT Nose-mounted forward-facing oblique F24 camera. *(airrecce.co.uk)*

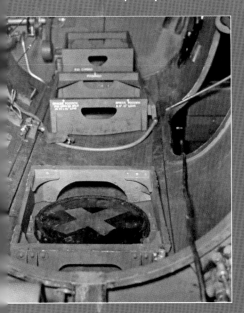

'The Mosquito was ahead of its time, but it was not a forgiving aircraft.'
George Lord, 235 Squadron

Chapter Six

The pilot's view

Light and responsive controls plus a big dollop of power from two Merlins made the Mosquito an extraordinary aircraft and a revelation to fly. It had terrific acceleration and top speed, was crisp and sensitive, and had superb harmonisation of the controls – qualities that made it an exhilarating experience. It was the perfect machine in which to go to war.

OPPOSITE View from the cockpit of Mosquito FB 26 (KA114) with pilot Keith Skilling at the controls. *(Gavin Conroy)*

In the driving seat

In a heartfelt letter to de Havilland, Wg Cdr John Wooldridge, CO of 105 Squadron, described the Mosquito as 'entirely free from unpleasant vices at all times', and said it could fly so well on one engine that his squadron felt it must have been designed originally as a single-engined machine with another engine stuck on for luck. And Flt Lt P. Hansor Lester, writing in *The Aeroplane* of 29 June 1945 of his experiences as a Mosquito pilot, said it was his opinion that there was no aeroplane more delightful to fly.

But the Mosquito was not one for the inexperienced, for it had something of the thoroughbred racehorse about it and, like a thoroughbred racehorse, it demanded careful handling and respect, otherwise it could turn and bite the pilot very hard – and it wasn't entirely free from vices.

The first obstacle was climbing aboard, which was quite a challenge if wearing a seat-type parachute – particularly on fighter variants which had the door on the side instead of underneath. The practical answer was to climb up the ladder, haul the 'chute up, and then position it on the seat before climbing back down to do a few ground checks. These included making sure that the undercarriage locking pins had been removed, that the pitot tube on the fin was uncovered, and that the rear hatch was secured. This was especially important, as loss of this door in flight could cause serious damage.

The difficulty in getting in, even slowly, inevitably left crews with one uncomfortable thought: what about getting out in a hurry? Baling out of a Mosquito has been described as 'slightly tricky'. The drill was to jettison the door and, if possible, feather the starboard propeller – especially on fighter versions, which had the side-opening hatch. A quick glance at any picture showing the proximity of entrance and propeller will confirm that this was sound advice, and another piece of useful guidance was contained in the manual on parachute drill: 'Should the navigator find it difficult to pass through the exit, the pilot should assist by giving him a good push with his foot.'

It was also possible to leave the aircraft through a jettisonable roof panel, but this was intended primarily for use after a crash. To escape safely from a Mosquito, plenty of height was needed: anything less than 5,000ft was considered virtually the kiss of death.

Cosy cockpit

Once settled in, the pilot felt immediately at home: the seat was comfortable, there was excellent all-round visibility, and all the controls were easily accessible. The fact that the pilot's seat on the left was angled slightly inwards towards the centre could cause some discomfort on long missions, and space was pretty tight for the crew – almost cosy.

The side-by-side seating was generally welcomed – but there was always the odd exception. As Dave McIntosh, a Canadian navigator with 418 (RCAF) Squadron put it: 'Once pilot, navigator and their war impedimenta were stuffed into the Mosquito cockpit, there was still lots of room – if you did no more than inhale and exhale. Long confinement in this office was not conducive to an atmosphere of fellowship but led, rather, to hours of silence punctuated by pilot–navigator bursts of crankiness, bitchiness, cursing and personal invective.'

The cockpit was fitted with a heating control that was situated behind the pilot's seat, and rotating it forward introduced hot air from the port radiator, while two adjustable ventilators, known as Punkah Louvres, allowed cold air into the cockpit. 'It was a good-tempered aircraft,' remarked 105 Squadron observer Mike Carreck, 'it kept you nice and warm – not too hot, not too cold.'

Operation of the fuel cocks was particularly simple and intuitive on basic Mosquitoes that were not fitted with drop-tanks or fuselage tanks, as just behind the pilot's seat were two cocks marked 'Left' and 'Right'. If these were turned so that they pointed towards each other, the inner tanks were selected. If rotated outwards, the outer tanks were in use. The procedure was that take-off and landing was done on the outers, everything else on the main, or inner, tanks.

Starting up

Once the usual cockpit checks were completed it was time to fire up the Merlins with the following settings selected: main fuel cocks switched to outer tanks: throttles half open; RPM control levers

at maximum position; superchargers on 'Moderate' (low-gear) setting; radiator shutters closed; pressure venting cock on; fuel transfer cock off; immersed fuel pump switch off; bomb doors shut with the selector at neutral.

Aircraft that did not have electrical priming operated from the cockpit were started by groundcrew using an external battery. The pilot then went through the cockpit checklist while the engines were idling and reaching 40°C for coolant and 15°C for oil. Supercharger operation was tested by opening up to static boost reading, setting the switch to 'Auto' and getting the groundcrew to push the test buttons on each engine.

This was followed with a full-power check before taxying out to the holding point. The engines were

ABOVE Cosy cockpit. No 604 Squadron's CO, Wg Cdr Michael Constable-Ward with his navigator, Flt Lt John Quinton. Mosquito fighter-bomber crews boarded and vacated their aircraft through a hinged entry hatch in the starboard side of the nose, which could be jettisoned in flight in an emergency. *(Andy Thomas)*

Cockpit and pilot's instrument panel in Mosquito FB 26, KA114. *(Gavin Conroy)*

1 Control column
2 Propeller speed control levers
3 Friction adjusting knobs
4 Throttle levers
5 Airspeed indicator
6 Altimeter
7 Direction indicator
8 Turn indicator
9 Rate of climb indicator
10 Artificial horizon
11 Boost control cut-out
12 Instrument light
13 Combined oil and fuel pressure gauges
14 Coolant temperature gauge
15 Oil temperature gauge
16 Boost pressure gauges
17 RPM indicators (behind control column)
18 Landing light switches
19 Propeller and carburettor de-icing control
20 Oxygen flow and cylinder pressure indicators
21 Triple pressure gauge
22 Undercarriage and tailwheel control
23 Flap control lever
24 Bomb doors lever
25 Aileron trimming tab control and indicator
26 Windscreen de-icing pump
27 Rudder pedal
28 Compass
29 Magneto switches
30 Engine prime and start buttons
31 Propeller feathering buttons
32 Outside air temperature gauge
33 Air vent
34 Instrument lights
35 Rudder trim tab control handle
36 Rudder trim tab indicator
37 Engine bay fire extinguisher handles
38 Bomb fusing and selector switches
39 Morse signalling unit
40 Downward identification lamps switch
41 Navigation headlamp switch
42 Fire extinguisher switches
43 Fuel tank contents gauges
44 Oxygen demand regulator
45 Cockpit entrance door
46 Not known
47 Not known

ABOVE Inside
the cockpit of the
bomber version of the
Mosquito. Note the
pilot's 'spectacle grip'
control column. (USAF
Museum)

was between +8.25 and +12lb, depending on the mark of Merlin, but mixture control was automatic, so no check was needed on this.

As there was no hydraulic pressure gauge, cycling the flaps on each engine in turn was a simple but important method of ensuring that both hydraulic pumps were operating correctly. This was a vital system, as it governed the undercarriage gear, flaps and bomb doors.

The radiator shutters were opened for take-off. These worked from the brake pressure system and were operated by two small switches that were usually sited next to the rudder trimmer, although on some marks of Mosquito two hand cranks were used. The shutters were either fully open or fully closed.

After the generator, driven by the starboard engine, was switched on, the gyros were uncaged and each engine was cleared with a quick two-second burst before lining up on the runway and moving forward a few yards to straighten up the tailwheel. With the awesome sound of two Merlins in stereo, it was time to go.

Take-off

There were two potential problems on take-off, and a pilot could see one of them even before he had climbed aboard: ground loop. Two big engines acting like giant gyros, combined with a spindly rear end supporting a small fin and rudder, caught out many a crew during the war, with the aircraft executing an unintentional 180° turn on the runway and left stranded ignominiously with the undercarriage ripped off and sometimes its back broken. The

very responsive to the throttles, and once the pilot had got used to them he would not need to use the wheel brakes much. When he did, the best method was short, sharp squeezes on the control column-mounted brake lever to avoid the aircraft swinging about untidily.

Time for a final check and settings for take-off, familiarised by the initials TTMFCOBRF – Trim, Throttles, Magnetos, Fuel, Coolant, Oil, Brakes, Rudder, Flaps. The elevator trimmer was set to 1.25° down to give a little nose-heaviness, rudder trim at neutral or slightly right, ailerons neutral, flaps up or 15° down. Propeller pitch controls were in the fully forward position to give maximum rpm at take-off boost, which

RIGHT Tail up and
engines developing full
take-off power, pilot
Keith Skilling prepares
to rotate KA114 from
Wairapa's runway on
19 January 2013. (Paul
Le Roy)

throttles were very sensitive and had a short travel, and such mishaps were usually caused by them being opened too suddenly, with the result that a vicious and often uncontrollable swing to the left would occur.

The torque from the engines would give the Mosquito a tendency to pull to the left, and the broad advice was to counteract this by leading with the port throttle and then bringing up the starboard one – but by exactly how much was down to practise, as over-correction could result in swinging the other way. This was not an aircraft for the heavy-handed.

Engine failure

The second potential danger on take-off was failure of an engine. There was an uncomfortable 'graveyard zone' between take-off speed and being able to fly on one engine, and if a failure occurred in this period the pilot would have both hands full and his brain working overtime. Although the speeds varied a little depending on the mark of Mosquito, the aircraft would need to reach about 180mph to fly safely on one engine, so it was important to accelerate as quickly as possible to be out of this dangerous envelope.

If an engine packed up just after taking off, there was little option but to close both throttles, keep going straight ahead and crash-land, the pilot being sure to pull his feet back smartly, as there were instances of propellers breaking up, slicing through the fuselage and causing horrific foot injuries – even amputating legs.

Attempting to turn would cause the aircraft to roll over and dive in, and many crashed in this way. If an engine failed a little later the choices weren't so clear; the important thing was immediately to reduce drag as much as possible, for a windmilling propeller – especially the paddle-blade type – and a lowered undercarriage would cause huge drag and handling difficulties, and the aircraft would not be able to sustain level flight.

The drill in an engine-out emergency was to retract the gear, feather the dead propeller and raise the flaps. The pilot would keep his left hand on the control column while using his other to raise the flaps and undercarriage, as the levers were in the middle of the instrument panel. Then

he would have to change hands to fly with his right hand while operating the throttle and pitch levers, which were to the left of the cockpit, before swapping hands yet again and flying with his left while using his right to actuate one of the two feathering buttons that were in front of the right-hand seat. This had to be held in long enough so that it stayed there by itself and released when the feathering was complete.

Doing all this in an emergency that could prove fatal required quick thinking and a cool head – but however quick he was, there was nothing the pilot could do to speed up the gear retraction process which, even with both engines running, took about 25 seconds. With one engine dead it took nearly twice as long, as only one hydraulic pump would be operating.

Getting the useless engine feathered would lower the critical flying speed on one engine by about 20mph, but the pilot would still be left with some juggling between rudder authority and power from the remaining engine. Basically, to have a chance of going round and avoiding a crash-landing the gear needed to be up, the speed not below about 150mph, the dead engine feathered and take-off boost available on the live engine.

However, with sufficient speed and in clean configuration with flaps and gear up, the Mosquito handled very well on one engine once

ABOVE Port feathered – the Mosquito was capable of flying on one engine in an emergency. *(Jonathan Falconer collection)*

the asymmetric forces were trimmed out. This would need a firm foot on the opposite rudder to counteract the initial swing as the dead engine feathered, and then two or three turns on the rudder trim wheel to hold the trim, after which the aircraft could be flown easily and without having to alter the throttle setting of the live engine.

The return legs of many wartime missions were completed successfully on one Merlin – but landing was the crucial phase, as with the gear down and flaps lowered it was impossible to go round again on one engine unless there was sufficient height and speed, so once committed there was no second chance. Losing control by not maintaining enough speed was one of the major causes of Mosquito crashes during the war.

All of this sounds very dark, but compared to most other twin-engined aircraft the Mosquito's single-engined landing characteristics were superb. Hansor Lester found that an approach on one engine, with or without the dead engine feathered, was easier to do well on a Mosquito than any other twin-engined type he had flown, even to carrying out an overshoot from as low as 500ft with gear and flaps lowered – but only as long as the speed was 145mph or more. He

had seen others try to do it with less airspeed and, without exception, they crashed.

Surprises

There were one or two surprises for a pilot getting used to the Mosquito's characteristics. Once comfortably airborne, he would brake the wheels and raise the gear, checking that it was locked, and then throttle to 150mph, which was the optimum climbing speed. When the coolant temperature had dropped to 95°C, a figure that could vary depending on the mark of Merlin, the pilot would close the radiator shutters. This resulted in a sharp nose-down pitch that required immediate correction.

This effect was so strong, that if the aircraft was trimmed with shutters open to fly straight and level 'hands off' and then the shutters were closed, the nosing down was strong enough to cause the engines to cut under negative g and, if unchecked, the aircraft would then continue into a steep dive. The usual shutter procedure was to close them with the right hand and re-trim with the left. Once trimmed for closed shutters, re-trimming was necessary when they

were opened again, as this time the aircraft would pitch up due to the trim-set.

However, this was not the only function that caused a change of trim: raising the gear would result in a slight nose-up tendency, while lowering it would have the opposite effect. With the flaps it was the other way round – nose-down when raised, nose-up when lowered. This nose-up effect was quite pronounced, and was considered 'objectionable' by NACA test pilots when assessing an F-8 in 1945. Opening the bomb doors would also cause a slight nose-up trim change, with nose-down when closed.

The Mosquito needed to be flown at all times: it was not one of those aircraft where the pilot could set the trim then sit back and relax. It was extremely manoeuvrable and capable of performing most aerobatics very impressively, but deliberate spinning was prohibited. Because of the responsiveness of the controls, care had to be taken to avoid excessive accelerations in turns and recovery from dives, while violent use of the rudder at high speed was also to be avoided.

Stalling

Normal stalling on the Mosquito with flaps and gear up was straightforward: to induce a stall the pilot would close both throttles and pull the stick back, trying to ignore the blaring of the warning horn, which could not be switched off. Being such an aerodynamically clean aircraft, speed fell off very slowly when compared to less slippery types, and there was little tendency for it to mush around and lose height.

As the stall was approached the needle of the airspeed indicator flickered around violently, so it was not easy to gauge the speed. This was the result of the pitot head being on the fin where the air was disturbed when nearing a stall. But the pilot had plenty of warning of what was going on, as at about 125mph the aircraft would start to shake and judder before finally stalling at about 115mph – yet there was still enough aileron authority to maintain lateral control during the buffeting stage. At the actual stall there was some snatching from the ailerons and then the nose would pitch down quite sharply with a tendency to roll to the left. Recovery was simple, with just a forward push on the stick to regain flying speed.

"Come out of the road—you'll get run over."

Landing

The landing approach was not difficult, but the aircraft's clean lines meant that the pilot had to allow more time than usual for speed to be lost. At about 1,500ft he would throttle back before lowering the undercarriage at around 180mph, and at that point the Mosquito lost its handling qualities and sensitivity. The gear caused so much drag and disturbance that an extra +2 or +3lb boost had to be fed in to maintain 160mph without losing height.

With undercarriage down, fuel cocks would be switched to outer tanks and radiator shutters would be opened, causing the nose-up effect. Then the flaps would be lowered, the pilot ready to correct the sharper nose-up pitch by pushing forward on the stick and holding this by winding forward on the elevator trimmer. Speed would be held at no lower than 140mph, as 145mph would be needed to maintain good control if an engine died.

At about 600ft altitude the pitch controls would be set to fully fine and the aircraft would be on final approach, still maintaining 140mph until crossing the hedge on the perimeter of the airfield. Then the throttles would be cut, speed would drop to 125mph and the Mosquito would sink gently on to the runway, either in three-point or tail-high attitude – there were pros and cons for both touchdown methods. With a smooth landing and no crosswind there was little tendency for any swing to port, but if there

ABOVE This superb Giles cartoon featuring the low-flying antics of the Mosquito appeared in the *Daily Express* on 5 March 1944.

was it could be easily corrected with short jabs on the brake. Then it was just a question of raising the flaps and taxying back to dispersal.

First solo

Those who flew the Mosquito never forgot the experience. The famous aerobatic pilot Neil Williams, who lost his life in 1977 when ferrying a CASA 2.111 (Spanish version of the Heinkel He 111), vividly recalled in *Aviation News* his first flight in a Mossie when he was asked to ferry TT 35 (TA634, now at Salisbury Hall) from Liverpool to Bovingdon for the filming of *Mosquito Squadron*. In the navigator's seat was the engineer who had worked on this aircraft. Neil didn't mention that this was his first Mosquito solo flight – but he noticed he was being watched like a hawk.

'We settled into the tiny cockpit, bulky in our flying kit and parachutes,' he wrote. 'With a whine the starter engaged on Number One engine, and as the prop started to turn I pressed the booster coil button. The massive blades rebounded slightly with the gears banging and protesting. I pulled the throttle back slightly and the engine immediately caught.

'I ran the engines up to to static rpm and checked CSU [Constant Speed Unit] and mags, the Merlins thundering deafeningly while the aircraft shuddered and jerked against the brakes.

'I taxied onto the long runway and let the machine roll forward to straighten the tail wheel, which was non-castoring, and increased rpm to

1,500 against the brakes. The aircraft trembled urgently, as though it was eager to be off. I released the brakes and she started to roll forward. Carefully, I used the brakes to keep exactly on the centre line.

Stupendous noise

'As she gathered speed I used coarse rudder, but this was barely effective. Now, as she was running straight, was the moment to increase power. I twisted my wrist slightly so that I led fractionally with the left engine. The throttles were very highly geared so that the slightest error resulted in a large alteration of power with the attendant possibility of a swing, and a swing on take-off in a Mosquito is incipient disaster.

'At 80 knots the tail came up and the throttles reached the gate. In the flying attitude she accelerated rapidly and now there was good rudder control, so I pulled the releases on the throttles and pushed them both fully forward. The noise was stupendous and my right foot was well forward to hold her straight – but now she was under control.'

Then Williams hit a problem: as he lifted off at 105 knots he knew that he needed to get up to a much higher speed as quickly as possible to be out of the danger zone if one engine failed, yet even with full power he couldn't get beyond 140 knots – though 'the strident roar of the Merlins was sweet and healthy'. Two amber lights gave the answer: the undercarriage was still down. 'Even those two magnificent engines at full power could only just hold the enormous drag of the undercarriage,' he wrote. 'Slowly, very slowly, the gear came up, pulling the doors closed by a very Heath Robinson system of cables and rollers.'

As the speed rose beyond 200 knots, the Mosquito's character began to change. 'Now it became a purposeful, shark-like creature, thrusting forwards and upwards – now it was coming into its element. It felt solid, and yet eager to respond to the touch – one sensed its lethal potential as a war machine. Now it had surpassed the Spitfire's cruising speed, and still it accelerated.

'It was light and sensitive on the ailerons, but strangely heavy and well damped in pitch. The rudder was extremely light and hardly needed to be used at speed, and in this it was very like a jet aeroplane.'

After a memorable flight in which Williams marvelled at the performance – 'the north coast of Wales flashed by at an incredible speed' – it was time to land: 'I kept the speed up and delayed selecting full flap until quite late – there was still time for an engine to fail. As the flaps went fully down I adjusted the throttles to allow the speed to reduce slowly. The note of the engines had subsided to a deep grumble which blended with the hiss of the propellers. The view was excellent, perched as I was so far forward.

'As the revs fell, the aircraft started to sink and I pulled back on the stick to control this. Down, down, and now there was concrete beneath the wheels; lower, lower, and then the squeak of protesting rubber as the wheels touched at 100 knots. I pressed gently forward on the stick and slowly throttled fully back with the characteristic Merlin popping and crackling.'

Williams held the tail up as long as possible, for he had been warned that when the tail wheel hit the ground the aircraft would try to swing. But, to his surprise, the Mosquito ran straight and true. He turned to his passenger and said: 'Well, that was a first solo.'

'Thought so,' was the reply. 'Mosquitoes never swing on a first solo landing!'

Like a lady

Bud Green, who joined 410 (RCAF) Squadron, had got used to Blenheims and Beaufighters, so the Mosquito was quite a shock after the Beaufighter, which was a heavy, solid aircraft that needed large movements to open the throttles. Like Williams, he was surprised by the Mosquito's short throttle quadrant: 'The effect was startling,' he wrote. 'An astonishing increase in power – faster, lighter. A bit touchy before you got used to the throttles, but then you could play them like organ stops. This was my initial impression of the Mosquito. My second impression was how responsive it was to aileron movements.

'The Mosquito was a superb design and a delight to fly. Like a lady, beautiful to look at, capricious, but if handled properly was a delight. Had vices, as all ladies have – stalling was one. But one can't dissociate the design concept from Rolls-Royce, because the engines were the key. No engine failed me in 1,000 hours. They were super engines.'

And the final word must come from the famous Eric 'Winkle' Brown, who has flown more types of aircraft than any other test pilot.

'I have a very high opinion of the Mossie,' he said, almost 70 years after he first flew one. 'As a pilot, you had to be on the ball, yes, but it was a wonderful warbird. The all-round view was superb, and it had what I would call a morale-building cockpit, with the crew seated side by side.

'The Spitfire, Mosquito and Lancaster were the outstanding British aircraft of the last war. The Germans were very worried about the Mosquito and tried hard to design an aircraft that would equal it, but they didn't succeed.'

BELOW No 81 Squadron's PR 34A (RG177) piloted by Flt Sgt Anderson makes a breath-takingly low beat-up of the airfield at RAF Seletar, Singapore, in May 1953.
(Copyright unknown)

'Ubendum, Wemendum.'

Unofficial motto of RAF groundcrew trades

Chapter Seven

Mosquito maintainers

—●—

Like the aircraft in their charge, the groundcrew trades who kept the Mosquito flying throughout the Second World War could be found in a diversity of locations around the globe – from Scotland to Cornwall, and overseas in Italy, Malta and the Middle East, to the Indian subcontinent and the far-flung Cocos Islands in the Indian Ocean.

OPPOSITE Inside a hangar at Gütersloh in western Germany, where only a few years earlier Luftwaffe mechanics had fixed Junkers Ju 88 night-fighters, RAF fitters and riggers are hard at work maintaining Mosquito FB VIs of 4 Squadron, October **1947.** *(Crown Copyright/AHB)*

Climate and weather affected the daily toil of Mossie groundcrews, be it the biting winds that reeled in from the North Sea on to cheerless East Anglian dispersals, or the sapping heat and humidity on dusty airfields in southern India. Like its human maintainers, the Mosquito was better suited to the temperate conditions of northern Europe, but when it was taken overseas on active service in the Middle East and the Tropics it suffered from the damaging effects of the climate.

Serving as it did with all three front-line commands of the wartime RAF, and in widely differing roles, the Mosquito groundcrew trades were equally as varied – engine and airframe fitters; electricians and photographers, radar technicians and instrument mechanics; and armourers who loaded and belt-fed everything from bombs and bullets, to rocket projectiles and air-dropped mines.

ABOVE No 627 Squadron, Oakington, Flg Off Eric Arthur, navigator, with the groundcrew of Mosquito B 25 'V for Victor'. *(www.627squadron. co.uk)*

ABOVE After a heavy tropical downpour, a Mosquito FB VI of 'A' Flight, 27 Squadron, taxies through rivers of liquid mud from its dispersal to the landing strip at Parashuram, eastern Bengal, during March 1944. Taking off under such conditions could be tricky. *(IWM CF114)*

LEFT Groundcrew carry a 100gal long-range fuel tank past a parked Mosquito PR 34 (RG203, 'E') of 684 Squadron Detachment at palm-fronded Brown's West Island, Cocos Islands, during July–August 1945. *(IWM CI1546)*

Cliff Streeter was a groundcrew electrician on 105 Squadron at Marham. He joined the squadron in early 1942 straight from 12 School of Technical Training at Melksham in Wiltshire.

'A typical day would start with the DIs [Daily Inspections] on our allotted aircraft. This would normally entail two of us going to each aircraft. One would be in the cockpit operating the switches etc, while the other would check from the outside, the navigation lights, landing lights, pitot head heater, bomb door and landing gear micro switches connected to warning lights in the cockpit. Also in the cockpit were such things as battery voltage indicator (24 volts), bomb release switch and selector, cockpit lighting and rheostats, and a few other things. If any faults turned up they had to be rectified. When all was satisfactory, one of us would sign the Form 700, signifying that everything electrical was serviceable. If a plane flew during the day after this, a similar between-flights check had to be made and, again, any faults found rectified. There were also Air Ministry modifications to be made as they came up. Any fault that occurred on an operation had to be traced and repaired, of course. When an operation was on, an electrician had to be on duty prior to take-off along with the other trades. Then the often long wait for their return and, hopefully, relief when you asked "Any snags, sir?" and he replied "No problems". Engine and airframe fitters always called electricians, wireless, instrument repairers and armourers etc, 'gash trades', although each flight was pretty close-knit. Your flight, whether A, B, or (as later) C, was, of course, the best!

'When an aircraft returned from an op, it opened its bomb doors, and when the engines had stopped the armourer would remove the fusing links from the bomb racks and show them. It was then known that the bombs had been dropped live. Sometimes it happened that the bombs were brought back and if the pilot said that they had been unable to drop them, the bomb doors had to be pumped by hand to the open position (not having been opened when the

ABOVE Wrapped up against the biting Fenland winds that lash their Oakington dispersal, these unidentified 627 Squadron fitters pause momentarily from their labours to glance at the photographer. The aircraft in their charge is B IV, DZ615. Minor engine inspections were normally carried out in the hangars, but circumstances often dictated that they were done out on the dispersals as soon as an aircraft had landed back from ops. *(www.627squadron.co.uk)*

BELOW No 627 Squadron, 'A' Flight dispersal at Oakington during March 1944. In the centre is DZ353, 'B', which was much photographed in 1942 while serving with 105 Squadron as 'GB-E'. DZ353 was lost on a visual marking operation to Rennes on 8 June 1944. *(Brian Harris collection/ www.627squadron.co.uk)*

engines were running). Then, with the pilot present, an attempt had to be made to drop them safe (un-fused). If they did drop, the electrician and armourer who had signed the Form 700 were very relieved; the aircrew presumably were not.

'Working at dispersal was great in fine weather, but on a hot, sunny day the cockpit of a Mossie could become almost unbearable. When working outside an aircraft on an icy, snowy winter's day, there would be a few curses flying around, especially from engine fitters, as frozen fingers grappled with small screws, nuts and bolts. However, whatever it was it had to be done, and usually was.'

Refuelling

Fuel for the Mosquito was contained in four pairs of CIMA-protected aluminium-alloy tanks, all of which were housed within the wing. The total capacity was 407gal.

Each pair of fuel tanks was provided with a filler cap under the wing top skin, accessible through flush-fitting doors. All wing tanks could be over-wing refuelled through their filler necks via these caps, one filler to each pair of tanks. The long-range tanks in the ventral compartment (if fitted) were refuelled through the filler cap on the port side of the fuselage above the wing.

Only the two inboard pairs of wing tanks could be pressure-refuelled via the fuel gallery. The fuel was delivered under pressure from the bowser at 50psi, which saved time and effort. The outer pairs of tanks were refuelled through the filler necks (that is, by gravity fuelling), which was a longer process.

The fuel gallery was mounted internally on the aft right-hand side of the ventral/bomb-bay compartment, and was accessible through the ventral/bomb-bay The gallery provided points for two refuelling hoses and incorporated three manually operated valves. The two outer valves were used for the inboard pair of tanks, and either pair could be selected for filling. The gallery also incorporated disc-type non-return valves to prevent flow from one pair of tanks to another during flight or while on the ground. Each pair of tanks was provided with a drain cock, and a check valve permitted uncoupling of the delivery pipes without loss of fuel.

The oil tanks were filled from inside the wheel

well by removing the filler cap. A dipstick was provided in each tank to measure the oil level.

Strict safety precautions were always followed when refuelling. Both the bowser (or trailer tanker) and the aircraft had to be properly bonded and earthed to prevent a surge of static electricity causing a spark that could ignite the petrol vapour. In common with other aircraft of the period, the Mosquito was earthed through its Dunlop 'Ecta' (Electrically Conducting Tyres for Aircraft) tail wheel tyre of metal-impregnated rubber. The static electricity picked up by the airframe during flight, often many thousands of volts, was earthed through the tyre the second the aircraft touched down.

The bowser itself was earthed by a metal chain, which it dragged behind it along the ground, but as an added precaution before refuelling began an earthing rod was driven into the ground. Wartime regulations also stipulated that, when refuelling, the bowser should be so parked that it could be quickly and easily driven away in an emergency; trailer tankers were kept attached to their prime mover (eg, a tractor) for the same reason.

Over-wing refuelling was a lengthy process that needed the involvement of several men or women, often using access ladders. It was also potentially risky because the fumes created an additional health hazard to the refuelling crews, not to mention the dangers of slipping on an icy wing surface or being toppled off the wing by high winds. The fuel itself was also prone to contamination by dust and water through the open filler necks.

Leading Aircraftman Francis Cooper was an electrical assistant on the ground staff of 230 Operational Conversion Unit at RAF Lindholme and Scampton from 1949 to 1950, which at that time was flying Lancasters, Lincolns and Mosquitoes.

'As a National Serviceman I did my trade training at 12 School of Technical Training in Melksham in 1948. Being in the RAF for the short-term (20 months) I spent eight weeks on a special shortened course for National Service electrical mechanics. I passed out as an AC1 electrical assistant and was posted to

ABOVE A Mosquito F II of 157 Squadron is refuelled from a Butterfield's Prime Mover petrol bowser at Hunsdon on 16 June 1943. The bowser chassis is a 3¼-ton Brockhouse, the fuel tank is by W.P Butterfield with pump gear by Zwicky, powered by a Lister 3hp petrol engine. *(IWM CH10313)*

LEFT One did not always have to fill a tank right up since the amount required was measured by a gauge on the bowser and double-checked with a dipstick placed into the tank. However, a gauge could sometimes develop a fault, but a dipstick never did. *(IWM CH10312)*

ABOVE Francis Cooper, on the right, spent most of his National Service as a 'sparky' with 230 Operational Conversion Unit (OCU) at Swinderby and Scampton. *(Francis Cooper)*

RAF Lindholme in Yorkshire where I joined 230 Operational Conversion Unit (OCU). When I arrived they were operating Mosquito NF IIs on fighter affiliation with Lancasters and Lincolns. Soon these older Mossies were replaced by brand new B 35s that were flown up from Hamble. There were three on our flight coded YW-A, YW-B and YW-C, but the unit code was later changed to IC-.

'As an AC1, for the first five months I worked alongside "Blondie" Taylor, an RAF "regular", pre-flighting the Mossies and doing the daily and weekly inspections. As we were a small flight all the different trades tended to muck in and work together. When "Blondie" was demobbed they left me on my own to carry on.

'I sometimes helped with the refuelling. The Mossie had two pairs of fuel tanks in each wing. A petrol bowser supplied fuel to the aircraft from a hose on a boom that swung out. You'd be on top of the wing where you'd lift a little hatch, then clip an earthing lead to the rim of the filler neck before unscrewing the filler cap (fuel flowing through a hose creates static so the bowser had to be earthed). Another earthing lead was run from the bowser and clipped onto the undercarriage leg. Once this was done we'd "fire away" into the fuel tank. When refuelling was complete we'd take out the nozzle, replace the filler cap then remove the earthing leads.

'A trolley acc [trolley accumulator] was used to supply electrical current for normal start-ups. When the acc was plugged into the aircraft's starter socket a switching mechanism automatically disconnected the aircraft's internal

battery. Once the pilot was ready to start up you pressed a button on the trolley acc to put its electricity supply through to the aircraft.

'Underneath a little flap on the outboard side of each engine nacelle was a Kigass priming pump. You'd push the plunger in, turn it anti-clockwise, then you'd give two or three strokes to prime the cylinders before the pilot turned the engine over. If the engine didn't fire first time you'd give it a few more pumps. Something you had to watch out for, though, was if you over-primed – you'd get flaming petrol spurting out of the exhaust ports above your head! Once the engines had been started you'd cover the pump with the little flap and wait for the pilot to give the signal to pull the chocks away.

'One of the difficulties with working on the Mossie was that some equipment was difficult to get at. If you ever had to change a Mossie's batteries you'd know! You had to climb up and squeeze in through the hatch into the rear fuselage to get to the battery tray on the top surface of the wing (which ran through the fuselage in a single piece). And I mean you really had to squeeze in and out! There were two 12-volt batteries linked together at their forward ends. The crew dinghy stowage was overhead the batteries.

'The Mosquito was built in the days when plastics were first being used for cable covering. A number of fires in the area of the engine were caused by splits in the plastic cable coverings. The heavy electrical cabling that ran from inside the cockpit to the engine starter motors passed through the wings, into the undercarriage bays and behind the oil tanks before reaching the engines. The cable was forced to take a fairly tight bend around and through the back of the engine bulkhead, which made the plastic pull away from the wires it was enclosing. Because the Mossie was all-wood construction all of the metal parts were earth-bonded. On some Mossies the bare copper cable running to the starter motors vibrated and touched the bonding wires, starting fires, although this didn't happen on our unit.

'Even so, an instruction came through saying that all Mossies were to be grounded until the cables had been checked. This meant the oil tanks located inside the undercarriage bays had to be drained, and then airframe fitters removed the tanks before the electricians could check the cables.'

AIRCRAFT RECOVERY

On 20 June 1947, 58 Squadron's Mosquito PR 34, RG206, had flown from RAF Benson to make a photographic survey north of Lisbon in Portugal when its crew were diverted to US Naval Air Station (NAS) Port Lyautey in Morocco. Some 800yd along the runway the port wheel brake failed and the port undercarriage and propeller were damaged when the aircraft fell off the runway into a 3ft ditch. The Mosquito's crew, Flt Lts Thomas and Northcott, were unhurt. Seaman First Class Aerial Photographer Jerry Zimmerman, US Navy, photographed the result of RG206's unscheduled landing. *(All photos courtesy of Jerry Zimmerman)*

ABOVE The pilot, Flt Lt Thomas, and NAS officers survey the damage to RG206 immediately after the crash.

BELOW Navy Seabees manning the base crane prepare to move the damaged Mosquito to the west side of the main hangar apron for repairs.

RIGHT An RAF repair crew was flown out from England and after a couple of weeks of work the Mossie was back in the air again.

Leading Aircraftman Craig Reid, RCAF, from Mattawa, Ontario, was a radar technician at Middle Wallop in Fighter Command from 1942 until his posting to 6 (RCAF) Group, Bomber Command, in early 1944.

'From the time I arrived on Fighter Command in 1942 until the end of the war our trade, of radar technician, had lived with many incongruities and contradictions. It was the high-tech stuff of its day – hush-hush and so on. It was a high status deal, yet our section never had an officer to speak for us until late 1944. All other sections – electrical, fitter, rigger, etc, had an officer to whom they primarily related. We didn't. The Engineering Officer was our boss and always he was unhappy about it. The Radar Officer at Group Headquarters was always in the position of overruling him, thus we belonged to nobody.

'On top of that our section hut was not usually adjacent to other section workshops. It was off by itself, usually next to the control tower. This put us in association with the big-wigs, senior officers in command, so you can see this was a source of resentment for other section personnel.

'When one considers that radar equipment was always just the next step beyond the prototype stage, whereas other equipment, engines, compasses, bombs, etc, had a proven record of performance, the comparative pattern of performance contrasted greatly at times. Radar manifested itself as fickle and erratic at times, and was the cause of 'scrubbing' a kite when all else was okay. Not a happy position to be in as a radar technician.

'Then there was at least one modification per month, meaning the riggers had to find a new spot for it, the electricians had to run new wires, all at the orders of the radar section. This moved the natural state of rivalry between sections to animosity at times. So, the modification would be put in, found to be ineffective, and Group Headquarters would order it removed. That kind of inconsistency did not make friends.

'Occasionally, we were asked to go for a flip, the "air test". The main reason was to do with a little matter of "finger trouble" by aircrew. Imagine yourself being given a one-hour orientation on a bench, set up with one of our present day high-tech units, and then you get sent off on operations. You have to do your own job as navigator and run the new toy as well.

'The result? Often the aircraft returned, radar U/S. So we'd check it out. Okay. So why the discrepancy?

'The tension around resolving this, you can see, was heavy. Remember, we didn't have an officer to represent us. The Engineering Officer wasn't particularly interested in defending a trade for which he had no fondness, and was often more a perceived irritation than a tangible asset; and a Navigation Officer who didn't like his navigators emerging as fumbling idiots.

'The result? Many a test run-up on the hard standing dispersal pad resulted in an onboard "lesson" by the technician for the aircrew, and they ate it up. They came to understand the vibration of a running aircraft caused natural variations in performance of a radar set, and they learned how to deal with them. This helped and went on for some time, but imagine how the powers-that-be felt when information of these illicit sessions leaked out.

'If that was not enough, there was a whole set more politics amongst the technicians.

'We had to sign the DI sheet as a result of our Daily Inspection. Sometimes a kite was on the perimeter getting ready for take-off, only for us to get a signal that the radar was U/S. Upon arrival it was not unusual to find the power plug

RIGHT LAC Craig Reid, RCAF. *(Courtesy the Reid family)*

RELOADING THE .303IN GUNS

- Remove the cover under the fuselage nose and clear all empty cases and links. (Note: a suitable container, such as a bag with a sewn-in hoop to keep the mouth open, should be held ready to catch the cases and links.)
- Remove the two nose compartment doors. Disconnect and remove the belt chutes.
- Remove the locating tube at the front of the ammunition boxes and pins at the bulkhead, and lift out the boxes.
- Load each box with 750 rounds and refit the inboard boxes first to enable the inboard guns to be cocked.
- After replacing the nose compartment doors, see that the lock indicator discs lay flush with the skin.

RELOADING THE 20MM CANNON

Note: immediately after opening the ventral compartment doors and before rearming commences, the fire and safe unit at the rear end of the gun body must be put at SAFE.

- Open the doors underneath the fuselage and secure them with the front and rear stays.
- Remove the ammunition box lids and the curved belt chutes.
- Attach the hoist and feed 150 rounds, flaking the belt into the ammunition box during the process. Repeat for each gun.
- Attach the support strap to the outboard gun (the chutes on the inboard guns must

LEFT Armourers prepare a Mosquito FB VI of 23 Squadron for night operations from Pomigliano, Italy, on 29 November 1944. Lapping in belt ammunition for the nose Browning machine guns is Leading Aircraftman E. Hurst, while Leading Aircraftman T. Hamill uses a pull-through to clean inside the barrel of one of the 20mm cannons. Keeping the insides of the ammunition boxes scrupulously clean was an obsession for many armourers, who knew that accumulations of dirt could easily cause the guns to jam in action. *(IWM CNA2088)*

be removed), free the guns at the rear supports and remove the feed units.
- Prime the feed units with 18 rounds each and tighten the tension nut on each unit.
- Fit the feed units, reattach the guns at the rear support, and remove the support straps.
- Fit the primed feed units to the inner guns.
- Open the hinged doors in the curved chutes and fit the chutes, feeding into them the rounds which hang from the feed units.
- Draw the belt down from the ammunition box as it emerges at the chute door, connect it to the rounds from the feed units with a spare round. Draw the slack back into the box and close the chute door. Fully tighten the mechanism in the feed unit.
- Replace the ammunition box lids.

disconnected – this condition usually resulting from forgetfulness by the radar technician at the time of the DI. Being all of equal rank it made for difficult interpersonal relations when a technician reported the nature of the fault. The resultant fallout was serious.

'So, corporal rank was introduced to double-check the matter. Did this work? Well, there were times when we suspected cunning aircrew of being part of the problem.

'The second most common fault after lack of power was discontinuity (that is, proper

grounding of sets and units). Since all trays or platforms were rubber-mounted to eliminate vibration, this could be tricky. How the hell do you explain to aircrew that sometimes a good bash at a special spot completed continuity to ground? One can readily anticipate their nervousness and scepticism.

'As groundcrew we worked hard to get bugs out of the kites and trusted our aircrew to do their best. We knew that our best was necessary because their lives depended also on our competence.'

RIGHT Two-six! Groundcrew manhandle a 307 (Polish) Squadron FB VI into a hangar for some essential maintenance that cannot be undertaken on the dispersal. (ww2images.com/ A01321)

ABOVE Well wrapped up against the cold, an engineer officer examines the starboard Merlin of a 29 Squadron Mosquito on a freezing dispersal at Hunsdon in 1944. Among the most common snags experienced on Merlins by groundcrews were the everlasting glycol leaks from their radiators and hoses. (ww2images.com/A03226)

ROLLS-ROYCE MERLIN TWO-STAGE, TWO-SPEED SUPERCHARGED ENGINES

ROUTINE INSPECTION SCHEDULE

The following scheme of periodic engine inspections was recommended by Rolls-Royce. The intervals between inspections could be adjusted, depending on where in the world the Mosquito was operating (climate, weather), the type of operations being flown (high level, low level), as well as a unit's specific flying and maintenance requirements.

Up to 50hr

- Remove, clean and refit engine scavenge oil filters.

Up to 100hr

Repeat 50hr inspection.

- Remove, clean and inspect SU pump oil filter (SU single-point fuel injection pump only). [Merlin 113, 114 – PR 32, PR 34, B 35, NF 36.]
- Remove, clean and inspect carburettor fuel filter (SU Anti-G float-type carburettor only). [Merlin 61 – PR VIII; Merlin 72 and 73 – PR IX, B IX, FX VI, PR XVI.]

LEFT A busy hangar at RAF Gütersloh, Germany, during October 1947, where 4 Squadron Mosquito FB VIs are undergoing maintenance. 'GU-P' is FB VI, TA540. (Crown copyright AHB)

- Inspect impact tubes and boost venturi for cleanliness and freedom from damage. (Rolls-Royce Bendix injection carburettor only). [Merlin 76, 77 – F XV, PR IX, B IX, PR XVI, B XVI, NF 30.]
- Remove, clean and refit main suction filter in oil tank.
- Magnetos – clean breaker contacts, reset gaps and renew cam lubricating pads.
- Examine exhaust stubs and troughs for cracks and check for security.
- Pressure test cooling systems and apply coolant tests.
- Check main and intercooler pumps for gland leakage.
- Check engine holding-down bolts for security.
- Replace sparking plugs with a new or reconditioned set.
- Check all LT wiring harness connecting plugs, booster coil and starter motor connections.
- Remove cowling for general inspection of cowling and power plant.
- Clean air intake filters or renew if necessary.

200–250hr

Repeat 50hr and 100hr inspections.

- Check priming system and volute drain.
- Check engine control rod ball joints for excessive play and pinch bolts for security. Lubricate joints with engine oil and control shaft with anti-freeze grease DTD 143C.
- Lubricate boost control unit.
- Check valve tappets for locking and valve clearance. Examine camshafts and valve springs.
- Replace flame traps by new or reconditioned sets.
- Blow out vent gauzes on magnetos.
- Check oil control valve for cleanliness and serviceability, as required.
- Inspect condition of starter motor and generator commutators. If dirty, clean with rag lightly dipped in lead-free petrol. Inspect bushes for wear and freedom of movement. Check bush flexible for fraying.

Airframe maintenance

Water damage

Owing to its particular form of construction the Mosquito airframe was susceptible to damage from moisture – something that was not an issue with its metal-framed and skinned contemporaries such as the Spitfire, Lancaster or Halifax. Mosquito groundcrew were always on the lookout for tears to fabric sealing strips and split or damaged wooden surfaces on the wings and fuselage, no matter how small. The ingress of moisture into the wooden body of the aircraft could lead to serious structural problems, so any damage had to be made good without delay.

For Mosquitoes that were picketed outside in all weathers if hangar accommodation was not available, groundcrew were advised to follow these procedures to minimise water damage:

- Make sure that all exits, doors, windows and inspection covers are securely closed.
- Fit engine, cockpit and radiator covers.
- If the aircraft is to be left outside in wet weather for a prolonged period, lower the wing flaps a few degrees to allow water to escape easily from the wing shroud gap.
- In frosty weather, fit wing and tail unit covers. These should also be fitted if the aircraft is to stand outside for several days in wet weather.
- After the aircraft has stood out in the rain for several hours, inspect internally and remedy leaks as far as possible.
- Make sure that all drain holes are kept clear of debris.

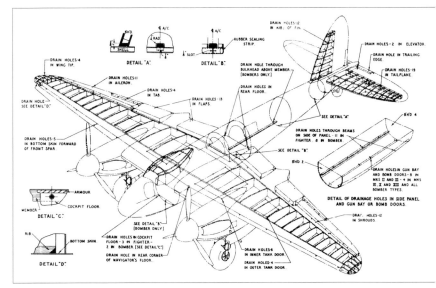

BELOW Location of water drain holes in the Mosquito airframe. *(Crown Copyright)*

AN OUTDOOR LIFE: WORKING AT THE DISPERSAL

1 Groundcrew of 110 Squadron 'ham it up' for the photographer as they 'service' the starboard engine of a Mosquito FB VI on the airfield at Joari in East Bengal during May 1945. *(IWM CF 586)*

2 A fitter attends to the exhaust stubs on a 464 (RAAF) Squadron FB VI at its dispersal at Hunsdon in 1944. Merlin exhaust stubs had a tendency to burn out like paper. With use, the studs securing them became more or less welded in the cylinder block, so that they had to be drilled out before oversize studs could be fitted when replacing a stub. You could only do the job twice or you were through the head and into the water jacket. *(BAE Systems/DH1846b)*

3 On a snowy dispersal at Castle Camps on 28 January 1945, 307 (Polish) Squadron's NF XXX, NT259/G, 'EW-W', receives electrical power from a trolley accumulator prior to engine start-up. The 'G' suffix to the serial number stands for 'Guard', meaning the aircraft must be guarded when on the ground because it is carrying secret equipment – presumably the SCR 720/AI Mk X radar. *(ww2images.com/A10201)*

4 Groundcrew hard at work preparing a B IV for ops. The corporal lying on top of the Mossie's nose is using a soft cloth to polish the Perspex. At night a speck of grime on the windscreen could easily be mistaken for an enemy fighter closing in for the attack. *(ww2images.com/A0545)*

5 One for the album: smiling 627 Squadron groundcrew take a break during fitting larger wing drop-tanks to one of the squadron's Mosquitoes. *(www.627squadron.co.uk)*

6 Using Type A 'hockey stick' hand winches, armourers hoist a 500lb MC bomb into position on the under-wing pylon of Mosquito FB VI, MM403, 'SB-V', of 464 (RAAF) Squadron at Hunsdon on 25 February 1944. On an intruder mission almost one year later MM403 suffered engine failure in the early hours of 18 January 1945, north-east of Merville, near Béthune, and the aircraft was abandoned to crash. The pilot, Flt Lt Richard Murray Trites, RCAF, was killed; the navigator, Flt Lt Donald McKenzie Shanks, RAAF, survived the incident. *(IWM CH12406)*

7 Loading 500lb bombs into the rear bomb-bay compartment of an FB VI. Note the outlets in the forward equipment bay doors (at the top of the picture) for ejecting spent cannon shell cases. *(ww2images.com/A13412)*

8 This happy-looking group of Polish air force officers from 305 (Polish) Squadron use a loaded bomb trolley as their prop to sit for the photographer. Behind them stands an FB VI on its dispersal, wearing protective covers over its cockpit canopy, wheels and engines. Even though the trees appear in full foliage, suggesting summer or early autumn, the Mossie's port wing is covered in netting that was used to prevent the accumulation overnight of frost and ice during cold weather. *(ww2images.com/A10071)*

Airframe repairs

When making good any damage to the airframe, groundcrew needed to give particular attention to the surrounds of windows (cockpit canopy, glazed nose and windows on either side of the fuselage in the nose), doors (crew access and equipment), filler cap apertures, etc, where a perfect seal had to be maintained. For this purpose marine glue was used.

To purge any water that had trickled into voids or internal spaces in the airframe or inside control surfaces, drainage holes and passages were incorporated into the Mosquito structure. Groundcrew were aware that these drain holes and passages had to be frequently checked and cleared of debris if they became blocked.

Edges of Madapolam strip (or fabric edging), which occasionally 'lifted', needed to be securely doped down again, otherwise moisture could become trapped behind the material. (Madapolam is a soft cotton fabric made from fine yarns with a distinctive weave pattern. It has two particular qualities that made it useful in the construction of the Mosquito. Its equal warp and weft means the fabric's tensile strength and shrinkage is the same in any two directions at right angles; and it also absorbs liquids such as paint and aircraft dope equally along its X and Y axes.)

PROTECTIVE TREATMENTS

External fuselage
Madapolam
3 coats of red dope
2 coats of aluminium dope
Camouflage or matt black top coat
Internal fuselage
1 coat of primer
1 coat of cellulose enamel, grey-green
1 coat of hydraulic fluid-resisting paint (DTD 399)
1 coat of acid resisting paint (BSX 19)
Wing, tailplane and fin, external
Madapolam
3 coats of red dope
2 coats of aluminium dope
Camouflage or matt black top coat
Wing, undercarriage and wheel well
1 coat of primer
1 coat of hydraulic fluid-resisting paint

ABOVE RAF Alipore, West Bengal, February 1945. Fitters prepare for the physically demanding job of installing a new Rolls-Royce Merlin 76-series engine in 684 Squadron's PR XVI, NS645, 'P' (see also page 53). The Merlin was a heavy lump of metal at about 1,645lb (roughly ¾-ton) dry weight and required craning into position.
(IWM CI1084))

Rubber mats, or other suitable protection, were laid on top of the wing for walking on, and care needed to be taken to avoid damage to the Madapolam covering when laying down tools, cowling panels etc.

Protective paint and dope treatments were affected to some extent by the corrosive effect of the various fluids used in the aircraft, such as fuel, hydraulic fluid, liquid for windscreen de-icing, etc. Any surfaces that were affected (except for those painted matt black on night-bombers and some night-fighters) needed to be lightly rubbed over with a paraffin-soaked cloth and then washed off with soap and water. The edges of the fuselage structure near the tailwheel unit needed to be cleaned periodically and treated with marine glue as necessary.

The internal protection of the fuselage also had to be maintained in good condition. Use of a protective material, such as sacking or felt, was advised when walking inside the rear fuselage to carry out maintenance.

Metal fittings bolted to wooden parts needed to be treated with marine glue on the contact surfaces before fitting. Parts liable to come into contact with hydraulic fluid also required treating externally with oil-resisting paint. Bolt holes through wooden members were treated with lanolin (DTD 279). Edges of windscreens, windows etc had to be sealed with Bostik Compound C (a bonding compound).

Aircraft servicing in the Far East

Whether you worked on a Mosquito or any other aircraft type in the Tropics, the problems associated with their maintenance were severe. Living conditions for RAF personnel in most locations were basic. Tents were pitched under trees, and the harsh heat, graphically described by some airmen as being 'furnace-like', added greatly to their general discomfort.

Daytime temperatures of up to 120°F and high humidity made heat exhaustion a constant threat for those who worked on aircraft, particularly if outside. Many airmen suffered from prickly heat rash while others were admitted to hospital suffering from heat stroke and dehydration. In such sweltering conditions it was necessary to drink up to 12 litres (21 pints) of water a day for the body to stay hydrated. Hot sultry nights under canvas after a day's hard physical work offered little in the way of respite for tired groundcrew.

For Mosquito squadrons operating in India and Burma most routine maintenance was conducted outside and squadron aircraft were picketed down in the open at night. Violent dust storms, the occasional severe thunderstorm with high winds, and heavy monsoon rain in season meant that flying would often be postponed.

Every breeze or gust of wind carried with it sand, which made life difficult for most of the groundcrew trades, particularly engine fitters, riggers, electricians and camera fitters. To make matters worse, billowing clouds of choking sand and dust were raised when aircraft ran up their engines before taking off.

After midday the metal of an aircraft exposed to the ferociously hot sun burned whoever touched it, and anyone working inside an aircraft cockpit would strive to get everything

right first time. In temperatures of 120°F no-one wanted to come back again to sort out any snags.

Groundcrew worked hard to protect their aircraft from the tropical heat and used the following procedures to help reduce the chances of airframe damage:

■ As far as possible, aircraft should be parked in the shade. Some form of grass or rush matting offers a good protection, particularly if an air space of a few inches is maintained between the matting and the surfaces.

■ If other conditions allow, the aircraft should be kept facing towards the sun.

■ If the usual cockpit and engine covers are fitted, a small air space should be maintained between the covers and the structure. The cockpit windows should be left open during daylight when conditions allow, but should be closed at night.

Climate damage

When the Mosquito was deployed to the Middle and Far East theatres towards the end of the war its wooden structure proved unsuitable in the harsh climates. Whether it was a good idea deploying the Mosquito overseas may be a matter for debate, but the fact was that many RAF squadrons previously equipped with American aircraft under the Lend-Lease programme had to return their aircraft to the USA when the war ended, and the Mosquito was one of the few British aircraft that were available to replace them.

In the Middle East the intense dry heat caused shrinkage in various vital components, which eventually resulted in Mosquitoes being grounded and the squadrons re-equipped with metal aircraft such as the Beaufighter Mk X. Meanwhile, in the Far East during late 1945 several months of heavy monsoon rain and high humidity began to take their toll on Mosquitoes. A shortage of suitable hangar accommodation had meant the aircraft were often left out in the open and constantly exposed to the worst possible conditions for their wooden construction.

Running repairs

The high humidity soon revealed weaknesses in the main spars and glued joints, and made the plywood skin covering warp – events which would have been unlikely or certainly very rare in the temperate conditions of north-west Europe. Repairs to an airframe required highly skilled tradesmen, but were practically impossible under such conditions, so the best that could be done was for ground staff to patch up an aircraft and keep it serviceable for as long as possible.

By the middle of 1946 great efforts were being made by the staff of 390 Maintenance Unit (MU) at Seletar in Singapore (the RAF's main aircraft servicing base in the Far East) to repair the decaying Mosquitoes that were arriving in their dozens. It was a highly labour-intensive activity that tied up specialist manpower for weeks on end but eventually proved to be a losing battle for the RAF, which instead instructed 390 MU to concentrate on keeping only the PR 34s of 684 Squadron flying (mainly because their specialised camera installations could not be replicated in any other aircraft).

ABOVE During 1946 much of 390 MU's heavy maintenance and rectification work at RAF Seletar in Singapore involved the repair of dozens of Far East Air Force Mosquitoes, whose wooden structures had failed to stand up to the humid climate. Particular emphasis was placed on keeping the long-range PR 34s serviceable. Here, engineer officers of 390 MU, commanded by Grp Capt Perkins, are pictured at Seletar with 81 Squadron's PR 34, VL615, on 17 July 1946. Co-author Jonathan Falconer's grandfather (Flt Lt 'Lofty' Owen) is in the front row, second from right. *(Jonathan Falconer collection)*

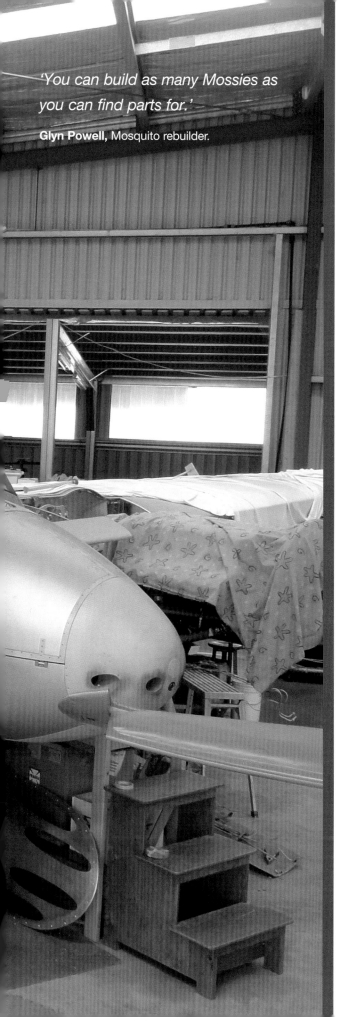

Chapter Eight

Mosquito restoration

──(●)──

When Mosquito T 3, RR299, was lost in a tragic accident in 1996, the chances of seeing a Mossie fly again were slim. Its wooden construction and the non-existence of vital fuselage moulds presented rebuilders with insurmountable challenges. Or so it seemed, until one man on the far side of the world took on the task of scratch-building a mould. Years later his perseverance has returned a Mosquito to the skies – and more will follow.

OPPOSITE From wreck to rebirth: Mosquito FB 26, KA114, seen when its restoration to flying condition was well under way in January 2011 at Avspecs' workshops in New Zealand. *(Avspecs)*

The raw power and graceful lines of the British Aerospace-owned Mosquito T 3, RR299, made it many people's favourite air show performer. For thousands of enthusiasts it was the highlight of the Fighter Meet at North Weald airfield in Essex on 15 May 1996, when their senses were treated to the Mossie's breathtaking display routine. Then, two months later, RR299 was gone for good.

Radio and television news bulletins on 21 July 1996 broke the tragic story that the world's only airworthy Mosquito had crashed at Barton air show near Manchester, claiming the lives of its crew, pilot Kevin Moorhouse and flight engineer Steve Watson. For some there was a touch of déjà vu, for only a week before at Duxford's Flying Legends the crowd had gasped in disbelief when The Fighter Collection's P-38J Lightning crashed and exploded, killing its pilot 'Hoof' Proudfoot. It had been a bad year, both in human and aviation heritage terms. Displaying vintage military aircraft could be an unpredictable and dangerous business.

As an ironic footnote to this sad tale, RR299's owner, British Aerospace, had planned to donate the aircraft to the RAF Battle of Britain Memorial Flight at the end of the 1996 air show season.

After the loss of RR299 the skies fell silent to the snarl of a Mossie's twin Merlins. It would be another 16 years before the beautiful form of a 'Wooden Wonder' took to the air again, only this time it would be on the far side of the world in New Zealand.

THE END OF RR299

Although she didn't have a particularly interesting service history, RR299 had become a star, not only for her regular air show displays, but also for her active roles in the film *Mosquito Squadron*. Built at Leavesden in 1945, she was a dual-control T 3 trainer and operated in the Middle East until 1949, before serving with a number of Maintenance and Operational Training Units.

Her final posting was to 3 Civil Anti-Aircraft Co-operation Unit in Exeter, and in March 1963 she was declared surplus to requirements. After being acquired by Hawker Siddeley Aviation at Chester, she received her Civilian Certificate of Registration as G-ASKH on 9 September 1963 and began a new career as a film star and public attraction.

For the rest of her life she was lovingly and professionally maintained by a small number of enthusiastic personnel from British Aerospace.

What went so tragically wrong at Barton?

There were no aerobatics involved in the display – just climbs, descents, medium turns and level flights in front of the crowd line at 250 to 275mph. As RR299 neared the end of her routine, she did a flypast along the line of the

BELOW RR299, coded HT-E, seen at Hatfield in July 1977. (Keith Wilson)

runway and then pulled up into a steep climb, followed by a wing-over to the right. The manoeuvre was not completed: when the wings were well over the vertical the aircraft slowed, lost height as it yawed, and then pitched nose down into an uncontrolled tumbling sequence. Seconds later control was regained in a dive, but too much height had been lost and RR299 crashed into a wood, instantly killing the crew and wrecking the aircraft.

Good amateur footage was studied by the Air Accident Investigation Board, and under analysis it showed that the port propeller began to slow just before the apex of the wing-over and moments later appeared to stop completely. With only the starboard engine delivering power, the pilot had no way of completing the wing-over or maintaining speed. It appeared that power to the port engine was regained in the latter stages of the dive, but by then it was too late for the pilot to pull out.

The port engine was a Merlin 25, and the starboard one a Merlin 502. Mechanically these were identical, the only difference being in the installation details. Engine maintenance and overhaul was subcontracted to specialist concerns and was not carried out by the aircraft's British Aerospace personnel.

Three weeks before the accident a different pilot doing a display at Lille experienced rough running of the left engine at zero g, and it did not recover immediately when 1g was applied. However, no fault was found and attempts to reproduce the problem in flight failed, so the aircraft was cleared to continue flying.

Even though the Merlin's problems in the war of fluffing and spluttering under negative g had been cured, the AAIB found that its early reputation persisted and was still thought to be a characteristic of the engine, with the result that any cut-out under reduced or negative g was not entered in the technical log.

After a thorough examination to eliminate as many causes of the accident as possible, attention turned to the SU carburettor. Both engines of RR299 had been fitted with the anti-g modification, but a number of faults were found in the carburettors – particularly in the float settings. The adjustable stops, which governed the lowest float height, had not been set correctly, with the result that at its lowest point in the chamber the float would have caused serious fuel starvation.

A fuel flow test with the floats at their lowest, and incorrect, point would have allowed 35 pints an hour on the port engine and 158 on the starboard. The correct flow figures for the same setting should have been 330 to 350 pints an hour – or roughly ten times as much on the port engine.

But the investigators stressed that it was not possible to relate the as-found condition of the carburettors to the likely effects on the engines during the final wing-over, a manoeuvre that had been carried out many times before with no problem. It was not feasible to isolate the many variables involved – nevertheless, the carburettor was the prime suspect in the death of two men and the loss of a beautiful historic aeroplane.

Mosquito survivors

With 7,781 aircraft built, the Mosquito is almost three times less numerous than the Spitfire at more than 22,000. Being a robust all-metal aircraft, dozens of examples of the Spitfire have survived into the 21st century, so much so that in Britain and further afield a multi-million pound industry has grown up around restoring and rebuilding them. Owing to the Mosquito's wooden construction the story for de Havilland's 'Wooden Wonder' has been very different.

Once a Mosquito was deemed surplus to service requirements, disposal of the wooden airframe was a relatively simple matter. All useful parts were stripped for reuse or salvage and the rest of the aircraft was either sold off to a scrap merchant for a matter of pounds, or doused in petrol and burned where it lay. For those Mossies that avoided the flames or dodged the breaker's axe, many were simply left outside to rot. The Mosquito's airframe had never been good at withstanding prolonged exposure to moisture or bad weather, which is one reason

SERIAL	MARK	STATUS	REMARKS
A52-319	PR 41	Static display	Australia, Australian War Memorial, Canberra.
HR621	FB VI	Under restoration	Australia, Camden Museum of Aviation, Harrington Park, NSW. Restoration to static display standard only.
A52-600	PR XVI	Under restoration	Australia, RAAF Museum, Point Cook, Victoria. Built at Hatfield as NS631. Restoration to static display standard only.
MB24	NF 30	Static display	Belgium, Royal Museum of the Armed Forces and Military History. Formerly RK952.
KB336	B XX	In storage	Canada, Canadian Aviation Museum, Ottawa, Ontario.
VP189	B 35	Static display	Canada, Alberta Aviation Museum, Edmonton. CF-HMQ. Modified to represent FB VI.
RS700	B 35	Under restoration	Canada, Calgary Mosquito Society, Alberta. CF-HMS. Moved to Bomber Command Museum of Canada, Nanton, AB, for restoration, 11 Aug 2012.
VR796	B 35	Under restoration	Canada, Vancouver, BC. Under restoration to flying condition by Victoria Air Maintenance Ltd for owner Bob Jens. CF-HML.
KB161	B 35	Under restoration	Canada, Windsor, Ontario. Under restoration by the Mosquito Bomber Group.
W4050	Prototype	Static display	England, de Havilland Heritage Centre, Salisbury Hall, Herts.
TA122	FB VI	Static display	England, de Havilland Heritage Centre, Salisbury Hall, Herts.
TA634	TT 35	Static display	England, de Havilland Heritage Centre, Salisbury Hall, Herts.
TJ118	TT 35	Under restoration	England, de Havilland Heritage Centre, Salisbury Hall, Herts.
TJ138	B 35	Static display	England, Royal Air Force Museum, Hendon, London.
TA639	B (TT) 35	Static display	England, Royal Air Force Museum, Cosford, Staffs.
TA719	B (TT) 35	Static display	England, Imperial War Museum, Duxford, Cambs.
HJ711	NF II	Static display	England, Yorkshire Air Museum, Elvington, Yorks. Composite restoration.
TE758	FB VI	Under restoration	New Zealand, Ferrymead Aviation Society. NZ2328/NZ2382 composite.
TE863	FB VI	Under restoration	New Zealand, RNZAF Museum, Wigram.
TE910	FB VI	Private collection	New Zealand, John Smith, Mapau, Nelson.
NZ2308	T 43	Under restoration	New Zealand, under restoration to flying condition by Mosquito Aircraft Restoration for owner Glynn Powell
NZ2305	T 43	Static display	New Zealand, Museum of Transport and Technology, Auckland. Formerly A52-1053.
TW117	T 3	Static display	Norway, Norwegian Aviation Museum, Bodo. Displayed as an FB VI.
LR480	PR IX	Static display	South Africa, National Museum of Military History, Saxonwold, Johannesburg.
PZ474	FB VI	Under restoration?	USA, Jim Merizan, Chino, California.
RS709	B 35	Static display	USA, National Museum of the USAF, Dayton, Ohio. Displayed as a PR XVI.
RG300	PR 34	Under restoration?	USA, Jim Deerborn, California.
RS712	TT 35	Static display	USA, EAA Air Venture Museum, Oshkosh, Wisconsin. On loan from owner Kermit Weekes. N35MK.
TH998	B (TT) 35	In storage	USA, National Air & Space Museum, Washington DC.
TV959	T 3	Under restoration	USA, Flying Heritage Collection, Everett, Washington State. Owned by Paul G. Allen, co-founder with Bill Gates of Microsoft. Under restoration to flying condition by Avspecs, Ardmore, New Zealand.
KA114	FB 26	Airworthy	USA, Military Aviation Museum, Norfolk, Virginia. Owned by Jerry Yagen, restored to flight by Avspecs, Ardmore, New Zealand. First flight 27 September 2012.

(Sources: Ian Thirsk, de Havilland Mosquito; www.mossie.org; various published and internet sources)

why so few are left today. It is a minor miracle, therefore, that any at all have survived into the 21st century.

Almost 300 Spitfires can be seen in museums and private collections around the world today, with another 50 or so Spitfires and Seafires that are airworthy and about a further 20 undergoing restoration to flying condition. By comparison the numbers for the Mosquito are tiny.

At the time of writing (2013) there were 31 survivors in all – 24 displayed in museums worldwide or under restoration to static condition; Jerry Yagen's FB 26 (KA114) rebuilt in New Zealand by Avspecs Ltd, and returned to the air in 2012, and at least three more airframes under restoration to fly. These are a T 3 (TV959) for owner Paul G. Allen by Avspecs, Ardmore, New Zealand; B 35 (VR796) for owner Bob Jens by Victoria Air Maintenance, British Columbia, Canada; and Glyn Powell's T 43 (NZ2308), which he is rebuilding himself at Drury, New Zealand.

It is also rumoured that American warbird collector Kermit Weeks is considering returning to flight TT 35 (RS712), which is part of his Fantasy of Flight collection in the USA, but on loan to the EAA Museum, Oshkosh, at the time of writing.

The most famous of all, however, is one that will never fly again: the first prototype (E0234/W4050), which has been on public display at the de Havilland Aircraft Heritage Centre since 15 May 1959, just yards from where it was built. At the time of writing, this aircraft was undergoing extensive refurbishment back to the configuration in which it last flew.

Rebuild for flight

When it comes to building or restoring a Mosquito, the process is unlike that for an all-metal aircraft such as the Spitfire. With wooden construction it is not possible to reuse parts of the original wood in the restoration, so the only option is to build the entire wooden airframe from scratch.

People have asked why some of the best-restored museum examples of the Mosquito cannot be brought up to an airworthy condition. There are three answers: the first is because of doubts over the structural integrity of the wooden airframe, its original glues, and the difficulty in getting access to inspect the condition of vital components such as the wing spar; the second is often to do with the cost; and the third is the availability of parts.

Thus, in order to build and fly a Mosquito that will satisfy the stringent safety requirements of the various international airworthiness bodies, the best solution is to start again from the beginning, providing you have enough components from a 'known' donor aircraft.

During the Second World War a variety of complex moulds, jigs and templates were the basis of the complex construction of the Mosquito. None has survived and it was believed that there were no extant plan drawings showing how they were constructed. For anyone today thinking of scratch-building a Mossie, these vital jigs are an absolute necessity and up until only a few years ago their non-existence was the insurmountable obstacle to fabricating new fuselages and wings.

Wooden wings over New Zealand

Glyn Powell, master mould and jig-maker

When New Zealander Glyn Powell became the owner of the hulk of a former RNZAF Mosquito T 43 in 1990, his intention was to restore the aircraft and return it to flight. But he discovered this was easier said than done.

'The fuselage of the Mosquito is built in two halves on wooden or concrete moulds. This is the only way you can get the double-curvature in the ply. As the moulds had all been scrapped after production ceased in 1950 I was faced with the problem of building them. I was told

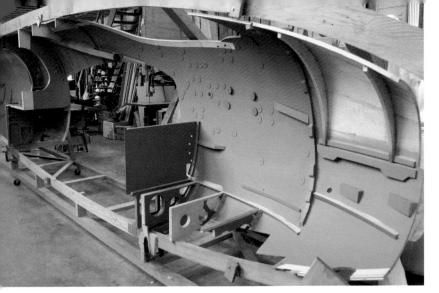

by people who knew about these things that it was impossible. Well they were nearly right! It certainly was not easy.'

But Glyn didn't give up. He formed Mosquito Aircraft Restoration Ltd and decided to build a Mossie in his workshop in Drury, Auckland. He scoured the world for original drawings and manuals to help him reconstruct the vital moulds and jigs. With the aid of leading Auckland boat-builder Chris McMullen, he lofted the designs for the two 36ft-long Canadian Red Cedar wood fuselage half-moulds, which then took him five years to make.

'The mould itself is not too much of a problem, it is the positioning – very accurately – of the bulkheads and numerous other members, including the main wing pick-up fittings in slots in the mould. I had to position them in space and build the mould around them. Working with a 36ft-long wooden mould with the natural atmospheric conditions made a difference to measurements, depending on which day you measured them. This is why the Canadians first used concrete moulds.'

Then over the ensuing six months he built the wing assembly jig. 'The jigging for the wing is an enormous job; the main wing assembly jig took six months to make and involved some very accurate engineering, especially with the drill plates for drilling the spars for the engine and undercarriage brackets, etc, which must be drilled absolutely precisely.'

A painstaking part of this process was the high level of accuracy required – in some cases the tolerances were to within 1/50,000th of an inch.

Enter collector Jerry Yagen

The visit to New Zealand in 2000 of American

warbird collector and businessman Jerry Yagen to review progress on the rebuild by Avspecs Ltd of his P-40 Kittyhawk, was the catalyst that brought together Glyn Powell, with his specialist skills and knowledge of moulds, jigs, and airframe building, and Warren Denholm of Avspecs, with his experience of historic aircraft restoration and rebuilds. It was at this meeting that Warren asked Jerry if he had ever considered adding a Mosquito to his Military Aviation Museum at Virginia Beach in the USA, because he knew of a derelict Mosquito airframe in Canada that was available for acquisition.

Later, Jerry visited Glyn's workshop at Drury and saw for himself what the former electrician and real estate agent-turned Mosquito restorer could bring to the party, realising that if anyone could return a Mosquito to flight then Glyn and Warren were two such men. In any case, Yagen wanted to fly a Mosquito and he knew that the only way he was going to achieve this burning ambition was to restore one.

Avspecs – New Zealand's world-beating aircraft restoration company

Avspecs Ltd was formed in 1997 by father and son partnership Colin and Warren Denholm. Originally based at Rotorua in New Zealand's North Island, the company was established to provide a fully dedicated restoration facility for warbird and vintage aircraft. The staff at Avspecs (there are normally about eight, but this can vary according to the volume of work on hand) have a wide range of expertise rebuilding vintage and warbird aircraft and have experience on the Spitfire, P-40 Kittyhawk, Sea Fury and Venom to name only a few.

The company relocated to Ardmore, South Auckland, in 2000 and is now run by Warren and his wife Shona. In 2003, Avspecs moved into their own new premises in Kittyhawk Lane, Ardmore airfield. Located on the southern edge of Auckland City, this facility allows for future expansion of the business and affords good access to all of the essential support services required by the company, such as heat treatment, NDT (non-destructive testing), electroplating and foundry services, all of which exist within 40 miles of Ardmore.

Mosquito FB 26, KA114

The derelict Mosquito in Canada to which Warren was referring was KA114. Built by de Havilland Canada at its Downsview plant in 1945 as an FB 26, it was too late to see any action in the closing months of the Second World War. In 1948 it was sold as surplus by the RCAF to a farmer at Milo, Alberta, where it was left in a field on the prairies to rot slowly in the freezing winters and baking summer heat until in 1978 it was acquired by a Canadian museum. Jerry Yagen's Military Aviation Museum in Virginia Beach, USA, purchased the sorry-looking hulk in 2004 and shipped it to Avspecs for rebuilding to airworthy condition.

The brainchild of Gerald 'Jerry' and Elaine Yagen, founders of Tidewater Tech and the Aviation Institute of Maintenance schools, the Military Aviation Museum at Virginia Beach, USA, is home to one of the largest private collections in the world of First and Second World War-era military aircraft. It has more than 30 aircraft, most if not all of which are certified for flight, with many others under restoration. The museum is constantly growing as they add new aircraft and aviation-related ground equipment to the collection. KA114 joins two other iconic British combat aircraft of the Second World War – Spitfire IXE (MJ730) and Hurricane XII (5667, registered N2549).

When the remains of KA114 arrived at Ardmore from Canada in June 2004 it was realised that the aircraft was actually in better condition than was first believed. Work began the following year with Glyn Powell supplying a number of parts he had built for his own Mosquito project that included ribs and bulkheads, plus the use of the all-important moulds and jigs. It took Glyn and his team almost three years to build the complete airframe, with the wings test-fitted to the fuselage in March 2008. There followed the complex jobs of fitting out the wings, airframe and cockpit with the fuel and hydraulic system, electrical wiring, control runs, engines and undercarriage.

Warren and Glyn have remained faithful to de Havilland's construction techniques and materials except for the glue. Instead of the original organic Casein adhesives, modern West System Epoxy has been used, which has

the added benefits of superior strength and waterproofing qualities – two factors that caused problems for the Mosquito when it was in service.

During the war de Havilland built the Mosquito using three-ply plywood. Aircraft builders today use thicker five-ply, which is unsuitable for the Mossie, so a three-ply birch was specially made for the KA114, cut in Germany and laminated by British Plywood Manufacturers at Ponders End (which is where some of the original plywood for the Mossie was made during the war).

ABOVE The sorry remains of KA114 in June 2004. It must have seemed an impossible dream to return this tangled heap of wood and metal to the beautiful aircraft it once was. *(Avspecs)*

BELOW TT 35, RS712 (foreground) is now displayed in the EAA Museum at Oshkosh, Wisconsin, courtesy of its owner, Kermit Weeks. In the background is T 3, RR299. There is talk that RS712 could be returned to the skies in the future. *(Jonathan Falconer collection)*

ABOVE Almost 18 months later the wooden fuselage has been covered in ceconite, a deviation from the original madapolam, April 2007. *(Avspecs)*

ABOVE The undercarriage assemblies have been installed and spinner back plates attached, 1 December 2011. *(Avspecs))*

ABOVE KA114 stands on her own undercarriage, 21 December 2011. *(Avspecs)*

ABOVE RIGHT KA114 is towed outside the hangar, 21 December 2011. *(Avspecs)*

RIGHT The partially completed cockpit, still awaiting the control column and full instrumentation. *(Avspecs)*

A pair of Merlin engines for KA114 was a lucky find in Australia. Not Merlin 225s as originally fitted to the FB 26, but British-built Merlin 25s complete with engine bearers and most fittings. They were bought from a collector in Melbourne who had planned to run one of the engines at shows, mounted on a trailer, but this had never materialised. Like the Victoria Air Maintenance B 35 in Vancouver, the engines were shipped to Vintage V12s at Tehachapi, California, for a complete rebuild.

A dream fulfilled

In September 2012 the skies over Ardmore airfield on New Zealand's North Island reverberated to the sound of KA114 getting airborne. It was watched by crowds of enthusiasts, many of whom had travelled from far away to witness this historic occasion. It had been more than 16 years since the world's last airworthy Mossie had crashed in England in 1996 and it marked the culmination of an ambitious eight-year rebuild programme that reputedly cost its owner, Jerry Yagen, the thick end of $4 million.

As a tribute to Warren Denholm, Glyn Powell and the many other New Zealanders who had brought KA114 to life, the Mossie was finished in a colour scheme representing an FB VI of 487 (RNZAF) Squadron and was painted as 'EG-Y' – also Elaine and Gerry Yagen. It was 487 that had flown on the Amiens prison raid in 1944.

Enthusiast Paul Le Roy from Wellington was one among many who thronged to watch KA114 put through her paces in front of an appreciative audience:

'When I first heard that a Mosquito was being restored here in New Zealand I was sceptical, knowing a little about the history of the aircraft and the complex moulds that would be needed to recreate it. I thought that it would be some sort of replica. However, after a bit of research I realised that I was totally wrong and that this was indeed a genuine restoration project and that somehow I had to see it fly. I had discovered that ultimately it would be going to live in the States.

'Following the progress of the restoration was a little difficult because details were hard to come by. Eventually I heard that, with luck and plenty of hard work, it would be complete and should debut at the 2011 Classic Fighters Air Show in Omaka, New Zealand.

ABOVE AND BELOW KA114 is put through her paces to the delight of thousands of onlookers. *(Gavin Conroy/Gavin Conroy/Paul Le Roy)*

'This never happened and I feared that unless I travelled to Auckland I would not get the chance to see it fly. When it finally took to the sky in late 2012 all I could do was record the TV coverage to keep as a memory. Then to my amazement the owner Jerry Yagen decided that it would be made available for display at the Wings over Waiarapa Air Show in January 2013, before being dismantled and sent on its way to the USA. I had already decided to go to the show, but now there was no way that I was going to miss this opportunity.

'The day arrived, the weather was perfect, and I decided to go to the airfield a day early to get a look at the Mosquito. When I arrived there were a few cars parked at the end of the runway and I stopped to chat with those who were waiting around. I discovered that the Mosquito was not yet on the ground but was due at any moment. I couldn't believe my luck – I was going to get a chance to see it ahead of time!

'A few minutes later – it seemed to take ages – I heard the unmistakeable sound of Merlin engines as the Mosquito came in low and fast in a sweeping left-hand turn and we were treated to a five-minute impromptu display. It passed just a few feet above my head before making a perfect landing. Having taken my camera with me I was able to capture this incredible event.

'The day of the air show was amazing, with all the vintage aircraft to marvel over, but nothing could compare with the Mosquito – its shape and distinctive sound is just awesome and I feel privileged to have been able to see it fly.

'When finally it landed at the end of the day and taxied to the parking area I was filled with emotion and came close to shedding a few tears. My feelings at the time were that I was so lucky, yet so sad that I would not get the chance to see it fly again.

'I've been to many air shows, and will go to many more, but nothing will ever compare with the way that I felt after seeing the Mosquito.'

In February 2013, KA114 was carefully dismantled and packed into three metal freight containers for shipping to the USA. It arrived at Jerry Yagen's Fighter Factory on 15 March, accompanied by two Avspecs engineers, to assist the American team reassemble the Mosquito. Warren Denholm flew out to the US in April to supervise the final preparation of KA114 before she took to the air again for Federal Aviation Administration (FAA) inspectors on 7 May, followed by her first public display at the Military Aviation Museum's Warbirds over the Beach Air Show on the 17th.

BELOW Keith Skilling brings in KA114 for a neat wheeled landing. *(Paul Le Roy)*

Mosquito T 3, TV959

The next Mosquito to emerge from the Avspecs workshops is likely to be a T 3 (TV959) owned by the American millionaire and co-founder of Microsoft, Paul G. Allen. David Braks is one of the carpenters at Avspecs who is working to return TV959 to flight. He is a furniture maker by trade and like his wartime predecessors at de Havilland in England and those further afield in Canada and Australia, he too has found his way into Mosquito building. 'Ardmore is a unique place. It's unusual that Mossies are being rebuilt here in New Zealand instead of somewhere like England, but it's exciting to be part of this history.

'The woodworking skills needed for rebuilding the Mossie are still the same as they were in the forties, but even so there are lots of little technical details to consider. It's been a steep learning curve. Luckily TV959 was stored inside before it came to Avspecs, so its airframe is actually in pretty good nick. I've been working with Corin McCrae, who's in charge of the wing-building. We built the wing pretty much from scratch as the original had been sawn off. Fortunately, we've got working plans and TV959 itself, which we've used as a pattern to copy. Corin has designed the wing for TV959 on a computer and cut the parts using a CNC machine.'

The condition of the fuselage has not yet been determined, which could mean a new one may have to be built if the original is found to be beyond repair. If this is the case, then it will add several more months to the project's end date. Whatever the outcome with the fuselage, it will be a few more years at least before TV959 is

ready to follow KA114 along Ardmore's grass strip and up into New Zealand's skies.

'Glyn's own' – Mosquito T 43, NZ2308

When work had finished on KA114, Glyn Powell returned to his own Mosquito, T 43 (NZ2308), which he hopes to have flying in about 2015.

'The Mosquito we [Glyn and his work partner Mike Tunnicliffe] are restoring is an Australian-built T 43, which is a dual-control Mosquito, the Australian equivalent of the British T 3. It began life on the Bankstown assembly line as an FB 40 (A52-20) and was converted to T 43 status as A52-1054. It was one of four purchased by the RNZAF in June 1947 and flown across the Tasman Sea in four hours. Not bad for an aircraft type which first flew in 1940! Its RNZAF number is NZ2308. It was disposed of in 1955 and ended its days on a farm at Riwaka in the north of the South Island, but at least it was saved from th⋯⋯⋯⋯the fate of most of the 80-odd other F⋯⋯⋯Mosquitoes.

'I acquired the ⋯⋯ns of this Mosquito in 1990 as the basis ⋯⋯ restoration. Because of its poor condition due to many years out in the weather, I decided that its wooden airframe would have to be rebuilt. As already mentioned there were no fuselage moulds, these had been disposed of after the war, and as it is not possible to build a fuselage to flying standards without them, I decided I would have to make them. This proved to be a lot more difficult than I thought. Eighteen years later I had built a prototype fuselage, which went to the Mosquito Bomber Group at Windsor, Ontario, and a

ABOVE LEFT Hardly recognisable as an aircraft, TV959 was moved from the Imperial War Museum in London to the IWM's Duxford site in 1988 where it was stored pending restoration. Here it is in March 1991, looking pretty sorry for itself. *(A. Allen)*

ABOVE In 2011, TV959 arrived at Avspec's workshops in New Zealand for restoration to flying condition on behalf of its new owner, Paul G. Allen, co-founder of Microsoft. *(Peter Lewis)*

complete wooden airframe for Jerry Yagen's Fighter Factory in Virginia, USA (it was fitted out at Avspecs at Ardmore Airport). And now I have started on my own Mosquito T 43 – NZ2308.

'It is basically of standard wooden construction but the detail, accuracy and tolerances required are mind-boggling. However, as I keep reminding myself, it's all been done before. When the wooden airframe is finished then comes the assembly of the thousands of metal parts and fittings. You just wouldn't believe how many metal parts there are in an aircraft "built entirely of wood". We have six shipping containers full of them, which I have accumulated over the years from around the world. And we still don't have all of them!

'We are looking for any Mosquito parts – engine cowlings, spinners, ailerons, radiators and lots of smaller items. Each one has to be cleaned up, inspected and NDT'd, repaired where necessary, the paper work written up, and a "serviceable" tag fitted – and the reject rate is high. However, almost all of these metal parts will be original and will form a large percentage of the completed aircraft. My plan is to fly this Mosquito back across the Tasman to Bankstown where it was born all those years ago.'

Glyn was asked what he considered to be the high point for him so far: 'There are several, but I suppose it would be when we pulled the prototype fuselage off the jigs. We tested it to make sure everything fitted and worked – and it did. It's no good doing anything else until you've got the fuselage made. That's the key to the whole thing.'

BELOW At Victoria Air Maintenance in Vancouver, British Columbia, B 35, VR796, has been stripped to her bare essentials for restoration and is about to lose her engines, February 2008. *(Victoria Air Maintenance)*

BELOW RIGHT Pre-refurbishment, one of the Merlin 113/114 engines from VR796 that went to Vintage V12s in Tehachapi, California, for complete restoration. The firm has more than 30 years' experience in providing restoration services for Merlin, Griffon and Allison engines. *(Victoria Air Maintenance)*

Canada's Mossies

Robert Jens – Mosquito B 35, VR796

Far away across the Pacific on Canada's north-west coast at North Saanich in British Columbia, a Mosquito B 35 is under restoration to flying condition by Victoria Air Maintenance.

Built in 1948 as a B 35 by Airspeed at Portsmouth, VR796 went straight into storage at an RAF maintenance unit until it was purchased in 1954 by Spartan Air Services of Ottawa as one of a batch of ten and was given the Canadian civil registration CF-HML. For nine years the aircraft was used by Spartan for high-altitude air mapping of northern Canada, making its last flight in June 1963. Between 1966 and 2002, VR796 had two different owners – Don Campbell and Ed Zalesky, to whom Campbell sold the aircraft in 1986. Both intended to make the Mossie airworthy, but this was not to be.

In 2005 the Mosquito was acquired by Robert Jens, owner of the Million Air corporate aviation service franchise at Vancouver International Airport, who contracted Victoria Air Maintenance to complete the restoration and return VR796 to the skies. Jens already owns a Spitfire XIVe and had worked on the restoration of a P-51 Mustang.

VR796 was in fairly good condition and did not require a major restoration, but it took another four years before the aircraft was finally delivered to Victoria Air Maintenance where

work began in April 2009. Within six months the engine firewalls and the radiator structures were installed, the cowlings fitted, and fuel lines and fuel selector cables put in place. The air filter system on the lower cowlings was removed and overhauled before reinstallation and the original engine mounts were paint-stripped and inspected by NDT. They were found to be in excellent condition. The two Rolls-Royce Merlin 113/114 engines were then shipped to Vintage V12s in Tehachapi, California, for complete restoration.

The engineering team at Victoria Air Maintenance was faced with many challenges, most of which stemmed from a shortage of reliable technical reference material for the Mosquito. In order to get a better insight into what they were up against, the engineers visited the EAA Air Venture Museum at Oshkosh, Wisconsin, to photograph Mosquito TT 35 (RS712) owned by millionaire collector Kermit

Weeks. There, the team took more than 500 detail photographs of RS712 to assist them in their restoration of VR796.

By the end of 2012 the restoration had made good progress. The canopy glazing had been installed along with the cockpit wiring; the warm-air pipework that kept the canopy windows ice and mist free had been furnished, and the air drier positioned; wheels and tyres had been fitted, along with the gear doors, and the gear swing had been completed satisfactorily; and the pneumatic system had also been checked. The bomb-bay doors were fitted and plumbed, and the fire suppression lines on each engine were installed. The rear fuselage door was in place and the overhauled engines had arrived back from Vintage V12s and were in situ on the aircraft. At the time of writing (June 2013) Victoria Air Maintenance reported that the aircraft was in the paint shop, but could not give a date for ground running or first flight.

ABOVE LEFT Mel Johnstone of Victoria Air Maintenance surveys the bomb-bay interior, January 2010. *(Victoria Air Maintenance)*

ABOVE Mel Johnstone (facing) and Martin Howse prepare to fit the ventral fuel tank inside VR796's bomb-bay, April 2010. *(Victoria Air Maintenance)*

FAR LEFT It takes three men, a winch and steady hands to reinstall a Merlin engine. *(Victoria Air Maintenance)*

LEFT Aluminium silver dope is sprayed over an undercoat of red. On top of this will be applied the aircraft's final camouflage finish. *(Victoria Air Maintenance)*

The Mosquito Bomber Group – Mosquito B XX, KB161 (Reproduction)

The Mosquito Bomber Group of Windsor, Ontario, is creating a hybrid Mosquito using the remains of B 35 (TA661). Some parts from a number of original Mossies have been used, including one that went down in the Northwest Territories, but when completed less than 10% of the aircraft will be original.

New fuselage halves were built by Glyn Powell's Mosquito Aircraft Restoration (his prototype fuselage), and new wings were constructed by the Mosquito Bomber Group themselves. On 19 March 2013 the group marked a milestone in the restoration programme when the main wing, which had been built in a vertical position, was flipped over into a horizontal position to enable the top skin, nose ribs and flaps to be attached. The group's

assistant project manager, Guy Moore, has said it will be several more years before the wing is attached to the fuselage.

Aussie Mossie

The Royal Australian Air Force Museum, Point Cook – PR XVI, A52-600

Although the Mosquito PR XVI on display in the Royal Australian Air Force Museum is unlikely ever to fly again, it has been included in this chapter because of its uniqueness. A52-600 is believed to be the only surviving Mosquito with a wartime operational history of 21 missions, and the only PR XVI left anywhere in the world. Beginning in 2002, the aircraft underwent extensive restoration to static display condition by the RAAF and a volunteer restoration team of young service personnel and civilians, supported by the Mosquito Aircraft Association of Australia. 'No, it will not fly, it's too valuable,' said a spokesman for the RAAF Museum at Point Cook, Victoria.

The future is wooden

– if you have the parts and the money

Thanks to Glyn Powell and Warren Denholm and the experience they have gained in rebuilding KA114 and NZ2308, together with the tools, production facilities and the all-important skills of the craftsmen, it will now be possible to restore and build Mosquitoes to museum or airworthy condition. For the latter, Glyn qualifies this by saying: 'You can build as many Mossies as you can find the parts for. There's a fairly good supply of engines, but you're limited in what you can do by the availability of other parts – then you'll need to find someone with eight or nine million dollars to pay for it!'

BELOW The RAAF Museum's PR XVI (A52-600, seen here in February 2004) was the subject of an extensive restoration by the RAAF Museum, Point Cook, assisted by members of the Mosquito Aircraft Association of Australia. It is the only Mosquito survivor with a combat history. *(RAAF Museum)*

Bibliography and sources

Primary

AIR 27/2029 – 544 Squadron, A Flight, sortie record book June 1943–May 1945

Secondary

Birtles, Philip J., *Mosquito – The Illustrated History* (Sutton, 1998)

Bowman, Martin W., *The Men Who Flew the Mosquito* (PSL, 1995)

Bowman, Martin W., *The Reich Intruders* (PSL, 1997)

Cumming, Michael, *Beam Bombers: The secret war of No 109 Squadron* (Sutton, 1998)

de Havilland, Sir Geoffrey, *Sky Fever* (Airlife, 1979)

Ducellier, J.P., *The Amiens Raid – Secrets Revealed* (Red Kite, 2011)

Foster, Ronald H., *Focus on Europe: a photo-reconnaissance Mosquito pilot at war, 1943–45* (Crowood Press, 2004)

Franks, Norman, *Dark Sky, Deep Water: First-hand experiences of the U-boat war in WWII* (Grub Street, 2004)

Golley, John, *John Cat's-Eyes' Cunningham – The Aviation Legend* (Airlife, 1999)

Hardy, M.J., *de Havilland Mosquito – Super Profile* (Haynes, 1984)

Howe, Stuart, *de Havilland Mosquito – An illustrated history, Volume 1* (Crécy Publishing, 1999)

Leaf, Edward, *Above all Unseen: The RAF's photographic reconnaissance units 1939–1945* (PSL, 1997)

McIntosh, Dave, *Terror in the Starboard Seat* (PaperJacks, 1981)

McKee, Alexander, *The Mosquito Log* (Souvenir Press, 1988)

Pilot's Notes: Merlin Mk 61, 63, 64, 72 & 73 Engines (Rolls-Royce, Derby, 1944)

Pilot's Notes: Mosquito FB 6, 2nd Edition, January 1950 (Air Ministry)

Rolls-Royce Merlin two-stage two-speed engine maintenance manual (Rolls-Royce, Derby, 1946)

Scott, Stuart R., *Mosquito Thunder: No 105 Squadron at war, 1942–45* (Sutton, 1999)

Sharp, C. Martin, *DH – A History of de Havilland* (Airlife, 1982)

Sharp, C. Martin and Bowyer, Michael J.F., *Mosquito* (Faber, 1971)

Streetly, Martin, *Confound and Destroy* (MacDonald and Jane's, 1979)

Streetly, Martin, *The Aircraft of 100 Group* (Robert Hale, 1984)

Sweetman, Bill and Watanabe, Rikyu, *Mosquito* (Jane's, 1981)

Thirsk, Ian, *de Havilland Mosquito: An illustrated history, Volume 2* (Crécy Publishing, 2006)

Other

Hatfield RAeS, *The Mosquito 50 Years On* (GMS Enterprises, 1991)

Aeroplane – various wartime issues

Aeroplane magazine – Mosquito Special (Kelsey Publishing Group, December 2012)

Aeroplane Icons series, *Mosquito – Britain's World War Two Wooden Wonder* (Kelsey Publishing Group, 2012)

Flight – various wartime and post-war issues

Websites

www.vmarsmanuals.co.uk – AP1093D Part 2, Introductory Survey of Radar

www.avweb.com – AVweb: the world's premier independent aviation news resource

www.mossie.org/Mosquito.html

www.aaib.gov.uk/cms_resources.cfm?file=/dft_avsafety_pdf_501355.pdf

www.warbirdregistry.org/mossieregistry/mossie-n1203v.html

www.airforce.gov.au/raafmuseum/exhibitions/restoration/dh_98.htm

The de Havilland Aircraft Heritage Centre

All eyes, all cameras, all attention have been on KA114, the Mosquito that flew again on the other side of the world after 16 years of Mosquito silence. And rightly so, for this was a monumental achievement, and one that in the American ownership of Jerry Yagen, will continue to thrill with its sound and fury.

And yet the heart of the Mosquito will always lie in the quiet of the Hertfordshire countryside at the de Havilland Aircraft Heritage Centre in the grounds of Salisbury Hall, where the first prototype (W4050) was built in 1940 and returned to live in retirement more than 50 years ago.

At the time of writing she was in the process of being lovingly restored to her former glory for future generations to admire – and perhaps to wonder, a lifetime later, what it must have been like to go to war in such a machine.

Her space at the museum, just off Junction 22 of the M25, is shared with two other Mosquitoes, together with many other pieces of memorabilia, including the mighty Molins gun and some superb historic models.

The museum, steeped in tradition and nostalgia, is the true home of all things de Havilland and a pilgrimage for lovers of the immortal Mosquito.

www.dehavillandmuseum.co.uk

Appendix 1

Mosquito variants

Prototype: W4050.

PR 1: Prototype (W4051) and nine others (W4054–W4056, W4058–W4063). All had short engine nacelles and 2 x Rolls-Royce Merlin 21 engines with two-speed, single-stage superchargers and de Havilland Hydromatic propellers.

F II and NF II: Fighter. Developed from prototype W4052. 4 x .303in Browning machine guns and 4 x 20mm cannon. 2 x Merlin 21 and 23 engines. Two were built experimentally with a rotating dorsal turret equipped with 4 x .303in machine guns. Some converted to PR II.

T III: Trainer. As Mark II but with dual control and without armament. 2 x Merlin 21, 23 and 25 engines.

B IV: Unarmed bomber. Similar to the PR 1 but with longer engine nacelles. 2 x Merlin 21 and 23 engines. Capacity for 4 x 500lb bombs (with shortened fins) in the fuselage in place of 4 x 250lb bombs in the original design. Later modified to carry 1 x 4,000lb Blockbuster or Cookie with a bulged bomb-bay.

PR IV: Unarmed photo-reconnaissance. Similar to the B IV, but with provision for cameras instead of bombs. A variant of the PR IV was supplied to BOAC as the prototype Mosquito courier-transport. Accommodation for one passenger was on his back in the felt-padded bomb-bay.

B V: Prototype developed from the B IV with new 'basic' wing to take either 2 x 50gal jettisonable wing tanks or 2 x 500lb bombs. 2 x Merlin 23 engines. This aircraft was the basis of the Canadian B VII.

FB VI: Fighter-bomber with 'basic' or 'standard' wing. Developed from the NF II with 2 x Merlin 22, 23 and 25 engines. Same armament as the NF II plus 2 x 50gal jettisonable wing tanks or 2 x 500lb bombs (or extra fuel tank in the fuselage behind the cannon). Provision was made in 1944 to carry 4 x 60lb rockets under each wing in place of the wing tanks or bombs for attacks on shipping. Two Mk VI Mosquitoes were modified for deck landing trials and one converted to Sea Mosquito by adding an arrester hook, strengthening the rear fuselage, and fitting four-bladed propellers and AI XV radar. This was the basis for the Mk 33.

B VII: Bomber. First 25 Canadian-built Mosquitoes based on the B V, but with 2 x Packard Merlin 31 engines driving Hamilton Standard propellers.

PR VIII: Photo-reconnaissance and the first high-altitude Mosquitoes. The PR VIII was converted from the B IV by fitting special Merlin 61 intercooled engines with two-speed, two-stage superchargers and adding provision for 2 x 50gal jettisonable wing tanks. Only five were built.

B IX: First high-altitude unarmed bomber. Merlin 72 intercooled engines with two-speed, two-stage superchargers. Capacity for 4 x 500lb bombs in the fuselage and 2 x 500lb bombs on the wings, or extra fuselage fuel tanks and 2 x 50gal jettisonable wing tanks. A few were converted to take 1 x 4,000lb bomb in the fuselage with 2 x 50gal jettisonable wing tanks, which in 1944 were replaced by 2 x 100gal jettisonable wing tanks subject to a weight limitation of 25,200lb. A pathfinder version was developed by the RAF.

PR IX: Photo-reconnaissance version of the B IX, used by the RAF and PR XVI by the USAAF for meteorological and photo reconnaissance over Europe before all major day- and night-bombing raids.

FB X: Proposed fighter-bomber, as FB VI but with Merlin 67 engines. This version was never built.

Mk XI: This designation was never used.

NF XII: Four-cannon fighter developed from the NF II, but with the four machine guns and the AI Mk V radar being replaced by centimetric AI Mk VIII radar in nose radome. 2 x Merlin 21 and 23 engines. The 'basic' wing was not fitted.

NF XIII: Four-cannon fighter developed from the FB VI. The four machine guns in the nose were replaced by AI Mk VIII radar in 'bull' or 'thimble' nose. 2 x Merlin 21 and 23 engines.

NF XIV: Proposed fighter as NF XIII, but with high-altitude Merlin 67 engines. This version was never built.

NF XV: Special high-altitude fighter developed in only seven days from pressure cabin prototype PR VIII with extended wingtips, reduced fuel tankage and 4 x .303in machine guns in a blister under the fuselage, plus AI VIII radar. Only five were built.

B XVI: Bomber. Pressure cabin development of the B IX with 2 x Merlin 72, 73, 76 and 77 engines able to carry 3,000lb bombs. Most were converted in 1944 to take 1 x 4,000lb bomb in the fuselage and 2 x 50gal wing drop-tanks, or 2 x 100gal drop-tanks with 4 x 500lb bombs.

PR XVI: Photo-reconnaissance version of the B XVI. Three extra fuel tanks were fitted in the bomb-bay. As well as the cameras carried in the fuselage, one F52 camera could be carried in each drop-tank.

NF XVII: Fighter developed from and similar to the NF XII with American AI Mk X radar.

FB XVIII: Fighter-bomber known as the 'Tsetse'. Developed from the FB VI with the nose modified to take a six-pounder (57mm) anti-tank gun instead of the 4 x 20mm cannon. The six-pounder could fire 25 shells in 20sec. 2 x Merlin 25 engines. Used mainly by Coastal Command against submarines and shipping.

NF XIX: Fighter developed from and similar to the NF XIII, but with 2 x Merlin 25 engines and able to take either British or American radar sets. In 1948–49, 45 were overhauled and fitted with four-blade airscrews and supplied to the Royal Swedish Air Force who designated the aircraft the J 30, the ultimate single-stage Merlin night-fighter.

B XX: Bomber. Second batch of Canadian production. Similar to the B VII but with Canadian–American equipment and Packard Merlin 31 or 33 engines. Forty fitted with cameras were supplied to the USAAF (who designated them the F-8) and were used for meteorological and operational reconnaissance.

FB 21: Canadian-built fighter-bomber corresponding to the FB VI, otherwise as the B XX. Only two were built, one with 2 x Packard Merlin 33 engines, the other two with 2 x Packard Merlin 31 engines. It was replaced by the FB 26.

T 22: Canadian-built unarmed dual-control trainer based on the FB 21 with 2 x Packard Merlin 33 engines. Only six were built. Similar to the T 3.

B 23: Canadian-built high-altitude bomber, which was a development of the B XX to make use of Packard Merlin 69 engines. Not proceeded with.

FB 24: Canadian-built high-altitude fighter-bomber developed from the FB 21 with Packard Merlin 301 two-stage, supercharged engines. Only one was built.

B 25: Canadian-built bomber identical to the B XX, but with 2 x Packard Merlin 225 engines.

FB 26: Canadian-built fighter-bomber developed from the FB VI but with 2 x Packard Merlin 225 engines and Canadian–American equipment.

T 27: Canadian-built trainer developed from the T 22 with 2 x Packard Merlin 225 engines.

FB 28: Model number allocated to Canada, but not taken up.

T 29: Dual-control trainer development of FB 26 with 2 x Packard Merlin 225 engines. All were conversions from FB 26s.

NF 30: Fighter. Developed from the NF XIX with high-altitude Merlin 72 and 76 engines.

Mk 31: Reserved for a Packard Merlin-engined night-fighter variant which was never built.

PR 32: Photo-reconnaissance. Specially lightened version of the PR XVI with 2 x Merlin 113 and 114 (two-stage, supercharged) engines and extended wingtips for high-altitude operation.

TF/TR 33: Fleet Air Arm version developed from the FB VI for multi-role operation. 2 x Merlin 25 engines, manually operated folding wings and oleo-pneumatic landing gear with smaller wheels.

PR 34: Photo-reconnaissance. Very long-range development of the PR XVI with Merlin 113 and 114 engines. This was the fastest version of the Mosquito, achieving 422mph in level flight.

PR 34a: Modernised version of the PR 34 with a revised cockpit layout and additional internal equipment.

B 35: Bomber. Similar to the B XVI except for 2 x Merlin 114 engines in early versions, 2 x Merlin 114A engines in later versions. A total of 274 were built, including 65 by Airspeed Ltd.

PR 35: Photo-reconnaissance. Fifteen were built, converted from B 35s.

TT 35: Target-tug, modified from B 35.

NF 36: Fighter. High-powered development of the NF 30 with 2 x Merlin 113 engines and British AI Mk X radar. Armament consisted of 4 x 20mm cannon.

TR/TF 37: Torpedo fighter-bomber similar to the T 33 with British ASV Mk 13B radar fitted in an extended nose.

NF 38: Fighter. Similar to the NF 36, fitted with British AI Mk IX radar. 2 x Merlin 113, 114, 113A or 114A engines.

TT 39: Target-tug converted from B XVI.

FB 40: Fighter. First Australian-built Mosquitoes, based on the FB VI with Hamilton Standard or Australian-built de Havilland Hydromatic propellers. The first 100 aircraft were built with Packard Merlin 31 engines, after which Packard Merlin 33 engines were used.

PR 40: Photo-reconnaissance. Australian-built conversion of the FB 40 with 2 x Packard Merlin 31 engines.

PR 41: Photo-reconnaissance. Australian-built, similar to the PR 40 but with extra radio gear and 2 x Packard Merlin 69 two-stage, supercharged engines.

FB 42: Fighter-bomber. Australian-built adaptation of an FB 40 to take the Packard Merlin 69 engine. After testing, the project was dropped and the aircraft became the prototype for the PR 41.

T 43: Trainer. Australian-built conversion of the FB 40 and almost identical except for the addition of dual controls and dual elevator trim tabs.

Some Mosquito mark numbers are in Roman numerals, others in Arabic. Until the end of 1942, the RAF had a policy of always using Roman numerals, but 1943 to 1948 was a transition period during which new aircraft were assigned Arabic numerals, although older machines retained their original Roman numerals. From 1948 onwards, only Arabic numerals were used.

Appendix 2

Sample specifications

DH 98 Mosquito F II

General data	
Type	day and night long-range fighter and intruder
Crew	2: pilot, navigator/radar operator
Length	41ft 2in
Wingspan	54ft 2in
Height	17ft 5in
Wing area	454sq ft
Empty weight	13,356lb
Loaded weight	17,700lb
Maximum take-off weight	18,649lb
Powerplant	2 × Rolls-Royce Merlin 21/21 or 23/23 (left/right) 1,480hp (21 and 23) each

Performance	
Maximum speed	366mph at 21,400ft
Range	900 miles with 410gal fuel load at 20,000ft
Service ceiling	29,000ft
Rate of climb	1,740ft/min
Wing loading	39.9lb/sq ft

Armament	
Guns	4 × 20mm Hispano Mk II cannon (fuselage) and 4 × .303 in Browning machine guns (nose)

Radar	
AI Mk IV or Mk V radar (NF variants)	

DH 98 Mosquito B XVI

General data	
Type	bomber
Crew	2: pilot, bomb-aimer/navigator
Length	44ft 6in
Wingspan	54ft 2in
Height	15ft 3in
Wing area	454sq ft
Empty weight	14,600lb
Loaded weight	23,000lb
Max take-off weight	25,200lb
Powerplant	2 × Rolls-Royce Merlin 72/73 or 76/77 (left/right) liquid-cooled 12-cylinder, two-speed, two-stage supercharged engines, each rated at 1,680hp/1,710hp respectively at 21,000ft

Performance	
Maximum speed	(Merlin 76/77) 415mph at 28,000ft
Range	1,370 miles with full weapons load
Service ceiling	36,000ft
Rate of climb	2,850ft/min
Wing loading	39.9lb/sq ft

Armament	
No guns	
Bombs	Either 1 x 4,000lb, 4 x 500lb bombs, 4 x 250lb bombs, or 2 x 160lb small bomb containers in fuselage bomb-bay, plus 1 x 500lb bomb under each wing.

Radio-navigation and electronic countermeasures equipment	
Gee, Oboe, H2S, Boozer, Monica, Fishpond.	

Index